The War System

# BERT COCHRAN

# The War System

THE MACMILLAN COMPANY · NEW YORK

COLLIER-MACMILLAN LIMITED · LONDON

The Macmillan Company, New York
Collier-Macmillan Canada, Ltd., Toronto, Ontario

Library of Congress catalog card number: 65–16133

Printed in the United States of America

# CONTENTS

# FOREWORD

There has been a decline in war jitters in the past two years. The peace marchers are not so vociferous or numerous, and the news commentators are more relaxed. The greater calm is the product of the "peaceful coexistence" that was ushered in after the Cuba missiles crisis.

That that crisis should have led to another détente instead of an aggravation of the cold war is astonishing. After all, it was Russia that climbed down; one can almost say that she capitulated to the American ultimatum. She pulled her missiles out of Cuba and, following that, peremptorily stopped her tub-thumping about Berlin. The temptation for the White House to press its advantage must have been very great. General LeMay and other military spokesmen were publicly stating that Russia had backed off because of our vastly superior nuclear arsenal, that our counterforce strategy was paying off, and that we ought to try for higher stakes.

But these counsels of militancy were rejected. President Kennedy and his advisers obviously concluded that it would be perilous to try to ride this particular Cuban horse any harder and that we had got all the mileage out of it that we could reasonably expect. In other circumstances, the Russian retreat would have led to shifts in the correlation of forces. This time it changed nothing essential in the dispositions on the international chessboard. There are strict limits to the creativity of statesmen when opponents can threaten one another with nuclear extinction.

If we could believe that mutual terror is a reliable deterrent to nuclear war, we might conclude that while it is a terribly expensive and brutal way to deter war, it is better than more fanciful but unattainable methods. In the world of power politics, we have to be thankful for small favors, and have to settle for less than ideal solutions. Unfortunately, mutual nuclear terror is not only an unreliable deterrent; I have tried to demonstrate that sooner or later it will break down.

The present détente can be reversed overnight in today's politically surcharged world. Cuba can again become the focal point of a world crisis; or we can become embroiled with Communist China, with Russia thrust into support of her ally by the radiating force of events; or the hostile confrontation can again become explosive in Central Europe.

This fear of a nuclear war remains in the forefront of people's minds in this country despite official assurances, the test-ban treaty, and the cold war relaxation. Senator Goldwater did not understand that he was flouting the profoundest popular feelings when he proposed during the presidential campaign to hand over nuclear weapons to the generals. Very quickly it became apparent to him, as well as to his opponents, that the nuclear issue—the impression that he was "trigger happy"—was a heavy albatross around his neck. It was his greatest handicap in the race.

In common with other students of this question, I come to the conclusion that the nuclear peril cannot be shaken off short of scaling down and eventually reducing armaments to police levels. Such a transformation can only be envisaged as part of a near universal treaty that sets up a limited world authority to supervise, regulate, and administer the disarmament of nations. I do not attempt to blueprint the steps that should be taken to realize this grandiose objective, nor do I attempt to draw up precise constitutional or administrative provisions for the projected world undertaking. Although I am convinced that there are deep impulses in our modern history to create a world community, I do not believe it is possible for anyone to penetrate the fog of coming events to identify and seize the individual threads that will lead toward such a consummation.

My purposes in this book seem sufficient to me—and I shall have realized them if I have succeeded in analyzing the main forces at play, and how we may be able to achieve a semblance of a world order out of the political and moral chaos of our age. On the scale of day-to-day politics, nothing seems more illusory or impractical than the attempt to graft revolutionary changes onto existing social dispensations and arrangements. But great ideals and far-reaching projects also play their part in man's history. If they fuse with his wants, they become irresistible.

BERT COCHRAN

New York City
October, 1964

"As the arms race continues and the weapons multiply and become more swift and deadly, the possibility of a global catastrophe, either by miscalculation or design, becomes ever more real."

SECRETARY OF DEFENSE ROBERT S. MC NAMARA

"We must recognize that the peace of nuclear terror cannot endure for long."

RALPH E. LAPP

"The prediction of inescapable doom that now overhangs the world is not really persuasive; yet it is the logical outcome of everything we know about international society. If it is not to be realized, some elements in the modern predicament must somehow undergo alteration."

WALTER MILLIS AND JAMES REAL

The War System

CHAPTER I   The Suicide Pact

MAN's dreams have often, upon realization, turned into nightmares. For ages, he aspired to fly and thought he would be as a god when he wrenched this secret from the bowels of the universe. Icarus fell into the sea and was drowned, according to the mythologies of antiquity, when the sun melted the wax with which he had fastened his wings. Then came George Cayley and the Wright brothers, who outwitted the sun, and the winds, as well. But instead of resembling gods after we had acquired wings, we appeared more like forsaken and demented furies. The perfection of the airplane revolutionized travel, and it also revolutionized war. We were able to annihilate distance, and we were also able to demolish whole cities from the air and to blast and cremate the inhabitants thereof.

We learn in Scripture that at one point God had concluded that the creation of man, who even in those ancient times defiled the earth with his violence and contention, had been a mistake, and the Deity resolved to destroy His own handiwork. But after the Flood, His heart softened when He reminded Himself that man's imagination is evil from the seed, and He went so far as to promise not to smite living things any more. It is not related whether after further consideration, God modified His opinions again. It is possible.

Goethe was sure that He would have to smash everything all over again to rejuvenate His creation. In any case, modern man, turned demigod, has wormed even this secret from the depths of the eternal. He can will universal death. He now has the knowledge, and, it would seem, the frenzy, to put an end to himself and his progeny. It is recorded in the Book of Infamies that when man first stole the nuclear fire from the gods, he used it for destruction and war. The chiliastic visions of the early Christian sects that the end of the world was at hand have never before been so realizable and realistic.

Thermonuclear violence is the eschatological McCoy. It will do the job, certainly as thoroughly as the Genesis flood. Possibly handfuls of Noahs grubbing underground, and some peoples in unaffected countries, may escape the final disaster. If fortunate, these chosen ones, impelled by blind instinct, like worms and fish, may continue to cling to existence, and procreate degenerate and debilitated forms of life even though much of the reasonableness for doing so had been lost. If the climax of six or seven thousand years of civilization is to be horrible immolation, the survivors, if there be any, will be like the blind white cobra in Kipling's story, who continued standing guard in a city which, without his knowledge, had long since been abandoned and had fallen into ruin.

Descartes once said that it is easier to understand something when you are watching it grow instead of looking at it fully formed. So it is easier to grasp the import of the new calamitous technology by considering it in its flow.

In the Second World War, the big bombing planes dropped 5- to 10-ton "blockbusters" of TNT. From official surveys of the damage, it was found that a 10-ton high explosive bomb destroyed buildings within 400 feet of ground zero. It took the British ten days of incessant bombing, dropping 8,000 tons, to gut Hamburg. Seventy thousand men, women, and children were consumed in that blaze of Allied glory; almost half of the half million homes in the city were pulverized; a fire storm raged over a radius of three miles for a week; normal processes of urban living ceased. Wind velocity exceeded 150 miles an hour; burning gases rose to 15,000 feet; temperatures went higher than $1,400°$ F. People in shelters were cooked to death as if they were in an oven, or died of heat stroke, or were choked by carbon monoxide. It was one of the worst raids of that war. All in all, according to the United States Strategic Bombing Surveys, 1,300,000 tons of bombs were dropped by the Anglo-

American forces on Germany, resulting in the death of approximately half a million people.

A few years later, we arrived at the threshold of the nuclear age. The single bomb exploded over Hiroshima was one to two thousand times greater in devastating power than the Second World War blockbuster. Like a red hot iron applied to nylon, it burned out over four and one-half square miles of the city. According to Japanese estimates, it left 100,000 dead and missing out of a total population of 300,000; another 100,000 injured; another 100,000 requiring regular clinical examinations.

The official American survey reports supplied this dispassionate account:

> At the time of the explosion, energy was given off in the form of light, heat, radiation, and pressure. The complete band of radiations, from X and gamma rays, through ultraviolet and light rays to the radiant heat of infrared rays, traveled with the speed of light. The shock wave, created by the enormous pressure, built up almost instantaneously. . . . The duration of the flash was only a fraction of a second, but it was sufficiently intense to cause third-degree burns to exposed human skin up to a distance of a mile. . . . In the immediate area of ground zero, the heat charred corpses beyond recognition. . . . The blast wave which followed the flash was of sufficient force to press in the roofs of reinforced concrete structures and to flatten completely all less sturdy structures. . . . Of approximately 90,000 buildings in the city, 65,000 were rendered unusable and almost all the remainder received at least superficial damage.

The Indian government report stated that damage was complete (including collapse of earthquake-resistant reinforced concrete buildings) within a circle of one mile across. Most of the houses within a circle of three miles across were destroyed. Houses up to four miles across were badly damaged. Aside from the blast wave was the intense burst of heat radiation and of gamma rays. About a quarter of the deaths were due to instantaneous burns from the heat flash; about a sixth were due to radiation burns.

At both Hiroshima and Nagasaki the bombs were exploded well up in the air. Consequently, not too much residual radioactivity remained on the ground. It was a different story during the underwater test explosion at Bikini, when the United States exploded a bomb fifty feet below sea level that was as powerful as the one dropped at Nagasaki. A column of water with a straight stem and a mushroom head rushed upwards. In fifteen seconds it was a mile high, and the mushroom head was a mile and a half across. The column contained a million tons of radioactive water. From the base of the column there rolled out a white ring of mist traveling at fifty miles an hour and covering ultimately an area of more than five square miles. The waters, and the ships deluged with water, remained intensely radioactive for several months, and would have killed all living things that remained there for any length of time.

Residual radioactivity will be similarly intense with an atomic ground burst. The effect of blast and heat flash may be reduced, but the blast will pulverize buildings and earth and spread highly radioactive dust and rubble over a wide area for a considerable time. If, by chance, rain should fall through the radioactive cloud, large areas will be contaminated with radioactivity and all living things within those areas will probably be killed. In Hiroshima, where neither rain nor ground burst was involved, there were numerous reports of later deaths of victims of fallout.

Peter Burchett, the first Allied reporter reaching Hiroshima, wrote in the *Daily Express:*

> I found people who, when the bomb fell, suffered absolutely no injuries, but now are dying from the uncanny aftereffects. For no apparent reason their health began to fail. They lost appetite. Their hair fell out. Bluish spots appeared on their bodies. And then bleeding began from the ears, nose and mouth. At first, the doctors told me, they thought these were the symptoms of general debility. They gave their patients Vitamin A injections. The results were horrible. The flesh started rotting away from the hole caused by the injection of the needle. And in every case the victim dies

A special bedevilment was the fire storm, which consumed victims who had managed to escape the other cataract of horrors. A fire storm is a monster fire in which cooler air is constantly drawn to the center of the burning area, raising the heat and perpetuating the conflagration. With the explosion, the air sweeps in from all sides, whipping up the flames and pouring out the smoke far and wide. The tornado continually absorbs, fuses, and is fed by the innumerable fires. Trucks, cars, people, houses, get sucked into the vortex from the periphery and are picked up by the blast winds and hurled for miles through the air as deadly projectiles. Winds are of hurricane velocities, and even at the edge of the storm they blow with the relentlessness of a gale. The holocaust consumes the available oxygen, so that any persons in shelters who may escape being burned to death are likely to be asphyxiated by the exhaustion of air.

So it was that in 1945 the human race, or at least part of it, had attained the high pinnacle where one single bomb could be dropped which was able to spread more death and destruction than ten days of continual bombardment had done in Hamburg. The one bomb was nearly forty times as powerful as the heaviest attack which Hitler rained upon London in May, 1941. It was almost six times as powerful as the last major strategic bombing (old style) of the war, the raid on Tokyo on May 23, 1945. There, it took 520 planes to drop 3,600 tons of bombs on an area of about eleven square miles. And we are talking about the effects of the *Hiroshima* bomb, an outdated, obsolete, mere 20-kiloton propellant, practically a toy by today's standards. It would not be accepted into present arsenals of the United States, Russia, or Britain. Probably even a self-respecting power like France would turn down anything so inefficient and archaic.

From the atomic bomb of 20,000-ton power we moved on to the thermonuclear bomb of 20,000,000-ton power in less than a decade, and in the case of Russia, in less than half a decade. The 20-kiloton bomb multiplied the power of the conventional blockbuster by a factor of one thousand. The hydrogen weapon has multiplied the atomic weapon by an additional factor of one thousand. Compared to the TNT stage, power per pound of explosive has expanded by a factor of one million. One thermonuclear bomb in the 20-megaton range releases seven times more destructive energy than all the high explosives used in the Second World War on all the far-flung battle fronts, in the air, on land, and on sea. A National Planning Association study, in an attempt to bring the situation home, has figured out that TNT containing the equivalent energy of one 20-megaton bomb would fill 4,000 miles of freight cars—a line that would extend from Los Angeles to New York and back to Denver. This represents a scientific revolution of a new order of magnitude, and as we shall see, the accompanying technology is proceeding at an unprecedented rate of development, as well. We are in an accelerating phase of a geometric progression.

## II

The military use of gunpowder sometime in the fourteenth century was said to have revolutionized warfare. Every school boy has read how its introduction spelled the doom of feudalism, because the medieval barons could no longer install themselves in their towered castles and from there dominate and subdue the country-side around them. The obsolescence of the baronial fortification was one hundred fifty years in coming. In 1464 the British Earl of Warwick invested the strong fortress of Bamborough in a week; eighty years later Franz Von Sickingen's formerly impregnable stronghold was reduced to ruins in a single day's bombardment by the artillery of Philip of Hesse. Only then did the feudal fastness become an anachronism.

The armored knight on horseback and the single combat of the age of chivalry were not swept away with one stroke. Technology has a habit of subtly fusing with social drifts, while different social groups try to use new discoveries or inventions as instruments of their own ambitions. The plebeian infantryman had already forced his way into the battle line after the English archers mowed down the chivalric squadrons at Crécy, Poitiers, and Agincourt. The last feudal armies even made use of guns, as in the case of Charles the Bold against the Swiss. As time went on, the new technology became an indispensable part of the social complex which undermined and then wiped out the medieval order, since the manufacture of artillery and gunpowder was the task of the bourgeois craftsman, and military matériel became dependent on the towns.

Hans Delbrück, the German authority on the history of war, showed that firearms began to count in battle only toward the end of the fifteenth century. Even then, the new style of warfare seemed to the feudal gentry to be destructive of its style of life. Was it not reprehensible for an armored knight to be killed with a projectile released by a commoner? Gian Paolo Vitelli, an Italian mercenary knight, who was later accused of treachery and executed at the order of Cesare Borgia, was so incensed at seeing his companions killed by gunfire in battle that he proceeded to pluck out the eyes and chop off the hands of all *arquebusiers* whom he could capture.

When in 1498 he took Buti, a small town near Pisa, he had the hands of all the garrison's gunners cut off.

Not that that stopped the military revolution, but it proceeded very slowly, more as a gradual evolution; change was wrought by the piecemeal introduction of numerous small improvements and innovations. No one dramatic technological breakthrough reversed the rules abruptly. It took five hundred years after the first military use of gunpowder—the middle of the nineteenth century—to enter the age of firearms, in the modern sense of the term. Gunpowder finally gave the infantry the breech-loading rifle, cavalry the carbine and pistol, and provided the battle line with efficient artillery pieces discharging explosive projectiles. The gun and howitzer gradually displaced the bow and arrow, the lance, sword, and catapult by proving superior in the performance of similar functions on the battlefield. But infantry still deployed in the open, cavalry still charged with remodeled spears, battles and campaigns were remarkably similar until Bismarck's day to what they had been for two thousand years.

Krupp's steel guns that helped Prussia gain a quick and decisive victory over France in 1870 set off an intense weapons competition and creativity. The arsenals began to work feverishly to increase the speed of fire, the accuracy of aim, the range, weight, and explosive force of projectiles. By 1914, the European armies were equipped with Hiram Maxim's machine gun, with mobile artillery, and 8-inch and 12-inch howitzers. The Dreadnought, with a speed of 25 knots an hour, bristling with 15-inch guns, and flaunting 13-inch armor plate, took command of the seas. The submarine, first sold by Sir Basil Zaharoff to Greece to threaten Turkey, and then to Turkey to threaten Greece, was taken over by all the larger navies. The ensuing four-year deadlock on the Western front, the senseless mass butchery at Ypres, Champagne, Verdun, at the Somme, at Arras, on the Aisne, and at Passchendaele, dispelled the mystique of the bayonet offensive, and discredited the professionals who thought that the new machines of destruction were only meant to clear the way for the old-fashioned charge of massed knights with spears.

The airplane was used only peripherally in the First World War. When it was perfected and supplied with greater fire power, it profoundly changed the face of war. It drove the battleship off the seas and brought in the aircraft carrier. It became the chief hunter of the merchant ship and submarine. It altered the tactical shape of army maneuver and deployment. It called into being a vast arsenal of defense, including electronically controlled gun directors, the proximity fuse, radar, radar-carrying defense fighters, and later, guided self-propelled ground-to-air missiles and unmanned interceptors. But the airplane did not eliminate armies and navies, or take war away from the battlefield. What it did was to add a new dimension to war, and a new division to the science of war which had traditionally been divided between land and sea strategies.

The more or less methodical and paced evolution of war technology over the past six centuries, or for that matter, over the past three millennia, brings into heightened relief the revolutionary nature of the nuclear explosive. This is not a technological revolution of the genus inaugurated with the invention of the machine gun, the submarine, or even the airplane; it is of a different species than gunpowder, which modified the tactical environment, but could still be fitted into the existing social and technical structure of society.

Up to 1945 the rising havoc of war derived more from the increase in the mechanical efficiency of delivering the explosives than from improvements in the explosives themselves. The power developed by chemical explosives increased slowly. The energy released in the detonation of one pound of modern conventional explosive may be five to ten times greater than that set free in the explosion of one pound of black gunpowder.

Nuclearism is something else. It is a cataclysmic overturn of the previous measurements, arrangements, and techniques, and thereby it has become a challenge to the continuation of both war and society. If this is not grasped, then nothing is understood of the new reality which, outside of the volition of most of us, has reared its Gorgon head in our midst and cannot be spirited away by traditional genuflections and offerings. Albert Einstein, who thought in large terms and remained true to the spacious Enlightenment tradition, said right after the atomic bomb was exploded that a new type of thinking was essential if mankind was to survive.

The atomic explosion and the thermonuclear explosion are both part of the one revolution still in progress which unleashed the atom. But the increase in energy release in the thermonuclear explosion is as great over the atomic explosion as the latter was over the molecular explosion of trinitrotoluene. That is why, from a warmaking standpoint, the fusion bomb overturned completely any and all calculations based on the atomic bomb, and effaced such coherent landmarks and doctrines as military analysts thought they possessed during the interval between Hiroshima and Eniwetok.

The thermonuclear bomb is measured not by kilotons but by megatons—explosive power in millions of tons of TNT equivalent. The device tested in March, 1954, was a 15-megaton job; and the 10-megaton bomb is, or was, a standard model in the nuclear inventory bins. There is no limit to how powerful these weapons can be made. A few years ago, a 20-megaton bomb was thought the upper limit, since no one could think of any conceivable objective whose demolition required a larger explosive charge. Now the Russians have exploded one three times as powerful. Moreover, the hydrogen bomb almost immediately gave way to the super bomb, the fission-fusion-fission three-decker. By surrounding the hydrogen bomb with a shell of ordinary uranium, the explosive power of the bomb was doubled or tripled at little additional cost. The uranium 238, when it undergoes fission, also releases large amounts of radioactive materials, which can kill off additional millions of people. That was the kind of bomb we exploded in March, 1954, and the kind the Russians exploded in their subsequent tests.

No thermonuclear bombs have been dropped under actual war conditions on live cities. Hence, we have to rely on the experience of the tests. Since tests are the lifeblood of weapons development, it is easy to understand why military technicians are so keen on having more of them. They are simply showing attachment to their vocations. The test results make fascinating reading. The "Mike" shot of the Operation Ivy series set off on November 7, 1952, caused the complete disappearance of the mile-wide island of Elugelab on which the thermonuclear device was placed. In its stead was left an underwater crater over one mile across and about 175 feet deep in the center. Energy of over five megatons of TNT equivalent was released, and the fireball was three and a half miles across.

The "Bravo" shot in the Castle series set off a year and a half later was reported to have been several times more powerful than "Mike." Since the radius of destruction varies as the cube root of the explosive power, and the area of destruction varies as the two-thirds power of the explosive force, a fusion bomb of 10 megatons has a 12-mile radius and a 400-square-mile area of destruction— larger than London. Lewis Strauss, then chairman of the Atomic Energy Commission, stated at the time that the one bomb could wipe out any city in the world. The air chiefs admitted at the time that war with such weapons "would be general suicide and the end of civilization."

The public learned only by accident that the March, 1954, shot of a 12-megaton charge had also spread fallout of lethal intensity over seven thousand square miles downwind from the explosion. The crew of the Japanese fishing vessel—misnamed, as it turned out, *Lucky Dragon*—became severely ill when it was exposed to a rain of hot radioactive ashes. The *Lucky Dragon* had been seventy-five miles outside the testing zone. The testers had not foreseen the extent of the fallout.

The various test explosions have been polluting the atmosphere. Everywhere on the globe today the soil contains quantities of strontium 90 and cesium 137, which means the radioactive element will rise in all foods and in human and animal bone. The human body, not alerted to what is going on, mistakes strontium 90 for calcium. The radioactive poison thereupon bombards the human cells with high-energy particles that can produce leukemia and bone cancer. The human body, like a foolish virgin, also mistakes cesium 137 for potassium. Unfortunately, this radioactive substance emits gamma rays that are injurious to human genes and can produce genetic damage leading to stillbirths and malformations. Some believe that carbon 14, which takes 5,600 years for half of its quantity to decay, is a major hazard and its effects, if tests continue, will be cumulative. More recently, scientists have become concerned with iodine 131, at first overlooked because of a half-life of only eight days. After the 1961 Russian tests, however, they discovered an abrupt rise in the level of iodine 131 in United States milk supplies. Apparently debris from explosions in the Arctic region, where the Soviet Union conducted her tests, returns to earth more quickly than the debris from the equatorial region, where the United States had been conducting her tests.

Knowledge of the subject is very sketchy, and because the body absorbs a certain amount of radiation from natural causes, it is very difficult to trace the precise effects of radiation emitted from the testing of nuclear weapons. Nobody claims, though, that it is going to do human biology any good. There is a widespread belief that there is no safe threshold so far as genetic damage is concerned; that even small amounts of radiation can produce leukemia, bone cancer, and other diseases, and shorten life expectancy. It gives one pause therefore to observe how technicians who have no firm knowledge of the effects of their tinkering are prepared to gamble with the genetic future of the human race. For so many, astigmatic specialization seems to have replaced the humanist outlook of a Leonardo da Vinci who not only refused to publish his notebooks on weaponry, but was even unwilling to privately set down all he knew. Of his submarine he wrote: "This I do not divulge on account of the evil nature of men who would practice assassinations at the bottom of the seas." Or of a John Napier, the sixteenth century mathematician, who refused to reveal his secret artillery invention because he felt that "for the ruin and overthrow of man, there were too many devices already framed."

At the May, 1959, hearings on radiation before the Joint Congressional Committee on Atomic Energy, some of the scientists talked like nuclear politicians. At one point, Senator Clinton P. Anderson, exasperated by the casuistic explanations, had this exchange with Merril Eisenbud of the Atomic Energy Commission:

SENATOR ANDERSON: Mr. Eisenbud, we had some testimony at one time about how good it was that it [the fallout] stayed up there, and it came down gradually. Now we get testimony about how good it is that it comes down fast and does not stay up very long. What should a man believe, in your opinion?

MR. EISENBUD: You mean with respect to this particular question?

SENATOR ANDERSON: Yes. One time it is good because it stays up for ten years. That is wonderful. The next time it is good because it comes down in two years, that is wonderful. Which would you believe if it were your place?

MR. EISENBUD: I have been asked to summarize what the panel submitted yesterday.

SENATOR ANDERSON: I asked you what you thought, Mr. Eisenbud.

MR. EISENBUD: I think it has been clear from the very beginning that the stratospheric residence-time is short in relation to the radiological half-life [28 years] of strontium 90. This means that for purposes of computation one can neglect the residence-time and simply assume that it is all going to come down. Everything that goes up has to come down.

SENATOR ANDERSON: Now you are on a physics law that I can understand. What goes up must come down. Does that apply also to these claims about how it does not damage . . .?

No wonder that the mass image of the scientist has changed so drastically since Victorian times! The scientist used to be thought of as a benevolent dreamer, a healer, a salutary scholar. Now in popular fiction he is more often than not portrayed as a demented wizard, a tyrant without soul or conscience, who possesses dangerous other-worldly powers.

This particular problem may appear to be academic since July 25, 1963, when the three major nuclear powers initialed a treaty to discontinue nuclear testing in the atmosphere, under water, and in space. It is not. Not only because France and China have spurned the agreement and may set off shots of their own at any time; but also because a resumption of testing by the United States and Russia is inevitable so long as the arms race continues. Hans J. Morgenthau remarked at the time, "It was nothing more than a ratification of what both sides would have done anyway—to stop after a series of tests had been made to evaluate the results." It was not the initial step toward disarmament or even an abatement of the arms race. It was a détente.

Khrushchev needed to make a political demonstration against his Chinese opponents, and accepted an agreement that had been there on the table for the taking for several years. Although at no immediate cost to themselves, the Russians, by signing the test ban treaty, tacitly accepted American nuclear superiority. At a later juncture the Russians may decide that such a status quo is no longer satisfactory to them. Or a prolonged series of American underground tests—in which the Russians have little experience and which may be too costly for their purse—may frighten them into renewing their own atmospheric tests. Once the knowledge accumulated from past tests is absorbed by the arsenals—and important new technical innovations require pragmatic confirmation before they can be readied for production—the pressures on both sides for a resumption of testing will become irresistible. Each side will be goaded by the inescapable logic of the arms race that if it permits "sentimental" reasons to stand in the way of its military progress, it will enable the adversary to run away with the show.


III


The technology of delivery has been able to keep pace and to accommodate the revolutionary advance in the destructiveness of fire power. When Albert Einstein wrote his now famous letter to President Roosevelt in August, 1939, which started the nuclear engines going, he hazarded the guess that while it would probably be possible to construct atomic bombs, they would likely prove to be too heavy for transportation by air. The bomb that finally emerged from the scientists' hatchery was heavy enough, to be sure, reportedly about five tons, but providentially the United States long-range bomber, the B-29, was able to carry it without any trouble. It was this plane that dropped the two bombs over Japan.

Military engineers saw at once that it would be a big advantage if the bomb could be made lighter and smaller. For then it could be carried in a faster and more maneuverable plane, or as the warhead of the then V-2 missile. They feared that not too much could be expected in this direction since the known physical principles underlying the critical mass of fissile material necessary for an explosion made unlikely an appreciable reduction. Again, good fortune smiled on us, and the scientists proved ingenious in reducing the size. Atom bombs were soon manufactured which weighed no more than half a ton, and some of the midget weapons were reportedly the size of a small grapefruit.

The same story was repeated in the case of the hydrogen bomb. As late as 1956, P. M. S. Blackett said he was skeptical that the fusion weapon could be made small enough to be carried in an intercontinental missile. Here, too, the difficulties miraculously melted away. The carrier has consequently been able to keep pace with the explosive projectiles through every stage of progress, the mutual support that one lent the other enabled the good work to move forward, and the military armorers could point with justifiable pride to their integrated and harmoniously balanced weapons systems.

Military technology has been exploding since Hiroshima far more rapidly than it ever did during the Second World War—a war so full of machines and labor-saving devices that it cost $65,000 to kill a man, two and a half times more than in the First World War, thirteen times more than in the Civil War. Two-thirds to three-quarters of all our research and development, and probably as large a percentage of Russia's, is being devoured by the military arts. Up to the outbreak of the second war, a weapons system would be the last word for a generation. Now a weapons system becomes obsolescent when it has barely gone into production. The B-17 Flying Fortress remained operational for a decade; the B-36 intercontinental bomber was obsolescent within seven years; the B-52 jet bomber became outdated in less time. Weapons systems now have an operational life of five to ten years, and closer to the former figure than the latter; in other words, there is a more or less thoroughgoing revolution in the art of war approximately every half decade.

The lumbering piston-engined bombers of the second war have given way to jets flying at supersonic speeds and to ballistic missiles of intercontinental reach. The B-29 used against the Japanese cities in 1945 could carry a 10-ton payload of which not more than a third was actually explosive, traveling 300 miles per hour over a radius of about 2,000 miles. The Titan missile can move the equivalent of several million tons of explosives at speeds up to 16,000 miles per hour over a range of 9,000 miles. This is also the announced range of the advanced Minuteman-2. Russian intercontinental missiles have similar operational ranges. Destructive power has multiplied by a factor of a million, delivery speed by 50, and range by 5.

Both sides are now putting into operation second generation missiles. Because these use solid fuel, or storable liquid fuel, and are of smaller size and weight, they can be produced more rapidly. They are sheltered in underground structures, or, as in the case of the Polaris, on atomic powered submarines, or mounted on mobile vehicles, or on planes in the case of air-to-surface missiles. The new improved models are the push-button affairs dear to the hearts of science-fiction writers. They do not require complicated last-minute preparations and long countdowns, and can be fired almost instantaneously. The planners already have their minds on third generation missiles which will have the ability to maneuver defensively. The pace moves ever faster. Manned aircraft did not break the sound barrier in level flight until 1947. By 1953 they attained twice the speed of sound, and three years later, triple the speed of sound. This country has just lifted the veil of secrecy from its latest manned all-purpose plane, the YF-12A, successor to the U-2, which reportedly flies at more than three times the speed of sound, attains heights above twenty miles, and can traverse vast stretches of the earth's surface in a single swoop. The TFX supersonic fighter in production can deliver 10-megaton bomb loads over intercontinental reaches. We are experimenting with a rocket plane traveling so fast—four times the speed of sound—that the air friction causes the paint on the nose to blister.

Every weapon demands another weapon. There is no end within the arms system itself. There is no point at which the system gains stability and the scientists inform the politicos, "This is the end of the line." From the primary means of explosion, the race proceeds to the competition for delivery vehicles. The experts no longer work with weapons but with systems. It is not the rocket alone, but its gantries, its oxygen supply, its down-range checkpoints, its supporting net of observers and computer posts. The bombers called into being the Bomarc-B, whose nuclear-warheaded "birds" fly at three times the speed of sound. Thereupon the big bomber was equipped with Quail, a little decoy jet plane which emits electronic pulses to mix up Bomarc's circuits. The big bomber also has ground enemies: the huge radar monsters like Dew and Pinetree which probe for him with their great antennae through the fastnesses of the deep. To counter these tentacles comes Shrike, an antiradar missile which the bomber releases. Shrike flies down the radar beam to explode and blind the radar set. The bomber can also let go with its own powerful missile like the Hound Dog, a small automatic jet plane which carries a nuclear bomb and permits the bomber to hit the target while still out of Bomarc's range.

The ballistic missile may make the bomber obsolete. That merely redirects the race in another direction. The first fruits of our antimissile research have been the radar establishments in Turkey and on Shemya Island in the Aleutians. From these electronic sentinels evolved BMEWS, the ballistic missile early warning systems, which sight rockets 3,500 miles above the horizon and cover all the approaches from the north. The Russians, having built rockets powerful enough to come over the South Pole, our Air Force has its "spy in the sky," Midas, a satellite system equipped with delicate infrared sensors that will give early warning of enemy missile firings picked up from the red glow of the hot rocket jet. Our U-2 plane became obsolete after the Russians built a rocket that can shoot it down. To fill the gap, we came up with Samos, our other "spy in the sky," a large satellite that takes pictures as it orbits the earth, equipped to obtain strategic knowledge of Soviet military activities and target information.

The far future is equally entrancing. We can look forward to new and more complicated satellite systems like Bambi, armed with antimissile missiles to explode right over the launcher's territory, and for which study contracts have been awarded. The moon also offers many intriguing possibilities, and Dr. Edward Teller has told Congress that we absolutely must gain control of it "for our own safety." Then, since we and the Russians are setting aloft satellites of all sorts, we have no way of telling presently whether the Russians will destroy some of our satellites. Our Air Force is consequently working on Project Saint (renamed Program 621A after protests from religious groups—apparently to the name only), an antisatellite inspection system designed to fly near orbiting objects and to determine, by methods to be perfected, if they are armed or unarmed, if their intentions are scientific or martial.

The opening up of space leads to the possibility of throwing nuclear bombs at each other out there. Michael Golovine, director of a subsidiary of the British Hawker Siddeley Aviation, has suggested in his book *Conflict in Space* that America and Russia may attempt to resolve their deadlocked conflict on earth with a full-scale trial of strength in space, and that the side that lost its "orbital cover" would have only the choice of a suicidal attack or a surrender. The Buck Rogers kind of warfare, though, is still the music of the distant future, and will have to await, if it ever materializes, the production of armored spacecraft.

Nuclear explosives have tipped the military scale overwhelmingly to the side of the offense. Especially since, from the age of nuclear scarcity where the new bombs were thought too precious to use for any but the highest priority attacks, we have arrived at the age of nuclear plenty. They can be used for any purpose, large, medium, or insignificant, so far as the supply is concerned. And from clumsy and slow-delivery bombers we have advanced to missiles that cover enormous distances with unbelievable rapidity and frightening accuracy. It is conceivable, of course, that the ancient law of militarism will reassert itself, and some childlike scientific investigator, immured among his test tubes and charts, will come up with a fantastic defense device to checkmate and immobilize all the missiles, all the planes, and all the bombs. David Low, the British cartoonist, has written in his autobiography, "It is no more unreasonable to expect a counter to the H-bomb than it would have been fifty years ago to expect a rocket to the moon. Science will have new wonders in its task of reducing war to an absurdity. Having already perfected explosives that shiver the heaviest armor to fragments, and airplanes so fast as to make combat impossible, we may hope they will pass on to a magnetic force, perhaps, that will boomerang missiles so that they turn in flight and whistle back to where they came from." We may hope, sure. But there is little belief among the specialists that the defense can gain the upper hand. The direction of technological development rules it out for the discernible future.

We and the Russians are doing a lot of research on the antimissile

missile. Already a billion dollars has been spent by the Army on the Nike-Zeus, "the bullet to hit a bullet," and additional billions of dollars are being spent on researching the Nike-X system. The Russians experimented with the effect of neutron heating on nuclear warheads at high altitudes in their 1961 test series, and there have been reports that they have an operational antimissile system around Leningrad. Whether such a defense against the missile will ever be practical, no one knows, and most are skeptical. Many like Hans Bethe believe the decoy problem is insoluble in a mass attack. Even were the antimissile missile developed to the point of partial effectiveness, where it could destroy a big fraction of the incoming missiles, inevitable counterweapons—radars to jam, saturate, or spoof; cleverer decoys to confuse; warheads capable of altering course during flight—would cancel out the defense. Even were all these stupendous difficulties successfully overcome, the cost of sending up a number of missiles to knock out one incoming enemy missile, and of building massively both blast and fallout shelters to protect the defended population, would be economically prohibitive.

Ironically, it is the United States which ushered in the nuclear age of technology, and thereby, with its own strong right hand, destroyed its military hegemony. At the close of the second war, the great powers had advanced into the last generation of the age of air power. Had we left well enough alone and permitted the cold war to mature within this environment, this country, with its superior strategic air forces, its command of the seas, able to rest on an unrivaled industry, and shielded by the immense distances of two oceans, might have remained the overwhelming military power of the postwar world. In time Russia would have certainly acquired the long-range air power to challenge our supremacy, but the advantages would have continued with us for many years.

By introducing an entirely new weapon, by childishly imagining that we could hold it monopolistically for ourselves alone, we, in effect, discarded the prenuclear military establishment where we were invincible and started on a brand new arms race with Russia from scratch. We gave up a bird in the hand for what we thought was a juicier one in the bush. We had a solid precedent for our stupidity. Britain had done a similar thing a half century earlier. In 1907 she produced the Dreadnought, which was faster, had guns of greater power and range, and carried heavier armor than any previous battleship afloat. The admirals were in seventh heaven, and the British press boasted that the Dreadnought was capable of sinking the whole German navy. Germany thereupon promptly set to work copying the new weapon, and within a few years the newly built German navy had done to the 75 British pre-Dreadnought warships exactly what the British thought to do to the German fleet. Because of their overweening ambition, they had made obsolescent their own navy—the most awesome battle line the world had known up to that time.


IV


There are several major estimates as to the number that will die in the event of a full-blooded thermonuclear exchange. In one of the earlier studies the Federal Civil Defense Administration studied the effects of a hypothetical attack employing 250 nuclear weapons of 5, 10, and 20 megatons, having a combined yield of 2,500 megatons, on 144 areas on the 1950 population of 151 million. In their testimony before the Holifield Subcommittee on Radiation of the Joint Congressional Committee on Atomic Energy in the 1957 hearings, Dr. William W. Kellog and Mr. Charles Shafer, who made the study, figured that on the first day there will be 36 million dead and 57 million injured; that by the sixtieth day, there will be 72 million dead and 21 million injured. Presumably, 58 million will be free and clear.

The figures updated for our population of 190 million read:

|              | Dead        | Injured     | Uninjured   |
|--------------|-------------|-------------|-------------|
| First day    | 45+ million | 71+ million | 73+ million |
| Sixtieth day | 90+ million | 26+ million | 73+ million |

In his answer to questions at the hearings, Charles Shafer further explained: "In this particular exercise, we dealt only with the immediate survival problem. We did not take into account the soil contamination, the uptake of strontium 90, and the long-term problem that certainly would be very much with us from an attack of this magnitude. We did not take contamination of water into account."

In *1970 Without Arms Control,* the National Planning Association analysts pointed out that the figures were incomplete. "In addition to the figure which the FCDA has been able to calculate for the radioactive deaths which might be expected within two months of the hostilities, there will be an undetermined number of further casualties during the following fifty years, caused by genetic effects, tumor induction, and the like. It is likely that in the countries in which the bomb explosions occur, these delayed casualties will equal the immediate ones."

At the June, 1959, Holifield subcommittee hearings, a hypothetical attack on the United States was analyzed which has become the basis for all sorts of studies and strategies, where 263 weapons ranging from one to ten megatons and with a total yield of 1,446 megatons were dropped on 224 centers and targets. This attack, it was estimated, would produce 50 million deaths and 20 million serious casualties, destroy or damage half of all homes, and leave the remainder radioactive from two weeks to a year. In this study too the statistical results of those 50 million deaths and 20 million serious casualties were obtained by limiting the study solely to the effects from blast, direct thermal effects, and radiation, and by ignoring fire storms, a breakdown in communications, disruption of urban organization, genetic damage, ecological damage, disease epidemics, or ingestion of radioactive isotopes—akin to counting up the casualties on a battlefield and disregarding all those who were burned to death, or who starved to death, or perished from disease, in the course of the campaign. The computations of Eugene J. Quindlen of the Office of Civil Defense and Mobilization, who submitted the figures, did show, however, that a large area of the country would be made uninhabitable, and severe food, water, and housing shortages might well kill off most of the remaining population.

For that matter, the 1,446-megaton attack figure was disingenuous in the light of today's nuclear stockpiles. In a study presented at the same Congressional hearings, scientists of the Rand Corporation and researchers of the Institute for Defense Analysis edged closer to reality. According to the Rand-Everett-Pugh studies, a 4,000-megaton attack would kill 130 million; if the nation were substantially bedded down in shelters, the dead would number 72 million. Relying on the same studies, but viewing the extent of probable attack as far too low, Linus Pauling projected an attack on the United States of 10,000 megatons. Updating his data for a population of 190 million, the figures read: At the end of 60 days, 179½ million dead, 8½ million injured, 2 million uninjured except for some effects of radiation.

Has the enemy got that many weapons, and can he deliver them?

According to the semiofficial figure used by the scientists at the Sixth Pugwash Conference, the world nuclear stockpiles of actual weapons stood at the end of 1960 at 60,000 megatons TNT equivalent. If we key the major strategic weapons to the delivery abilities of the two major combatants in 1963-64, while arbitrarily disregarding the smaller planes, naval planes, intermediate and short-range missiles, and other weapons, we get the following rough estimates based on the report of the London Institute of Strategic Studies and *New York Times* dispatches:

|  | **United States** |  |  |
|---|---|---|---|
| Delivery System | Total Megatonage | Megatons Per Vehicle | Number of Vehicles |
| B-47 Bombers | 4,000 | 10 | 400 |
| B-52 and B-58 Bombers | 17,500 | 25 | 700 |
| Atlas and Titan Missiles | 1,000 | 5 | 200 |
| Minuteman | 600 | 1 | 600 |
| Polaris Submarines (16 with 16 Missiles each) | 128 | ½ | 16 |
| TOTAL | 23,228 |  |  |
|  | **USSR** |  |  |
| ICBMs | 5,000 | 25 | 200 |
| Long-range Bombers | 3,750 | 25 | 150 |
| Medium Bombers (capable of refueling) | 1,500 | 10 | 150 |
| Missile-carrying Submarines (10 Missiles each) | 200 | 1 | 20 |
| TOTAL | 10,450 |  |  |

Thus, the United States can hurl a 23,000-megaton load at the heads of the Russians, and the Russians a 10,000-megaton load at us. Which makes the game more even than it would appear, because the experts figure that since the populated part of Russia is a whole lot bigger than the continental United States, an attack on Russia must be made with twice as many bombs as an attack on the United States in order to kill the same fraction of people.

Can the stuff be delivered? If we assume that the perfected ground-to-air defense against the bomber has reduced the figure to 70 per cent of the fleets that will penetrate enemy territory, and that for the missiles the number of duds, misfirings, and those disabled by enemy action is very high so that the percentage that hit some kind of target is also no greater than 70 per cent, our strategic cross-continental command alone can deliver a 16,000-megaton bombardment on Russia, and be the beneficiaries of a 7,000-megaton reception ourselves. In the Second World War it was rare for the defender to impose a 10 per cent toll on attacking bombers. The Battle of Britain was won by less than that; ninety per cent or more of the bombers always got through. Now these percentages spell suicide.

In 1954 the United States Air Defense Command admitted that even "a 90 per cent effective defense might not be good enough to guarantee national survival," and estimated that 50 thermonuclear bombs "could be enough to paralyze the country, its industrial machine, and its will to go on fighting." Before the bombers were equipped with missiles to deliver their nuclear loads from distances of 500 miles away, and it was thought that the newfangled defense devices—jet interceptors equipped with tracking and fire control radar, and ground-to-air missiles—might destroy a greater percentage of the invading planes, the Chairman of the Joint Atomic Energy Committee gave this going estimate of the situation: "At best—and this is very optimistic—we might intercept as many as one out of every four Soviet bombers." All the opponent had to do was to deliver 50 thermonuclear bombs of 10- to 20-megaton strength to knock us out of the war, and he could probably do that by sending over a force of 70 planes. The fact that one hydrogen bomb is enough to knock out any city makes all defense problematical.

It took one *20-kiloton* atomic bomb to kill outright 100,000 people at Hiroshima. On the assumption that a one-megaton bomb is the size most likely to be delivered to most cities of 100,000 or more population, and using somewhat more comprehensive figures of delivery capability than those quoted here, Professor Seymour Melman came to the following conclusions in his pamphlet, *A Strategy for American Security:*

> For the 370 major cities of the Sino-Soviet bloc, the United States has an overkill capacity of 41 times, allowing for a 30 per cent attrition of delivery systems.
>
> For the 140 major cities of the Soviet Union, the United States overkill capacity is 78 times, even allowing for a 50 per cent attrition of carriers.
>
> For the 404 NATO area cities of 100,000 people or more, the Soviets could deliver about 9 megatons per 100,000 city people,

allowing for a 30 per cent attrition of delivery systems. This is an overkill capability of 450 times.

For the 192 United States cities of 100,000 or larger, U.S.S.R. medium-range vehicles are excluded and an attrition of 50 per cent is assumed. Yet the Soviets could deliver about 2.9 megatons per 100,000 city people—an overkill factor of 145 times.

People were at first concerned with how much damage we could do to the Russians and how much damage they could do to us. The question has obviously shifted to a more exotic plane. The question now is: How many times more can we kill the Russians than they can kill us?

At least in the grisly realm of obituary statistics, we seem to be edging toward an area of agreement. General David M. Shoup, testifying in January, 1963, before the House Appropriations Committee, stated: "I have said for the last two years that when the nuclear exchange of the magnitude that is possible occurs—and there will be even greater capability later—that we will have not millions but 700 to 800 million dead. Although I did not give him the figures, that is exactly the figures Khrushchev used in the past month." Even in the more conservative view adopted by Secretary of Defense McNamara in his testimony before the House Armed Services Committee at this same time, this was the best he was able to offer concerning the results of a tremendous nuclear exchange: "This is a question we have considered. And I can't answer it. . . . I think probably the fatalities in Western Europe would approach 90 million, the fatalities in the United States would approach 100 million, and the fatalities in the Soviet Union would approach 100 million. Now when you consider on the order of 300 million people dead in those areas, it is very difficult to conceive of what kind of military weapons would continue to exist . . . and of what benefit they would be to our nation at that point."

Let us break down the grand statistical totals into some of their component specifics.

A 10-megaton burst on a clear day at an altitude of three miles would raze by fire an area of 5,000 square miles. It would produce thermal radiation to ignite dry deciduous leaves at a distance of 25 miles, shredded newspapers at 35 miles, highly combustible material at 40 miles. The instantaneous emission of radiation would be lethal at distances up to two miles. The heat flash could produce third-degree burns to a distance of 20 miles, and second-degree burns to a distance of 25 miles. If it was a surface burst, the bomb would leave a crater 250 feet deep and a half-mile across. The area of devastation would be smaller, but the fallout would be very severe. Fallout is maximized with the ground burst; blast, with a low air burst; heat, with a high air burst. If the enemy chose to explode several bombs at various altitudes, the chances of anyone or anything surviving within the 5,000-mile radius would be close to zero. In clear weather the explosion of a medium-sized bomb would cause all persons within view of the fireball to look at it by uncontrollable reflex action. Even at a distance of 40 miles from the explosion, these people would go blind instantly, whether the fireball arose out of an air or ground burst. The Atomic Energy Commission has reported that the light intensity of the initial burst and the later fireball is sufficient to damage or destroy eyes in the direct line of sight up to 350 miles away. In a 1958 shot, the eyes of experimental rabbits were burned 370 miles away.

Harrison Brown and James Real have tried in *Community of Fear to* reconstruct what would happen to Los Angeles if the downtown area were struck by a 10-megaton warhead. They wrote:

> The blast effects would exterminate virtually all but the most deeply sheltered living things within a radius of five miles. Blast casualties would be severe up to a distance of ten miles. But the phenomenon that would complete the devastation of life in the entire area would be fire. The area would be one great sea of fire, which would burn until there was nothing more to consume. A good proportion of the metropolitan area's three and a half million cars and trucks would be lifted and thrown like grotesque Molotov cocktails, to spew flaming gasoline, oil, and automotive shrapnel onto and into everything in their paths. In an instant most underground gasoline and oil tanks would rupture and explode within the blast area, and a large proportion of the remainder within the fire storm area would follow, each in its own particular manner—pumps and pipes sheared, and finally, higher and higher ambient temperatures which would soon expand, rupture, and explode the remainder. . . .
>
> It seems safe to speculate that at least a 25-mile radius and an unknown distance beyond would be, within minutes, engulfed

in a suffocating fire storm that would persist for a long time. . . .
It seems clear that in the event of such an attack there would be
virtually no survivors of the blast and thermal effects, with the
possible exception of a few persons who had made elaborate
preparations for surviving the catastrophe. Their shelters would
have to be very deep and provided with a built-in oxygen supply
and cooling system. Unless they were able to maintain themselves
in such a shelter for many weeks, their chances of making their
way to relative safety would be slim.

A 100-page paper on the effects of a 20-megaton explosion in
midtown New York, prepared by Dr. Tom Stonier for the Scientists
Committee for Radiation Information, was presented to the New
York Academy of Sciences on November 13, 1961. Here are a few of
the important findings: The explosion could start at least one
million fires within the limits of New York City alone. The fire-
fighting forces would be unable to cope with the conflagrations, even
if some of them were still able to function. The unchecked fires
would probably coalesce to form a fire storm which would cover
a circular area from 30 to 50 miles across, or even more. Almost six
million out of eight million New Yorkers would have died within
the first few days, mostly from blast and heat. If the burst occurred
on a weekday when 900,000 commuters were in the city, the
figure would be correspondingly higher.

At distances of up to 27 miles from ground zero an individual
might receive third-degree burns; second-degree burns may be
suffered by persons up to 32 miles away. First-degree burns would
occur at 45 miles. Second- and third-degree burns received under
such circumstances could well be fatal. The bomb could totally
destroy ordinary unreinforced brick or wood-frame houses 10 miles
away; such homes 20 miles away would remain standing, but would
need major repairs. Some damage would be incurred by most
structures 50 miles or more away.

The report hesitated to set down the precise effects of fallout for
man's immediate and long-term survival, and on plant and animal
life, since there is much that is not known, and what little is known
is classified. At any rate, those who managed to live through blast,
heat, direct radiation, fire, and fallout, would have a good chance
to succumb to disease epidemics, hunger, chaos. In the postattack
environment, transportation would collapse, power would cease,

water supplies would be contaminated, large areas of land would be ruined by radioactivity, civil organization would break down.

Will this devil's spawn be used? Will not both sides try to limit the attacks in their own self-interest? The experience of two world wars and the current arms race is conclusive that if the big war starts, each side will in desperation and mounting ferocity not cease to wreak its vengeance on the other while it has one remaining bomb or warhead in its bins, and one last ounce of vehicular strength left in its system to throw it. The intransigence of the conflict between East and West guarantees that if the works erupt, both sides will proceed on the assumption that the loser will be wiped out literally as a nation and people. That the "winner" will have a happier fate, no one is bold enough to assure us. The only restraint on exhausting all the weapons will be the probability that before the nuclear stockpiles are all used, and the delivery vehicles all out of commission, both sides will have been reduced to a state of chaos and disability, that coordinated activity will no longer be possible, and that the survivors will have become wolfish bands of marauders and refugees.

Now all the estimates and figures are speculative. No one can predict the exact dimensions of the disaster of a nuclear war because no one can know what would be dropped where, and how much, what the winds would be, and other circumstances. And the scientists are not sure about many of the effects. Possibly half the population of the world would survive. Possibly a quarter. Possibly only small groups. Possibly, as *On the Beach* pictured it, no one at all. Whether man—if there are enough survivors left—can maintain himself on any level in the wake of such a war, after the existent balance of nature has been destroyed, or whether the rats and cockroaches and ants, who are less susceptible to radiation, may not complete the job that the H-bombs have started, is anybody's guess. What is clear is that neither the Americans nor the Russians would realize their ambitions. Clausewitz's rule about war being the continuation of politics would be negated the first day of the encounter. The means of annihilation would have triumphed over the ends of dubiety. Both the Western and the Communist ideologies would be as irrelevant to the living as is medicine to the dead.

On the most favorable hypothesis, both belligerent countries would be reduced to polluted junkheaps, and the world would consist of dazed populations, wracked by hunger and disease, incapable of maintaining the complicated mechanism of industrial society, rapidly sinking to more primitive states. When, after the holocaust, the chieftains of both sides meet in the seventh circle of lower hell, reserved for murderers, suicides, and destroyers of their own substance, none will point with military pride to a Pyrrhic victory. They will probably want to avoid the subject altogether.

## V

The overefficient progress of the art of mass butchery has put our government in a dilemma. The United States Constitution says that one of the main reasons for the government's existence is to provide for the common defense. Every military establishment has heretofore promised to protect its people from the enemy. And since in the mythology of states one's own military is invincible, it has always been patriotic and proper to assume that it was the other side that would get clobbered and bear the woes of defeat.

In our nuclear age, the government and the military have had one of the psychological props of war knocked from under them. The can no longer hold out the prospect of victory, or of even saving most of the population. Since no one in high office has proposed doing away with the war system, a natural response to the black disaster threatening to engulf us has been to hide, run, or burrow underground. An Orwellian world of horror and double-think necessarily required Kafkaesque plots of incomprehensible activities and lunatic assertions. If you could no longer save the population, at least you could save most of it. If you could no longer save most of it, at least you could save some part of it. If you could no longer save some part of it, at least you could save a fraction of it—and that was better than nothing.

Such was the origin of civil defense, an offspring of bewilderment and duplicity. After the Russians exploded an atomic bomb in 1949, and the possibility of an atomic war became a reality, Congress passed the Civil Defense Act. The first responses were still suffused with bright colors and optimistic sangfroid suitable to a nation that dominated the world militarily and had won every war in which it had engaged. We were going to provide our hard-working citizenry with blast shelters, perhaps a bit more elaborate than the air-raid shelters used in Germany and Britain in the Second World War. The reports on Hiroshima had pointed out that only a sixth of the deaths had been caused by radiation. Therefore, it was facilely assumed that if most of the people could be protected from the big explosion, we could come through not much worse than the Londoners came through their ordeal of fire.

Before anyone began to get serious about building blast shelters, or could start asking embarrassing questions about how populations would survive fire storms and other related horrors, the Russians set off a thermonuclear explosion, which destroyed, along with some of our easy self-confidence, the whole of the blast-shelter program. That started the evacuation cycle, which went on until the experimental missiles began to fly over the horizon, and which doctrine was embraced with the same light-mindedness with which we had previously adopted blast-shelter defense. On many highways leading out of cities, you can still see posters designating roads set aside for evacuation in case of enemy attack. In October, 1961, Representative Kastenmeier demanded of the Defense Department that the evacuation signs be removed from Wisconsin highways because they were confusing people. The year before, mystified residents in major cities received in the mails a map to use in the event of evacuation, accompanied with a detail of instructions, directions, and exhortations. In the years when the Evacuation Program was in vogue, local and regional organizations issued thick manuals to enlighten the denizens of our large cities, packed with humanity and choked with traffic jams, as to how, in the event of an attack warning, they were to hop in their cars and zoom away by the indicated routes.

Even before the coming of the big missiles it was never made clear where the millions of city folk were supposed to go, assuming they could get there. Where were a hundred million, or a hundred fifty million refugees, to be housed? How would they survive for weeks and possibly months? The July, 1960, report on civil defense, issued by the House Committee on Government Operations, said, "The evacuation policy led to a simple designation of exit routes and evacuation-reception areas. No plans were made for provisioning these areas with the basic supplies and equipment which would be required to sustain an evacuated population at

even the barest level of subsistence." It is easy to imagine the results had there actually been an attempt at mass evacuation. The
roads leading out of our metropolitan centers would have resembled
the Belgian roads leading into France after Waterloo.

With the coming of the long-range rocket, and the reduction of
anticipated warning to fifteen minutes, the evacuation bubble burst.
There remain some military intellectuals who continue to advocate
it, but they are talking about a different kind of evacuation. What
they are proposing is that if the Russians become provocative—in
other words, if they do what we don't want them to do—we will
proceed to clear out our cities and give the Russians an ultimatum
to stop doing what they are doing—or else. The clearing of the
population out of our cities will show them that we mean business, that we stand ready to shoot it out, if need be; it will make
our warning "credible," to use the jargon of the *cognoscenti*. Such
an evacuation does not really come under the heading of civil defense. Were it employed, it would have the same significance in
the world of the cold war as did the order for mobilization in the
world of 1914. It would probably be an opening gambit of a third
world war.

For the government planners, evacuation had become an untenable proposition, even though much of the civil defense bureaucracy
has continued to the present day to base its plans on evacuation,
out of inertia. The main line of policy consequently swung over to
fallout shelters. Beginning about 1958, Madison Avenue script writers, turned military architects, ground out copy on how, with a
pick and shovel and a couple of wood planks and some nails, every
home owner could construct his own serviceable little shelter, "to
save lives." The Gaither report strongly advocated a shelter program. Governor Nelson Rockefeller made it his special political
hobbyhorse. The glossy magazines, the newspapers, and the air
waves kept up a steady drumfire of warning and exhortation. But
all to no avail. The exhortations broke on the rock of mass indifference. The innate common sense, which the rank and file are
thought to possess, and very often do not, asserted itself in this case.

The saving grace about civil defense was that up until the
Kennedy Administration mounted its massive assault on the public mind, no one took it very seriously. The military chieftains were
not interested in it because they feared it might draw a lot of
money away from making planes and bombs, and might possibly
produce a Maginot mentality. For government decision-makers, civil

defense was a fifth wheel to the military chariot. It was left to the charge of former state governors who had been defeated for re-election and had been awarded the job for loyal party services. The personnel of the agency consisted of an assortment of minor bureaucrats and poltical hacks. It was, as Senator Stephen Young of Ohio called it, a "billion dollar boondoggle." It enabled local officials and aspirants for office to don steel helmets, stage exercises, put on martial airs, and get in their licks for coming election campaigns. It enabled political has-beens to belabor their fellow citizens with patriotic talk about survival, while drawing large salaries from the public treasury. Eisenhower, who had presided formally for eight years over civil defense and, for the last two years of his office, over the campaign to sell fallout shelters to the American people, said when he returned to his Gettysburg farm as a private citizen that if anyone asked him whether to build a shelter or not, he would not know what advice to give, and in any case, he had not built a shelter and was not going to.

There was one group, however, that took shelters with utmost seriousness and dedication—the military intellectuals. For them, it was an indispensable pillar of their games and strategies. Those that were wedded to the counterforce doctrine had to have shelters in order to give consistency to the theory of concentrating nuclear attacks on military targets, bypassing the cities, and ensuring that our system would "prevail" after the war. Those that were playing the limited deterrence field wanted shelters to give credibility to their deterrence, and insurance in case deterrence failed. But whether to "prevail" after a nuclear war, or to deter an enemy from striking or acting provocatively, they had all included it as a necessary prop in their strategic models.

They kept pounding away in reports and special articles; they berated and belabored government officials for their lack of foresight; they gave vent to scorn and righteous indignation concerning our people's emotional and intellectual immaturity. As a clincher, they fell back on the old but unbeatable argument that the enemy was doing what we were too foolish and complacent to do. As Rogers Cannell of the Stanford Research Institute warned us all a few years ago: "With Russian industry decentralized, with military targets empty of weapons, and cities empty of people, we would have difficulty inflicting a serious blow with our second-strike forces." In plain English, unless we were ready to undertake a spending program of $5 billion, or $10 billion, or $20 billion, or

$30 billion annually—depending on which expert we listened to—
we would be behind the eight ball. Our "second strike" would
lack targets; our deterrent would lack "credibility"—and the Russians could send over by wireless our marching orders.


## VI

After laboring in the wilderness for several years, the efforts of
the military intellectuals bore fruit when the Kennedy Administration, in the wake of the crisis over Berlin, decided to steal
Rockefeller's thunder, and to steel the American people for the
rigors of the nuclear age. Civil defense direction was taken out of
the hands of courthouse politicians and entrusted to live-wire administrators working under the Defense Department. An additional
$207 million was added to civil defense funds already voted by
Congress, to make a total of $306 million for the fiscal year 1962—
a 500 per cent increase over the amount allocated the year before.
And the power and prestige of the White House were put behind
the campaign.

The Administration experimented with two motifs, "insurance"
and "deterrence," to justify the campaign and interest the public.
According to the "insurance" theme, as explained by President
Kennedy, the strength and invulnerability of our retaliatory power,
and not shelters, will deter the enemy from attacking. But we
can never be sure what will happen. In the event of an irrational
attack, a miscalculation, an accidental war, shelters will be insurance to save millions of lives. While we trust the insurance will
never be needed, we could never forgive ourselves for foregoing it
in the event of catastrophe. According to the "deterrence" theme,
as explained by General Lemnitzer, "Any doubt in the mind of a
potential enemy with respect to his capability to deal us a decisive
blow makes less likely the possibility that he will initiate a nuclear
attack on us."

As a public relations proposition—and that is the way it seemed
to have been conceived—the campaign was a resounding success.
As a matter of fact, it was too much of a success, for it quickly
collapsed under the weight of the too great excitation it had
aroused. It was one thing during the Eisenhower era when the
pontifical warnings of civil defense politicos and the indignant denunciations of the civil defense critics were both lost in the sleepy

haze of Administration blandness and public apathy. But when President Kennedy got assertive about it, the hustling and bustling of the New Frontiersmen provoked an answering shout from non-government scientists and educators who proceeded to tear into a program that could not withstand critical examination.

At least there was a kind of lunatic logic to a Herman Kahn $200-billion shelter layout with caverns a thousand feet underground to take direct hits of bombs up to five megatons and near misses of larger bombs, and which would house an economic and indus-trial complex "to provide a base for rebuilding the country." In the Wagnerian netherworld where the science priests foregather to perform their voodoo rites, this made good sense in the context of a social order where to spend half of our national wealth for mili-tary preparations was the norm, where decision-makers rationally and sanely decided to go to war, and where, when all our major metropolitan areas were wiped off the surface of the earth, the village and farm population would rebuild the works in ten years and proceed to "lead normal and happy lives" in a postwar en-vironment which "would be more hostile to human life for some 10,000 years."

When this nightmare science out of the troglodytic caves was transposed into a politician program for fallout shelters in the American mass society, the result was bedlam. "The heart of the President's program," as Secretary of Defense McNamara described it at the August, 1961, hearings of the Military Operations Sub-committee of the Committee on Government Operations, was to provide fallout shelter for 50 million people by identifying, mark-ing, and stocking available space in existing buildings throughout the country. This was going to save 10 to 15 million lives. Where did the figures come from? It will be recalled that the 1959 Holi-field study had estimated that there would be 50 million dead in the event of a 1,446-megaton attack on 224 areas. Three-quarters of these would have resulted from blast and thermal effects, and the shelters would be of no help here. But the other quarter that were scheduled to die—12½ million people—could be saved by be-ing sheltered from fallout, and this, freely translated, added up to 10 to 15 million people. Holifield reminded McNamara that "this leaves, out of 185 million people in the total population, 170 mil-lion people subjected to the hazards of the attack. You are aware of that, naturally." To which the Secretary responded, "Well, it leaves only the 140 million, approximately, that are not in the shelter spaces, subject to the fallout hazard." Secretary McNamara got his 140 million figure by deducting the 30 million people who were positively going to die, so there was no point in including them in the computations.

Thus far, the program rested on three assumptions that ran from the shaky to the spurious. First, on shelter space. The Holifield committee had the year before reported that the "oft-repeated estimate that 25 per cent of the United States population can be sheltered in existing structures is not borne out by the pilot surveys," and concluded that "undue reliance on existing structures which afford only modest shielding creates an illusion of security and severely understates the magnitude of the civil defense requirements." The second assumption was even more arbitrary. The hypothetical 1,446-megaton attack was not a prediction, not an estimate, not a guess. It was just a figure pulled out of a hat and used for purposes of illustration, or orientation, or what have you. It could actually be predicted that a thermonuclear attack, whatever its exact dimensions, would not be that small, or anywhere near that small. The final assumption came out of counterforce theory, or enough of a bowdlerized version of counterforce theory to fit into the procrustean bed of a sideline fallout shelter program.

According to this theory, thermonuclear war will be very short, and civilian populations will not be important to the war effort once the war has started. The initial attack will therefore be directed at the weapons sites, not the cities. Both parties will fear that if the party of the first part attacks the other's cities and leaves his forces intact, then the party of the second part will retaliate with a return attack on the cities of the party of the first part, which will destroy his society. The implications of this counterforce theory will be considered later on; here it is sufficient to record that it was not much of a theoretical underpinning for an urban shelter program. It was a hoax to suggest that we could hole up in the cities because cities would not be prime targets in a war. It was impossible to separate populations from military targets, and everybody knew it.

Said Admiral Arleigh Burke to the Senate Armed Services Committee in April, 1961, "Many of these missile bases are right close to our cities, right close. So are many of our other bases. So an attack on our major bases would necessarily destroy a great many cities and a great many of our people. When these missiles start coming over you do not know whether the intent of the enemy was to hit or not to hit a city if he hits it. The same thing is true with the Russian military installations." Said General Thomas D. White, an Air Force advocate of counterforce, at the same committee hearings: "I cannot conceive of an all-out atomic war in which cities as well as bases are not going to be destroyed and subject to fallout." Our Secretary of Defense, who was in charge of the fallout shelters, thought no differently. The following exchange took place at the House Defense Appropriations Subcommittee hearings in the spring of 1962:

> REP. MINSHALL OF OHIO: Can you imagine any situation where the Soviets would attempt to spare our cities?
>
> SECRETARY MCNAMARA: I can imagine such a situation, yes. I am not suggesting that I think it highly probable.

The Air Force, which is the powerhouse of counterforce strategy, has not been, and is not, bothering to separate its missile bases from population centers. Neither is the Navy or Army. Titan missiles have been built in a complete ring around Tucson, Arizona. Plattsburg, New York, is ringed with missiles. Omaha, Nebraska, is Strategic Air Command headquarters. Charleston, South Carolina, is the Polaris home port. Plans call for the construction of 150 missile pads in New England, our densest concentration of population. Nike bases are built close to many of our major cities. According to Richard Fryklund of the *Washington Star,* a supporter of the Air Force line, "If the bomb alarm system said missiles also were falling on Brooklyn [New York City], Newport News, Washington, D.C., and Miami, we would still withhold our city force because the enemy might be going for navy bases and the Pentagon, or might be missing nearby air bases by more than had been expected." Clearly, counterforce theory is more potent in soliciting additional public funds for more "invulnerable" and "mobile" missile bases to build up a "second strike" than in resisting the claims of Congressmen who want installations built where their constituents need jobs, or the convenience of Air Force contractors who want missile bases built where there is a ready supply of skilled manpower and of materials, or the spiritual needs of Air Force officers who display a regrettable preference for stations within easy motoring distance of cities, bright lights, and night spots.

In any case, counterforce is not a game that can be played like solitaire. The Russians have to join in too, or the whole doctrine collapses. And the Russians publicly told us to go chase ourselves. Soviet Defense Minister Marshal Malinovsky made it very clear at the Twenty-second Communist Party Congress that in a nuclear war, targets would be enemy armed forces and installations, industrial and population centers, communications—everything that might contribute to the enemy's war strength. To lend emphasis to the potency of their posture of minimum-deterrence massive-retaliation—the threat to clobber us with everything they have—the Russians exploded a 60-megaton bomb and neatly placed 7 ICBM's on their target in the Pacific at a range of 7,000 miles.

No one doubts that they can rope up the monster warheads to their rockets. American rocketeers have calculated, based on the boosters that put Soviet spacemen in orbit, that they can make the rockets to loft 100-megaton warheads and get them on target. This escalation of weaponry makes invulnerable missile bases vulnerable. A 35-megaton bomb would tear up our 100-pound-per-square-inch missile sites now under construction. It makes previous calculations based on 5- to 10-megaton bomb falls on cities anachronistic. A 100-megaton air burst would burn to a cinder everything within 15,000 square miles. If our ability to destroy Russia was not enough deterrent against a nuclear attack, a public-relations shelter program was not going to salvage it. If war came, the fallout shelters would be largely academic. But we weren't listening to the Russians. We were listening to our computers.

It was on the plane of public relations, however, that the Kennedy program had its worst fall. The American people were not schooled in the mental gymnastics of our operational analysts. When they heard their President tell them that we must be ready to use force over Berlin, that the government was going to mark and store provisions in shelter spaces for 50 million people, and that all homeowners were urged to build shelters in their back-yards, they concluded that war was near and they had better get ready. With that, a wave of hysteria swept over the country, providing an inkling of the extent to which nuclearism has brutalized people, and giving us a slight foretaste of what things would be like in case of actual combat. It was given an especially ugly twist by the Administration's original unthinking emphasis. The initial pitch had consisted of free-enterprise, do-it-yourself, every-family-with-its-own-shelter-in-the-backyard. President Kennedy personally

endorsed a *Life* magazine layout which showed that life in a
family shelter could be adventurous and even glamorous.

According to *Life* magazine, never given to understating its
case, if each and every one of us took the necessary precautions
against fallout, only about 5 million—a mere 3 per cent—would die
in a nuclear attack. Dr. Willard F. Libby, whose own shelter
collapsed in a brushfire that swept the Los Angeles area, assured
the millions of readers of his series of articles, entitled "You Can
Survive Atomic Attack" and published in 400 newspapers throughout the nation, that 90 to 95 per cent of the population could
come through it if they built fallout shelters. *Newsweek* noted
that "The President's own eloquent statements about the duties
of every man to provide for his family—plus Khrushchev's trucu-
lence over Berlin—have vaporized as effectively as the latest Soviet
superbomb, the old foot-dragging indifference." Three-quarters of
the 30 million copies sent out, of the government pamphlet on how
to build a family fallout shelter, were shipped after the President's
July 25 television broadcast. The demand for another government
pamphlet, *Family Food Stockpile for Survival,* grew so great that
there were a million requests unfilled by the end of November.

The nation was not only responding with a vengeance, but in a
manner that quickly turned the enthusiasm of government officials
to ashes. We were preparing to fight a civil war among ourselves
within the larger war against the Russians. Without realizing what
they were about, the government planners, in pushing for the
family shelter, pushed a program that favored the rich over the
poor, the house dweller over the apartment dweller, the home
owner over the renter. When it was broadcast over the air waves
that it was up to every family to protect itself, the me-first-and-
devil-take-the-hindmost spirit was given full rein. A class and
regional struggle for survival was about to commence. The county
civil defense coordinator warned all citizens of Beaumont, a city
standing at the pass between Los Angeles and the Imperial Valley, to arm themselves with guns to repel the hundreds of thousands of refugees who would flee that way if Los Angeles was
bombed. The citizens of Nevada were equally quick to see the
danger and resolved that an armed militia was to seal off the
northeast route out of Los Angeles. In case of war, said the Nevada
civil defense head, they "would come into Nevada like a swarm
of locusts." A Chicago suburbanite told *Time* magazine reporters
that he planned to mount a machine gun in front of his shelter

and mow down those who tried to force their way in. In Hartford, citizens were advised to equip themselves with firearms in order to repel those who might be running around "like madmen" after an attack. A Jesuit priest gathered together all the threads of thought to generalize them into a creed of Christian brotherhood with his proclamation that self-defense was traditional Catholic morality, and that a person had a right to use violence to keep his unprotected neighbors from breaking their way into his family shelter.

The program to arouse the American public had obviously gotten out of hand. By the end of the year the Administration tried to forget the millions of words that had been rained on powerless heads, and to shift attention away from the trim, cozy family shelter to community shelters in schools, public and office buildings, dual-purpose structures, such as undergound garages that could be used as shelters in an emergency. The Administration also decided to damp down what had proven to be too ebullient and jarring an orchestration. In December the Deputy Secretary of Defense announced that less than $700 million was to be asked of Congress for the next year's civil defense, half of the estimated cost to stock and ready 20 million shelter spaces—only two-fifths of the original 50 million program. Of this money, moreover, not more than $500 million was to be for community shelters, and then to be spent only if others—schools, hospitals, other non-profit organizations—put up a third of the cost.

By the beginning of 1962, when the much-touted government booklet, *Fallout Protection, What to Know and Do About Nuclear Attack,* was issued, everything was being conducted *sotto voce.* The *Time-Life* Madison Avenue crowd that had been called in to write the original draft had been fired; their document, considered "too optimistic" in tone, had been discarded; after many rewritings, a final version described as "bland" had been approved. Now the other plans were dropped which called for a copy of the pamphlet to be mailed to every family, with a covering letter by the President, and for the President to address the nation on it over the television networks. The pamphlet was simply made available free at all post offices. By spring, as the war scare over Berlin died away, interest in civil defense faded.

The indifference was the more profound after the nation's anxieties and hopes had been excited and exploited to no purpose. The same legislators who the year before had voted millions practically out of hand, now quietly reversed themselves. When in July, 1962, the House Appropriations Subcommittee slashed the next year's request by almost four-fifths, the civil defense program was already buried under an avalanche of public reaction and the ridicule of independent scientists and investigators. The next year, civil defense took another jolt when the City Council of Portland, Oregon, which had been the first city to build an underground civil defense operations center, and had staged the largest population evacuation exercise, voted to drop the entire pretense. The Oregon legislature thereupon followed suit and abolished the state program. Senator Wayne Morse explained that the people of his state were "sadly disillusioned"; that when a typhoon had swept in off the Pacific Ocean in October, 1962, and paralyzed most of the state, the civil defense setup proved helpless and worthless.

Civil defense was back in its accustomed role of fifth wheel of the military carriage. That does not assure that there will not be other hysterical campaigns to go underground. Where the military mystique is concerned, there are few guidelines, and no rules. But the Kennedy fallout shelter program was overtaken by the same skepticism that has riddled all previous civil defense panaceas.


VII

If we were interested in a real shelter program, we would have to excavate huge caverns deep in the underlying rock. We would have to provide them with ventilation, fallout filters, food, sanitary and medical facilities, light, power, oxygen. It is probable that people would have to stay in them for months on end. If they managed to keep alive—and it is problematical that even such lavishly constructed and equipped underground cities could survive the fire storms, the burning heat, the radiation, the wreckage— millions of people would come up to find a shattered and poisoned world, and possibly an uninhabitable one. No one is willing to spend the kind of money that even a half-effective program would consume.

If one proceeds more or less on the assumption that thermonuclear war is inevitable, and wants to prepare for some kind— any kind—of survival, one has to discard the peripheral solutions. None of these bargain-basement programs can withstand scrutiny. What the more comprehending military planners are then driven

to are proposals to dismantle our present industrial civilization, and
to re-create a new one specifically and primarily designed to fight
a nuclear war, after which they hope to salvage enough pieces to
be able to rebuild something—just what, no one can be sure.

Nothing less will do than to build up a complete subeconomy
deep underground. This has already been adumbrated by the military intellectual avant-garde. But were we to proceed with this
scheme, it would be merely a question of time before we found
that there were not enough resources and personnel to keep two
economies going—one would have to be discarded. Were we to
steer our course by the light of the military metaphysics, there
would be no question as to which one that would be. With computing machines at our head, like tribal deities, and with para-
military physicists for our guides, the armies of industrial society
would be triumphantly headed for the caves and catacombs.

Harrison Brown and James Real, reading the unpropitious signs,
have projected this dismal future:

> If the arms race continues, as it probably will, its future pat-
> tern seems clear in broad outline. As a result of the emergence
> of the current tremendous capabilities for killing and destroying,
> programs will be started aimed at the evacuation of cities, the
> construction of fallout shelters in regions outside the major
> metropolitan areas, and the construction of limited underground
> shelters. Increased offensive capabilities will then emerge which
> will to some extent neutralize these efforts. Larger bombs will
> be compressed into sufficiently small packages to be carried by
> ICBM's. Very large bombs (about 1,000 megatons) will be built
> which, when exploded at an altitude of about 300 miles, could
> sear six Western states.
>
> The new developments will cause people to burrow more
> deeply into the ground. Factories will be built in caves, as will
> apartment houses and stores. Eventually human life will be un-
> derground, confronted by arsenals capable of destroying all life
> over the land areas of the earth. Deep under the ground people
> will be relatively safe—at least until such time as we learn how
> to make explosives capable of pulverizing the earth to great
> depths. . . . Tens of thousands of years ago our Mousterian and
> Aurignacian ancestors lived in caves. The vast knowledge which
> we have accumulated during the intervening millennia will have

brought us full cycle. The epic of man's journey upward into the light will have ended.

Withal, our industrial civilization is not headed for the underground. The plan will not be taken up. Not because of its whackiness; humanity has not shrunk away from equally insane notions, especially in recent times, and other circumstances being propitious, that might even be one of the sources of its appeal. Nor will this project be rejected because of its costliness or wastefulness; where military considerations can be dangled before our eyes, cost is no consideration; we love to waste. But the scheme cuts across the political and social realities. Even the military metaphysicians, who dwell in a tightly insulated world of their own fanatical creation, have had the vague premonition that nothing very much will come of this particular offspring. That is why the note of embitterment, as in plaints of rejected suitors, has crept into their writings.

Were we to entomb ourselves and our cities, we would be handing the prizes of the current world contest to our rivals without a struggle. We would guarantee our elimination as a world power while we were busily cutting into deep rock. Neither we nor others are free of psychosis, but it is psychosis of a special kind; it is psychosis moving along rigid lines of functional rationality. Hence, the underground brainstorm doesn't fit in. Since our adversaries have not become converted to the new doctrine, it would permit them to penetrate new territories above the ground while we were staking out our claims beneath the ground. The arms race will undoubtedly go on for years. Our generation will continue to live on the volcano's edge. If, as the climax of this race, we and our opposites blow ourselves to pieces, we can rest assured it will be done in strict accordance with the stylized rules of the suicide pact. We have this consolation, however. As George Steele and Paul Kircher assured us in a recent book, "If we lose and die, we are still much better off than the Communists. Forlorn atheists, the world is all they have. We have eternity."

THE mounting tension between us and Russia has been likened to the growing conflict between England and Germany before the First World War. Then, as now, there was a geometrically rising arms race; there was a proliferation of incidents, each one more hysterically pursued than the one preceding; there were the compulsive exhortations of patriots on both sides urging their governments to stand firm, to talk tough, and to give not a jot or tittle away. Whether war could be avoided was uncertain, the realists explained, but if there was any chance of avoiding it, only a stiff-necked implacability, and arming to the teeth, would deter the other side from aggression.

There is the surface similarity, and the symmetry of fanatical attitudes, self-righteous assumptions, and evangelical phrase-making. In retrospect, we can see that the Allied conflict with *Junker* Germany had mitigating features which the present cold war lacks. There was no ideological conflict with the Kaiser's Germany. The Western nations all had a common cultural tongue. The academic communities of both England and this country were beholden to German scholarship; they were frank admirers and often avowed disciples of the German schools of history and philosophy; promi-

nent and influential public personalities on both sides of the Atlantic visited with associates in Germany until almost the very
outbreak of the war, hobnobbed with members of the royal family
and military staffs, and returned with glowing accounts of German culture, German science, German industry, German organization, German discipline.

Once the war fevers began to rage, the fear of a competitor
was escalated into a pseudo-ideological fervor. We may recall that
during the war it was even prohibited to teach the German language or to play German music; and people with Germanic names
proceeded, in feeble gestures of self-defense, to anglicize them. But
the anger had a synthetic quality about it. Beneath the surface
ran an appreciation of the strong intellectual bonds between the
two sets of nations. Many continued to hope during the worst
days of embitterment that the break was temporary, and that
once the tragic war was over, amicable relations would be re-
established. If without substantial clashes of ideology, Anglo-
American hysteria against the Boche, the Hun, could reach the
heights that it did, we can fathom what fierce fires are stoking
the hatreds between the Western and Soviet worlds.

The present conflict is bedeviled by ideological antipathies and
intransigencies as well as imperial rivalries. From the day in 1917
the Bolsheviks set up a government over the territories of the
Czar, to the present, East and West have exhibited toward each
other a pronounced allergy. Relations have run the gamut of overt
hostility of the early twenties to the hypocritical cordiality during
the Second World War alliance. There have been a number of
adaptations on both sides, and as many attempts to temper the
dislikes, fears, and sensitivities. But throughout the forty-five-year
history, in days of forbearance and in days of wrath, neither the
Soviet nor the Free Enterprise stalwarts have modified their original view that the two systems were corrosive to each other's well-
being, and that at some point or other the rival system would
have to be denatured.

That such hostile states managed to sink their differences during
four years for the sake of a war alliance against naziism, which
both the British and Russians had only recently tried to appease,
will long be recorded as one of the anomalies of history. Only the
fear of a common enemy was the bond; the shared ideals were
not there. In the midst of the war, while the leaders of the three
Allied powers were toasting each other's health and assuring the

world of their everlasting friendship and mutuality of aims, suspicions, fears, and intrigues were never far below the surface. Stalin
was convinced that the long delay in opening up the Western
front was a plot to bleed Russia so that she could not participate
as an equal in the victory. Churchill, as is well known, campaigned
from 1943 on for military operations in the Balkans, and hoped
to invade Austria through the Ljubljana Gap to reach the Danube
valley ahead of Soviet forces. After he was frustrated in his major
design by American insistence on a cross-Channel invasion of the
continent, he continued to urge Eisenhower to move rapidly on to
Berlin. "I deem it highly important that we should shake hands
with the Russians as far east as possible," Churchill told him. In
the pursuit of this design, Churchill was not preoccupied with pet
military projects. He was trying to forestall postwar Soviet extension
into Europe.

The absence of common aims became painfully apparent the
moment sonorous generalities had to be translated into practical
terms. In theory, the three partners were committed to joint
decision-making within every European country, regardless whose
armies were occupying it. In fact, East and West kept each other
at arm's length. When the Anglo-American forces conquered Italy,
they ran things to suit themselves and kept Russia out of their
counsels. When Russia overran Rumania and Hungary, she followed the identical procedure. Stalin, whose thinking was heavily
weighted with old world power notions and *condottieri* predilections, assumed this was the tacit arrangement. It seemed to him
a piece of churlishness and bad faith for the Westerners to make
a moral issue of Poland after he had scrupulously carried out his
part of the bargain in turning over Greece to Britain, in telling
the Communists of Yugoslavia and China to accept subordinate
positions in coalition governments, and in giving his allies a free
hand in France, Italy, and Belgium.

The atom bomb, which was at first thought to destroy the
previous power balance and establish American hegemony, showed
that the marriage of convenience lacked not only affection—that
had been understood—but respect, as well. In the Oppenheimer
hearings of 1954, General Groves, head of the Manhattan Project,
when questioned about security regulations, testified: "I think it
important to state—I think it is well known—that there was never
from about two weeks from the time I took charge of the project
any illusion on my part but that Russia was the enemy and that

the project was conducted on that basis. I didn't go along with the attitude of the country as a whole that Russia was a gallant ally. I always had suspicions and the project was conducted on that basis. Of course, that was reported to the President."

On the eve of the atomic test, President Truman's first thought was about the Russians, not the Japanese. "If it explodes, as I think it will," he remarked, "I'll certainly have a hammer on those boys." His Secretary of State, James Byrnes, told one of the scientists that the bomb was needed to "make Russia manageable in Europe." Field Marshall Allanbrooke related in his diary Churchill's first spontaneous reaction: ". . . With his usual enthusiasm for anything new, he was letting himself be carried away by the very first and rather scanty reports of the first atomic explosion. He was already seeing himself capable of dominating all the Russian centers of industry and population without taking into account any of the connected problems, such as the delivery of the bomb, production of bombs, possibility of Russians also possessing such bombs, etc. He had at once painted a wonderful picture of himself as the sole possessor of these bombs, and capable of dumping them where he wished, thus all-powerful and capable of dictating to Stalin."

So the strange demiurge of human affairs, which pushes events in directions that neither kings or captains can foresee, directed that the atom bomb, initiated by European refugee scientists to defeat Hitler, was to be dropped instead on two Japanese cities. Then caught up in the mounting struggle between the erstwhile allies, the bomb became for the Anglo-American statesmen a weapon against Russian communism.

Not surprisingly, each side blamed the other for the bad relations. The West ascribed them to the paranoia of Russia's leaders, who needed to create the myth of a garrison country surrounded by ravening foes in order to justify their tyrannous regime over their own people. The Soviet rulers ascribed them to the rapacity of Western imperialism, and capitalism's inherent hatred of socialism. The explanations were at variance, but both parties affirmed the reality of the tension. And both explanations were right. Communism was a messianic movement of international dimensions, whose existence and activities tended to erode the foundations of the Western order. And the going creed of Wilsonism—which Walter Lippmann called American fundamentalism stretched into a universal order—was wont to identify American national interests

with the universal and eternal principles of the good society, and
to confuse the massing of American might against its rival with
a moral crusade to bring an international outlaw before the bar
of world justice.

## II

With the end of the war, public leaders in this country were
thinking in terms of an American Century. The temptation to do
so was irresistible. This country stood triumphant, unspent amidst
shattered enemies and exhausted allies—"the highest point of maj-
esty and power ever attained by any community since the fall of
the Roman Empire," Churchill had said. At Bretton Woods and
San Francisco we proceeded to lay down the lines for the new
world dispensation, sure of our destiny to exercise world leadership, and of our power to assert it where challenged. Russia, by
contrast, had emerged from the war with immense losses of blood
and treasure. By any reasonable calculation, she was an inferior
power that could either be forced into taking her assigned place
in the blueprinted world order, or could be pressed into changing
her government if her rulers proved recalcitrant.

George Kennan's "containment" thesis of July, 1947, was the
scholarly rationale of preponderant American estimation of the
power balance between our two nations, and of the perspective
we could reasonably hold for the immediate future. The West's
diplomatic campaign to undo the consequences of Russia's victory,
to push her out of Eastern Europe and back to her prewar frontiers, started almost with the conclusion of the war in Europe. It
has been pursued with greater or lesser vigor for a decade and a
half under a variety of reasonings, explanations, and expectations. In
the first optimistic days, it was pursued as a realistic short-term
goal. "A policy of firm containment, designed to confront the
Russians with unalterable counterforce at every point where they
show signs of encroaching" upon Western interests was going to
"promote tendencies which must eventually find their outlet in either
the breakup or the gradual mellowing of Soviet power." All this
could be confidently assumed and acted upon since Russia was "in
a certain sense an impotent nation." At that time Kennan was sure
"that Soviet power bears within it the seeds of its own decay, and
that the sprouting of these seeds is well advanced."

This was the American springtime of soaring visions. As with all springtimes, we were not only self-confident and conscious of our superb powers; we exaggerated them, and were unrealistic in what we could prudently project. The possession of the atom bomb gave us the "Jupiter complex," where the airman from the empyrean would deliver with his bolts of lightning godlike retribution on the forces of evil. Both we and Britain had rapidly disbanded our huge wartime establishments, all the while basking in the imagined superiority afforded us by the atom bomb. Our armed forces of twelve million had shrunk by 1948 to less than a million and a half, and Britain's five million to three-quarters of a million. Not that these were insignificant numbers. The combined forces were almost three times as large as those that England and America had on the eve of the Second World War. But Russia had not demobilized to the same extent. Of her wartime forces of twelve million, she kept five to six million. Lacking a strategic long-range air force, with no sizable surface navy, and with her army not up to Western standards in mobility, she sought to overcome inferiority in armor by superiority of mass.

The swift reduction of Allied military manpower has in later years been offered as a sure demonstration of the West's pacific intentions as contrasted to Soviet bellicosity. This is an oversimplification which ignores the rose-tinted spectacles through which Western governments viewed the world in those days. It was politically difficult, of course, for Britain and the United States, operating under democratic regimes, to maintain the swollen wartime armies. The political pressures for demobilization were considerable. American troops abroad became demoralized once the fighting had stopped, and the cry went up on all sides to get the boys back home. But before government officials yielded to populist *force majeure,* they had already succumbed to the seductive glitter of the atom bomb. It was thought that the slogging foot-soldier had become almost obsolescent, and that with the bomb alone the United States could dictate terms to any would-be challengers.

Not that our superior might was only in our heads. We had a strong edge. Our mammoth industrial plant, freed by the war from its straitjacket of the thirties, dominated the world markets. Our battle fleet of aircraft carriers commanded the seas. With our strategic air force, we could strike at the Russian heartland, and the Russians had no way of getting back directly at us. Bringing our superior weight to bear, we were able to press the Russians back at several points. Thus, in the Middle East, faced with a virtual ultimatum from President Truman, Russia pulled out of Iran, while Anglo-American oil interests entrenched themselves. In the center of Europe, the Potsdam arrangements broke down almost at once. Stalin was intent on squeezing out of prostrate Germany the full measure of reparations that the bond called for—which the Americans quickly became convinced was going to come out of their own pockets. In any case, the antithetic social aims of the two parties blew up all efforts to set up a unified rule. The West halted reparations, scrapped the Potsdam disabilities, and united its own zones into a West-oriented Germany. Stalin could only protest and counter by consolidating a puppet regime in the smaller and less important Eastern zone. But these two instances virtually exhaust the story of what America was able to do to restrain Russia. Aside from control of the Turkish straits, Russia's victory in the Second World War annulled the territorial consequences of the defeat of 1917, restored the geographical position held by the last Romanov, and realized the master plan of Czarist diplomacy which its secret agreements with the allies of 1914 were designed to effect. This the Soviet Bear was determined to hold, and neither threats, blandishments, nor warnings would make him budge.

As the truth of the stalemate sank into Western consciousness— that Stalin had neither belief nor trust in the Wilsonian vision, neither could he be persuaded nor pressured to go along with the message of Dumbarton Oaks—some Western leaders started toying with the idea of a preventive war, or of confronting Russia with a series of demands and diplomatic ploys, which would possibly lead to war. Churchill said, "The Western nations will be far more likely to reach a lasting settlement, without bloodshed, if they formulate their just demands while they have the atomic power and before the Russian Communists have got it too." To this day, one runs across statements of military and political writers in which it is reiterated that at least up to 1950 or thereabouts, the United States had the capability, had it chosen to exercise it, to impose its conditions, either by threatening to use the atom bomb against Russia, or the threat failing, to quickly knock her out militarily and topple Soviet rule. Is it really true that Stalin bluffed his way through in this difficult interim period? No one can be sure of the correct answer. Though there are coteries that have made a profession of venting bitter accusations at the powers that be for having missed a golden opportunity that may never return, the military issue was always in greater doubt, and the results far more unpredictable, than the enthusiasts for preventive war imagined. Wars have been on more than one occasion the graveyards of the doctrines with which they were started, and of the anticipations on which they were based.

The chance was most impressive during that fleeting moment at the end of the forties, or the beginning of the fifties, when this country had built up a stockpile of atom bombs, while the Soviet Union had either none or but a few, and the United States had the strategic air force and the nearby bases to deliver them on Russian cities and installations, as against Russia's lack of ability to strike with any effectiveness at us. But even when we had the upper hand, it is more than doubtful that American strategic bombing could have decided the issue. Despite the optimistic forecasts of extremists, official military thought in 1951 held that an all-out war would last from three to five years though initiated with atomic weapons. In the first years after World War II, the mainstay of the American bombing force was the slow piston-engined B-29, which could carry the heavy atom bombs of that period to an operational range of 1,600 miles. It was the late forties before the B-36, with its greater range, was introduced. We had only about eighteen Strategic Air Command bases in 1950, no warning system of any consequence by today's standards, and the Ground Observation Corps was still two years in the future. To counter our might, Russia already had in production the TU-4, a copy of our B-29; she had a first-class fighter plane, the MIG-15; and she had begun early after the war to invest heavily in warning systems and interceptors. Whether our base system could have long survived a Russian riposte was in the lap of the gods.

## III

What was Russia's theory? This cannot be deduced solely from her military doctrine, which, in Stalin's time, was a hopeless muddle. The need to square the repugnant reality of an Asiatic dictatorship with the libertarian rhetoric of the Marxian founding fathers and patron saints proved too heavy a burden for conscientious investigation and critical thought. The results were disastrous for her military theory no less than for her history or sociology. Russian military writing was reduced to barren quotation-mongering, sophomoric bragging, and schoolman sophistry. The inability of Soviet military writers to talk straight stemmed directly from the Stalinist mythology of the Russo-German war, fashioned by the need to conceal the weaknesses, derelictions, stupidities, and crimes of the regime.

The extraordinary Soviet performance in the latter part of the war diverted attention from her near collapse in the first two years. The tardy counteroffensives produced a final victory excessively costly in Russian treasure. The reasons for the disastrous Russian defeats which resulted in the German armies slicing their way to Rostov and the Don have never been satisfactorily explained. The Russian armies were as large as the German. True, they lacked the mobility of the Nazi Wehrmacht, but they were later able to win smashing victories despite that. The regime and general staff had been preparing presumably for just such an encounter for a decade and a half. Two questions consequently cried out for elucidation. Why did Stalin permit his armies to be surprised by Hitler? And why could they not stem the Nazi tide and halt the disorderly retreat for another two years?

The strategic surprise achieved by the German forces at the war's outset dealt an irreparable blow to Stalin's pretensions to generalship. How could he have been caught napping after he had been warned by Churchill, by Czechoslovak sources, and by his own espionage network, that the Germans were massing troops for an offensive in the East? Even without the specific warnings, such an eventuality was a distinct possibility in the military and political climate of that moment. It was a case of blindness brought on by oversuspicion, and overreliance on the diplomacy of trickery. His mind was so preoccupied apparently with the suspicion that England was intriguing to embroil him in a war with Germany that he ignored not only warnings from other governments, but the evidence reported by his own agents. The discipline and rigidity of a totalitarian regime then worked its worst to transform the obtuseness of one man into the obtuseness of a nation. Up to the last minute, he kept feeding Hitler with supplies and war materials. When Churchill, at one of the subsequent wartime conferences, asked Stalin why his warning had not been heeded, the latter could only reply lamely: "I thought I might gain another six months or so."

Even the original smashing blow is insufficient to account for the long period it took for the Soviet forces to rally their strength and take the counteroffensive. It is relevant to observe, though, that Stalin's cronies who were in the top military command, like Budenny and Voroshilov, proved incapable and were shunted aside as the war progressed. It was only when a new group of fighting officers emerged to take charge of military operations that the tide turned. To one degree or another, the blood purges of the thirties undoubtedly hobbled the Russian military establishment. Western general staffs at the time were inclined to discount Russian military effectiveness when they learned that the purges had swept away 3 out of the 5 marshals, 13 out of 15 army commanders, two-thirds of the corps commanders, all 11 Vice Commissars of war, 75 of the 80 members of the Supreme Military Council, 90 per cent of the generals; in total, about half of the entire officer corps. This internal bloodletting probably had a lot to do with the Russians suffering 4 million casualties in dead, wounded, and prisoners, the loss of two-thirds of their tanks and three-quarters of their aircraft, in the first few months of the war.*

Stalinist military doctrine was framed with the purpose of casting a discreet cloak of silence over this damning piece of history. It was designed to serve primarily political and propagandistic rather than military needs. In 1942 Stalin formulated the so-called immutable principles of war, termed the "permanently operating factors" which determine both its course and outcome. These highly touted novel principles turned out to be such unsensational matters as the stability of the rear, the army's morale, size, training, and equipment, the ability of the command. Since it was held that it was these "permanently operating factors," and not "transitory factors" like surprise or

---

* The publication in this country in 1963 of the authoritative Russian work, *Military Strategy* edited by Marshal V. D. Sokolovsky, gives added weight to this conclusion. The authors discreetly slip in the same explanation with this bit of bureaucratic jargon: "The Red Army had not enough trained cadres (particularly at the strategic level), which to a great extent was the result of repressions arising out of the cult of Stalin's personality."

The faults in organization and preparation added up to quite a list: the leaders badly miscalculated the time limit between the launching of hostilities and the actual commitment of the main mass of forces; they did not understand that large armored formations could pursue independent operations; they underestimated bombers and gave insufficient attention to their construction; their naval theory was antiquated and mistaken. Even where they had pioneered the concept of airborne troops for deep penetration and fast operation, they did not develop an air transport system to give weight to their theory. The authors come to this conclusion: "Despite the permanent threat of war, we did not have the necessary reserves of weapons and military equipment for the mobilization requirements of our armed forces."

blitz tactics that accounted for victory or defeat, and since by definition the Soviet regime was superior to any capitalist regime in the
enumerated virtues, it followed as inevitably as day follows night
that the Soviet Union was fated to come out eventually on top.

This may have been a morale booster during the war to the
sorely beleaguered Soviet masses, or it may have been accepted as a
species of gallows humor. Effective or not in steeling the Soviet
peoples for the implacable struggle, it did furnish a much needed
alibi, and switched the discussion after the war on to more favorable
ground for the regime. Stalin came up at a later date with a fanciful
pronouncement about "Parthian tactics" to weave the myth that the
1941–42 rout was not the chaotic affair that it was, but a carefully
executed withdrawal meticulously planned ahead of time by himself,
and designed from the first to exhaust the foe and ready him for the
well-aimed counterblow.

Stalin was always more interested in power than in doctrine, and
manipulated all doctrine as the rationale for his power. His new
great principles of war were no more than a schematization of the
unexceptionable Marxian postulate derived from the Napoleonic
era: that in contemporary war two sides pit against each other all
the material and spiritual forces of their people, that the war is a
contest in which all the strengths and weaknesses of the societies
remorselessly come into play, and war tactics and strategy are in
direct dependence upon the level of each country's economy and
culture. Where this had been viewed before as a sociological truism,
it was now propounded as a species of secret weapon or incantation
which only the Soviet leaders possessed, but which was denied to the
bourgeois militarists, and which consequently assured the final
victory of history's chosen people.

Even those who believe in absolute truths of war maintain that
the application of these truths has to be deduced on each occasion
from the circumstances—which are always different. The principles
of concentration, of the objective, of pursuit, of the offensive, of
security, of surprise, of the economy of force, do not contain a
single sure answer for a single decision in a single battle. A country
would be as well advised to hand over its military affairs to a staff
of medicinemen as to entrust them to a directorate which had no
greater resources with which to organize its establishment than these
immutable war principles. How then could a diffused sociological
proposition provide the nutriment for a military doctrine in the
nuclear age? It could not and did not. Soviet military writing in the

early postwar years remained a dreary, indigestible exegesis around its allegedly unique and superior principles and the West's fatal error in basing its calculations on the supremacy of any single weapon, which error flowed inevitably from a bourgeois strategy which could not count on the lasting morale of its society.

Western analysts read with stupefaction these bootless exercises, and could only conclude that the Russian militarists were preparing to fight the next war with the tools and ideas of the past one. But postwar Russia was not as hopelessly bogged down in dogma as its lacklustre writings made it appear. Stalinite Marxism has had always a considerable ritual quality about it, furnishing the rhetorical flashiness for policies empirically derived.

Stalin was fully cognizant of his weakness after the war, and of the special advantages that the atomic weapon bequeathed to the West. He set about methodically to overcome his weakness. The Soviet response was a combination of propaganda and redoubled technical effort to catch up. To its peoples at home and supporters abroad, the Soviet loud-speaker blared forth the reassuring news that the atom bomb was just another weapon. "The experience of the Second World War and the unsurpassed victories of the Red Army have clearly shown that success in war is not achieved by the one-sided development of one or the other weapon, but by the perfection of all arms and their skillful coordination." This proposition, enunciated in September, 1945, became the theme song of all subsequent orchestrations. A year later, the head man himself made the definitive pronouncement on the matter in his characteristic prose: "I do not consider the atomic bomb as such a serious force as several political groups incline to think it. Atomic bombs are intended to frighten people with weak nerves, but they cannot decide the outcome of a war since for this atomic bombs are completely insufficient."

While there was thus no need for panic, fear, or undue excitation, and the Soviet press assiduously maintained a matter-of-fact air of business as usual in its none too frequent discussions of atomic energy, Soviet leadership combined cunningly with this military stance a humanitarian propaganda to "ban the bomb" because it was so terrible. This fell on receptive ears. Throughout the non-European world the thought rankled that the new fearful weapon had been used by the white man against Asians, and the Russian pose as the champion of peace against the organizers of a new war got a sympathetic round of applause in the most far-flung quarters.

In the West there was also a lot of uneasiness that a new calamitous struggle was in the making. Consequently, the demand to ban, to outlaw, to do away, to destroy forever this fiendish device, earned its promoters sympathy and support, and by the same token built up a political atmosphere unfriendly to the employment of the weapon. Atom-bomb rattling became bad public relations.

But public sentiment is evanescent, changeable, subject to manipulation. Despite sporadic Soviet propaganda successes, peace sentiments swelled into political movements in only a few places, and even there, they formed but one strand of a confusing and conflicting mesh of attitudes and opinions. Stalin, an extraordinarily practical and cautious man, with little faith in ideas not directly backed by corporeal power, never put his main reliance on propaganda. The breaking of the American monopoly within four years makes it plain that immediately after the war, while propaganda hacks were deprecating the power of the new weapon, enormous resources were thrown into the fray to snatch the secret of the atom for Russia as well. The hard-bitten Kremlinites were well aware that bluff and bluster would not carry them too far or too long.

What about the fearful interim before Russia had produced the bomb? Was it just a matter of hanging on, talking tough, and hoping for the best? The Russians had a strategy going beyond the seminary dissertations on the "permanently operating factors." We know what it was in a general way. In the spring of 1947 the Soviet historian Eugene Tarlé described in a public lecture what a war between the United States and the U.S.S.R. would look like. As soon as the war started, he said, the Soviet Union would overrun Western Europe. The Red Army would meet little resistance, for one Frenchman in three was a Communist. The bombing of Moscow and Leningrad, or of Russian-occupied Europe, would settle nothing. The two sides would never be able to come to grips and would fall back on a war of nerves. The war would begin with the atom bomb but would not end with it, because American bombs could not eliminate the Russian army.

This was not an unreasonable strategy for a major war in the immediate postwar years. Given the geographical positions and equipment of both sides, and America's small number of atom bombs and limited delivery abilities, the Soviet Union could hope to overrun the continent, or as much of it as it wanted to, and knock out or immobilize Britain by a submarine war many times more destructive than the German one. When one senior Western officer was asked what kind of equipment the Russians would need in order to be able to reach the Pyrenees, he answered, "Shoes." The odds were in her favor that while sustaining bomb damage to her territories, she could stop the opponent from closing in for the death grapple. The two belligerents would be reduced to glaring and grimacing at each other across the ocean.


## IV

It took only a few years to puncture the chimeras of Kennan "containment," the "swift and condign punishment" of the Baruch Plan, the supreme illusion that the atom bomb had made it possible to fight an easy and irresistible war against another great power, or to manipulate the levers of history in a chaotic and revolutionary age. Despite the American monopoly of the atom bomb, the billions poured into China had not prevented the swift passage of that immense country under Communist control; the fierce fighting of the Korean War had done no more than to restore the *status quo ante;* the crackup of the Potsdam agreement had only frozen Europe into two hostile war camps. As the hopes for a postwar settlement went glimmering, both gladiators settled down in deadly earnest to the cold war.

America now thought to use her economic and technical superiority to construct a ring of military alliances and to amass formidable armaments and armed hosts to press her opponent into a position which her initial might had been insufficient to accomplish. Russia thought to catch up with her stronger rival, consolidate her own sphere, and to blow up the winds of history against her rival. Through all the successive phases of thrust and counterthrust, of diplomatic blackmail and arms buildup, both were to discover that the suicidal nature of the new weaponry made it unusable as a sanction of diplomacy or the basis of alliances. The nuclear arsenals paralyzed both sides even as it drove them deeper into the arms race, and made it impossible to formulate a coherent military strategy even as the armed forces became equipped with a superfluity of death-dealing devices.

Within a short time, the network of American alliances, what with the proliferation of pacts, presidential doctrines, and bilateral agreements, crisscrossed much of the globe except for those areas already locked inside the Soviet sphere. Never before had the world seen a coalition as extensive, as costly, and as bristling with arms. It cast into the shade the notorious coalitions of an earlier day with which Pitt tried to destroy Napoleon and which seem like an awesome collection of substantial regimes united in a common cause compared to the ragtag and bobtail that make up a disproportionate number of the clients and supplicants which we have assembled outside of Europe. Despite their bloodcurdling cries on behalf of freedom, many of our friends retain their primary loyalties for their private rackets. This motley and incongruous array of satellites, puppets, dependents, factions, tribes, cliques, military strong men, and adventurers on the make, is a military claim upon us rather than an augmentation of our armed strength. Politically, this coalition of rickety regimes is an encumbrance to our democratic protestations, and cuts across the main drift of nationalism sweeping through the Asian and African continents.

Our gimcrack diplomacy, which contrasts unfavorably with British Tory performance in the Napoleonic era, stems not from inferior talent but from changed circumstances. Pitt was operating from an inviolable island fortress blocked off by superior British sea power in a period which its contemporaries thought demonically revolutionary, but which, in comparison to ours, was feeble and parochial in its revolutionism. Even in the earlier, Republican part of his career, Napoleon could never incite revolutions in Italy or Prussia, and eventually the nationalist fevers that he induced were directed against him. The British were able to pour out their treasuries to the benefit of relatively responsible governments, who had the capability, by the standards of the day, to put impressive armies in the field. Our own statesmen labor in a cataclysmic epoch in which it is harder to find solid substance for their policies. The inviolability of Fortress America disappeared while two-thirds of the human race went into the throes of upheaval, with the dynamic for change directed against the past arrangements of the West. Hence, a good many of the alliances have the appearance of elaborate and expensive edifices set squarely on foundations of shifting sands. Through these alliances America secured far-flung bases to close the ring around Russia. But their military value has been fast decreasing in the frantic spiral of the arms race, and the political costs have long since offset their strictly logistic advantages.

However, the centerpiece of the military alliances is not our pact with Chiang Kai-shek or the Persian Shah, or with Turkey and Greece, but with the contingent of West European nations that are the substance of the North Atlantic Treaty Organization. Here are the old European powers that only a half century ago dominated the world, and after their recovery from the bloodletting of the war, make up again a series of strong industrial nations, rich in experience and skills, and with manpower and industrial complexes not far inferior to those commanded by Russia and her bloc satellites, and far superior when combined with the resources of the United States and Canada. NATO is a formidable military structure which must be reckoned with in any diplomatic and strategic calculation, and in a purely statistical comparison the West European nations might be thought the equal of their transatlantic partner.

The very lustre of NATO's real strength makes its impotence the more bewildering. NATO stands as a testimonial to the polarization of military strength to the two superpowers, and the inability of even an England or Germany to pursue an independent military course. It underlines how the nuclear bomb has sterilized militarism. In over a decade of existence, and after the expenditure of vast sums of money, NATO has been unable to push back the Soviet outposts of power by a square foot, or to lure any of the satellites into its own orbit, much less to erase the division of the continent. In the case of the one satellite country that left the Eastern bloc and became a neutral—Yugoslavia—it had nothing to do with NATO or its military buildup. It was due entirely to the internal developments within the Soviet bloc.

Neither has NATO been successful in formulating a coherent military doctrine. It cannot provide a satisfactory explanation of why it is in existence, and of what it is supposed to be doing. It continues to maintain and deploy considerable military forces on the vague assumption that as the years wear along, social changes will in some undefined fashion work to release the Soviet satellite countries from the Russian embrace, and NATO power-in-being will somehow permit the reassertion of Western power as of yore. In the meantime, the continent remains as divided as on the day of NATO's formation. Every twist and turn of the arms race sends NATO spinning into a new crisis of confidence, hastily papered over with a patina of rhetoric and patched up with parcels of arms sent over from America. With another revolution of the armaments wheel, the European powers scurry to a new round of anxious conferences, where they adopt yet another resounding strategy whose life tenure proves even shorter than that of its predecessor.

Every coalition has centrifugal tendencies, for within the common purpose of standing together against an opponent each member has his own aims, which at times are at cross purposes with the aims of other allies. It takes a certain amount of give-and-take to hold the thing together. But the members of military coalitions have a tradition, ruled by self-interest, of honoring their force commitments, and of clearly establishing the purpose of the alliance and their responsibilities and rights in it. NATO has blazed new trails for coalitions in muddle, cant, and duplicity. Nothing hangs together as it should.

Its declamatory purpose is to deter the Russian armies from sweeping westward, and in the event that they make the attempt, to defend every member of the alliance on the ground. It was in line with this that the United States made her offer to help the Europeans build up forces to required levels, figured at about a hundred divisions, for clearly we could not count on allies if the military balance of Europe was to be carried by our strategic air force, which could promise to liberate Europe only after its prior destruction by the enemy. Cutting across this declaratory aim is the general conviction that the main thrust of Russian policy lies outside of Europe, and that its military strength lends authority but does not supplant the political and ideological methods on which the Russians rely to effect penetration. There was a momentary fear at the start of the Korean War that the Russian armies might start marching, but it quickly passed when it became clear that the Korean War was a limited and local action. Consequently, premiers, defense ministers, generals, and admirals have ladled out with generous hands repeated and glowing tributes to the grand alliance but for whose existence Europe would long since have been overrun by the Eastern hordes. But their governments never get sufficiently exercised about the danger to build forces that could actually stop the Russian armies.

"But NATO," to quote Robert E. Osgood in *NATO: The Entangling Alliance,* "was not created to marshal military power, either in being or in potential, in order to deter an imminent attack on Europe. Like Russia's huge army, it was intended to provide political and psychological reinforcement in the continuing political warfare of the cold war. There was no significant fear of a massive Russian invasion." The European statesmen, not being credulous, or inclined to get carried away by the force of their own or Washington's rhetoric, never harbored misunderstandings on this score. That did not mitigate the contradictory pulls of the parties to the transaction. Ironically, Washington was transformed from the isolationist provincial who refused to become embroiled in old world quarrels into the rich and officious uncle goading, cajoling, threatening, begging, and bribing his lackadaisical nephews to show more militancy and make more sacrifices. The United States wanted NATO to be the instrument to redress the military imbalance on the continent. For the Europeans, NATO was the indispensable instrument to continue receiving American aid and to keep America bound to her European allies. The elaborate integrated structure of command and the ambitious strategic plans were more a matter of perpetuating a gigantic bluff and appeasing American pressures than the prerequisites for meeting urgent military requirements. At first, when American military supremacy was taken for granted, and her nuclear deterrent was a unilateral one, there seemed little urgency to match Russia's land armada. Afterward, when Russia entered the lists as a nuclear power, and the nuclear deterrent became a mutual one, it seemed futile.

V

By the end of 1953 the American leaders were in a high state of frustration, and an air of unreality hung over the Western military enterprise. Up to this time in history, nations had undertaken arms buildups on the scale that we started in the forties, either to go to war or to make irresistible their diplomatic demands. We were not doing the one, and our negotiations from strength were not getting us anywhere toward accomplishing the other. The vast rearmament from the time of the breakdown of the Baruch Plan had been for nought so far as redrawing the map of the world in our favor was concerned. Worse than that, while we were unable to push back Russia behind her prewar borders, Western power was continuing to crumble in Southeast Asia and the Near East.

The NATO effort ground to a halt at this time, as well. For a few years, while American help had been flowing freely into Europe, the governments seized the opportunity to rebuild their military machines for the broad NATO purposes, and to safeguard their own spheres of influence outside of Europe. Soon, the rearmament programs led to inflationary price increases of raw materials and balance of payments deficits, parliamentary oppositions became vocal in England and France, and the Dutch foreign minister warned the NATO Council that "any further lowering of the present living standard in Europe without the prospect of a rise in the near future will endanger the social peace on the home front which is so essential to our defense effort."

The European governments thereupon moved to reduce their swollen military budgets, and it was clear that the grandiose project that was approved, under American pressure, by the NATO Council at the 1952 meeting in Lisbon—for 96 divisions and 9,000 aircraft—was not soon destined to see the light of day. Since at this time NATO's 15 equipped divisions in Central Europe, stretching from the Swiss border to the mouth of the Ijssel, were facing a Russian and allied host ten times as strong, it was difficult to avoid the question of just how effectively the NATO divisions were guarding the gates of civilization.*

The theory that was adumbrated to explain NATO's military façade was that its armies were performing the function of a "trip wire" or of "plate glass." The fundamental deterrent against the Red hordes marching was the American strategic bomber force and the nuclear weapons. By challenging the Soviet armies on the ground, however, the *casus belli* would be dramatically established, and the alarm touched off to set the retaliatory forces into motion. Many military theories and plans are worthless because they are

* This does not mean that the Russian and satellite forces even a decade ago had ten times the manpower of the NATO forces. Western troop organization is exceedingly elaborate, bureaucratically overorganized, and wasteful. Liddell Hart, in *Deterrent or Defense,* has stated, "The present NATO-type divisions—a legacy of the last war's lavish standards—are so costly to equip that their number is restricted, so demanding in scale of supply that they would be easily paralyzed in nuclear warfare, so cumbersome in scale of road transport that they are unsuited either for nuclear or guerrilla conditions." According to Raymond Aron, *On War,* European rearmament "has set a record in cost and inefficiency; it would be difficult to imagine how more money could be spent for fewer weapons and weapons of more doubtful worth. The American division chosen as the standard for the European divisions represented an 'improved version' of the American division of 1944, with heavier tanks, more vehicles, and increased fire power, but also even more complex services and a smaller number of front-line troops in relation to the size of the division." The Soviet army raised 175 divisions from an approximate strength of 2½ million men, as against the 14 divisions that the United States raised from 870,000 men. The Soviet-and-satellite–West ratio of armed manpower for Europe in 1960 was less than 3 to 2, but Russia was able, using 1,770,000 of her own troops, to assign 120 divisions to the European theatre, while the Western powers, with 2,200,000 troops, earmarked 21 divisions for service under SHAPE (Supreme Headquarters, Allied Powers, Europe). This is also the view of Alastair Buchan in *NATO in the 1960's:* "There is probably less waste of resources in the Soviet defense effort than in that of the United States, and greater emphasis on the development and production of larger quantities of a few types of planes and other weapons than is the case within NATO."

impossible to put into practice in the turmoil and confusion of war. This one described the train of events on the hypothesis of a Russian invasion accurately enough, but it was deficient in common sense.

If that was the role of the NATO land forces, why could not border patrols, armed with nothing more expensive and complicated than regulation rifles, serve equally well? They could call on the invading armies to halt, and upon receiving a refusal, or their demand being rudely ignored, they could announce to the world that an invasion had started, and for the American retaliatory forces to please hurry over. At the most, the NATO forces would compel the aggressor to mobilize for the attack and thereby give advance warning to the nuclear retaliatory forces to get set. The same applied to deterring the Russians. The NATO forces were impressive enough to be provocative, but not large enough to halt a full-scale attack. This was understood even when the Lisbon program was being hailed by the government orators. The London *Times* commented that the NATO communiqué from the Lisbon conference was an unfortunate attempt at confusing military planning with political propaganda. The *Times* was convinced that the "imaginative" figures contained "the maximum amount of provocation with the minimum amount of deterrent effect," and would not impress the Russians.

The disarray of NATO's military position meant the unacknowledged abandonment of the "forward strategy" that had been adopted in 1950. At that time, Acheson told the Europeans that the price of continued American support was a rearmament of the Germans and their admission into NATO. Since the Germans would have no inducement to rearm if the consequence was to fight a war on German soil, the proposition was accompanied with the strategical plan to stop the Russians on the Eastern borders. This was part of the integrated design which included the dispatch of American troops to the continent, the setting up of a supreme headquarters headed by an American general to direct "balanced collective forces" for "integrated defense" of the North Atlantic area, and the buildup in Europe of indigenous land and air forces.

Three years later, France had not yet agreed to German participation; in England the desire to hold fast to American support was in uneasy balance with the fear of a new German ascendancy on the continent; and inside Germany the Adenauer government had to maneuver against popular opposition to rearmament. There was no

relation between NATO's military commitments and abilities—and
this was only one aspect of the dilemma that Western rearmament
had come to a dead end. The enormous outlays of money had not
shifted the power balance in our favor.

To get back on the high road, we adopted the strategy of the
"new look"—going off in the opposite directions of unlimited and
limited nuclear war at one and the same time—a strategic method
that was to become the rule rather than the exception in the age of
nuclear bewilderment. In October, 1953, President Eisenhower approved the decision to use both tactical and strategic nuclear weapons
against conventional attacks. On the basis of this decision, the
military budget was substantially reduced, and more of it was
allocated to enhancing our nuclear striking power at the further
expense of conventional arms and ground forces. Admiral Radford,
the Joint Chiefs of Staff chairman, announced that "atomic
weapons have virtually achieved conventional status within our
armed forces," and the way was cleared for Dulles's sensational
January, 1954, speech of "massive retaliation," where he propounded
the more important part of the new dispensation.

No longer would we meet local challenges with a defense confined to the area picked by the enemy; we would answer with
nuclear weapons, and not necessarily against the local authorities,
dupes, nationalist fanatics, civil war zealots, or allies of communism,
but against the instigators of the aggression, the original source of
the evil—we would "retaliate instantly, by means and at places of
our own choosing." In the Korean War, when the chips were down,
we had not believed it possible to use the atomic bomb when Russia
could not have had more than a few in its arsenal, and we shrank
from bombing enemy bases in Manchuria lest they retaliate by
bombing Japan or our aircraft carriers or supply ports. Now we had
disenthralled ourselves. Henceforth, the leaders of communism were
on notice that every local disturbance, every civil war, every dislocation, every attempt to aid allies or ship arms to purchasers
abroad who meant to use them for less than pacific purposes, could
mean stern retribution of retaliatory nuclear annihilation at whatever source we deemed proper.

It was a fearful warning, and the next two years were very
dangerous ones, although the doctrine of massive retaliation was not
as new as Dulles made it out to be. It had been implicitly our basic
military punch from the end of the war, and had been the governing
principle of the Air Force—the pampered darling of our postwar

military establishment. With the Dulles pronouncement, we simply threw all our eggs into the nuclear basket. When Robert Oppenheimer came to the realization that to bank everything on nuclear immolation was to paralyze military strategy, and advocated getting war back to the battlefield, the Air Force, utilizing the McCarthyite techniques prevalent at the time, set afoot the intrigue to disgrace him. The Administration got behind its military martinets, and drove home the lesson to any other scientists who might have big ideas: Supply us with the information we ask for, and work out the techniques we require; but don't meddle with high policy. That is not your province.

In the ensuing debate over the correct party line, Dulles gave the appearance of bowing to some criticisms that massive retaliation harbored within itself the danger of spiraling every incidental squabble into a nuclear world war, that because the President would hesitate to risk everything on secondary conflicts, it might make it harder, not easier, to stamp out local disturbances. We continued nevertheless to threaten massive retaliation with atomic and hydrogen bombs, and stripped other services to the benefit of an enlarged Air Force. This all-or-nothing strategy was close to the heart of our national thought. It fell in with our penchant for simplistic solutions. It offered an easy-to-understand, sure-fire way to halt the disintegration of a familiar world. It pushed to the fore our strong suit of letting the machine rather than the man carry the brunt of the burden. It appeased our resentment against evil, ill-disposed men abroad, but for whose sinful ways the world would have gratefully accepted our own values and leadership. It fed our self-righteous hunger for playing the world umpire. And to top off these advantages, it promised to save money. A bigger bang for the buck! Who could resist it?

Unfortunately, Dulles's war of nerves was more successful in frightening our allies than our adversaries. In an era of unprecedented upheavals, a strategy which would expand any local challenge or commotion in any part of the world, no matter what its cause or who its participants might be, into a nuclear war that was likely to incinerate Europe held little appeal for the Europeans. By 1954 it was not credible even for the United States, because our territory was no longer a privileged sanctuary. In the summer of 1953 the Russians had exploded a thermonuclear device of a more advanced design than we had at the time. And just a few months after Dulles's broadside, Soviet Bison jet bombers, corresponding to our

B-52's, and Badger medium bombers, corresponding to our B-47's, demonstratively flew over Red Square. The realization dawned that "massive retaliation" was a two-way proposition. Even while he was approving the "new look," Eisenhower sadly announced that "our former unique physical security has almost totally disappeared before the long-range bomber and the destructive power of a single bomb. . . . In its wake we see only sudden and mass destruction, erasure of cities, the possible doom of every nation and society. . . . The Soviets now have the capability of attack on us, and such capability will increase with the passage of time."

As critics had foretold, when confronted with an actual decision, the United States backed off from its threat of massive retaliation—although Dulles and many of our militarists had the courage of their convictions, and wanted to go through with it to the bitter end. The United States rejected French requests and the proposals of Dulles and Radford in 1954 to use nuclear bombs at Dien Bien Phu when the French were facing defeat in the Indochina war. The next year, the President supported General Ridgeway against the other chiefs of staff in opposing the use of nuclear weapons to defend Quemoy and Matsu off the China coast. Several years later, when we landed troops in Lebanon, the Army was not even permitted to bring an Honest John ashore.

A 1959 study on developments in military technology prepared for the Senate Foreign Relations Committee by a Johns Hopkins University group, made this appraisal of the changed balance: "Soviet counterdeterrence began to affect the actions of the United States and its allies. . . . Britain and France appear to have taken Khrushchev's Suez 'bomb rattling' seriously, and the United States might not have disavowed any intention of intervening in the Hungarian revolt as categorically as it did had Soviet nuclear strength remained at its 1953 level. Faced with the damage this nation might suffer in the course of a 'punitive' strike against an opponent who was himself capable of massive retaliation, the United States strategy of nuclear deterrence began to disclose its limitations."

"MASSIVE retaliation" convinced many that the militarists had lost their bearings, and if left in control, would lead the nations down the road to perdition. Those who feared that the threat would lead to action saw the strategy as one of mutual suicide. Those who were convinced that the threat could not be carried out saw the strategy as ineffectual bluff, requiring a voracious military establishment which was immobilized by the preposterousness of its own vehicles of violence.

Liddell Hart, Britain's foremost military analyst, wrote in an article for the March 3, 1956, *Saturday Review*, "The time has come to ask whether the military men who are advising our governments about defense are giving good advice—or whether our governments are justified in following it." He recalled Clemenceau's aphorism that war is too serious a business to be left to the generals, and he thought it had to be used again because the military men had not adjusted their thinking to new conditions. The very constitution of the military hierarchy, with military chiefs, who are promoted in one great emergency, staying on for a long time, ossifies the establishment. He recalled how the British generals in the First World War resisted the machine gun and tank, and the admirals opposed the convoy system, until Lloyd George forced their hand. The long addiction to the big bomb, of which Eisenhower's "new look" was little more than a return to the unalloyed theories of 1945, was a recrudescence of the same kind of military astigmatism. American declarations sounded as though we were saying in effect: "If the Communists tread on our toes, we must immediately commit suicide by blowing ourselves up along with them."

Military writers on both sides of the Atlantic, aware of the cogency of the criticism, felt called upon to reestablish a relevant military doctrine. It was in an attempt to work their way out of the existing cul-de-sac that they devised a theory of limited war. The British admiral, Anthony Buzzard, was the most forceful and prolific advocate of something called "graduated deterrence," an attempt to find a middle-of-the-road haven of atomic safety between the Scylla of thermonuclear annihilation, and the Charybdis of slow strangulation. He accepted the growing opinion of the time that hydrogen bomb warfare to stop a local aggression was suicidal. Its unthinkability, however, left an enemy with the conviction that piecemeal aggression could be committed with impunity. On the other hand, the return to conventional warfare was excluded because it would necessitate matching the East man for man, and this, for reasons too difficult to follow, was held to be impractical since it was claimed that it would economically bankrupt the West, or in another argument, leave the West open to nuclear blackmail. The intermediate and judicious course was to make the punishment fit the crime: to counter aggression with just the right dose of tactical atomic bombs and shells, no more and no less, to make the enemy abandon his wicked purposes and return to the ways of virtue, or at least, abandon the ways of vice. "The foreign policy of the West," declared Buzzard, "seems therefore to require a defense policy which, while continuing to maintain the deterrent against deliberate world war, can also provide the local tactical strength necessary to negotiate from local strength, to deter limited Communist aggression, and to deal with the local nationalistic quarrels of third parties." (*World Politics,* January, 1956.)

The discussion was taken up in this country, and the limited-war concept was given its most comprehensive theoretical gloss by Henry Kissinger. In the British atmosphere, the new doctrine appeared as an attempt to ease matters and to supplement the thermonuclear stalemate with an atomic stalemate. Buzzard even suggested that graduated deterrence would lead to ultimate disarmament. Once the idea had traveled across the ocean and found an abode in our more forbidding climate, limited war abruptly dropped its benign mien, and tried to hire itself out as a more effective gladiator for the cold-war battlefields. Where the British emphasized the deterrent aspect of tactical atomic-war doctrine, Kissinger and others stressed our advantages in the tactical atomic battle.

By fighting only for specific political objectives, by trying to affect rather than to crush the opponent's will, by meting out only graduated amounts of destruction for limited aims, we would all but seduce him to acquiesce in our plans, since we would "make the conditions to be imposed seem more attractive than continued resistance." Our opponent was going to have to dance to our tune, he was going to have to fight local actions on our terms, and if things went beyond a local war, we would shift the onus and the risk for that to the other side.

Kissinger waxed increasingly lyrical about the theory he had devised, or borrowed, as he explored the hidden beauties of its many unsuspected surfaces. He saw in his mind's eye a return to the stylized contests of the feudal period, with military operations conducted in stages, and time taken out chivalrously by both sides to evaluate the results before it was decided to begin the next engagement, or to initiate parleys to consider the advisability of a settlement. The tables were triumphantly turned, and instead of the Soviets nibbling us to death, as Vice President Nixon had phrased it, we were going to nibble them to death.

It seemed to the apostles of the new doctrine that we had trapped our opponents: they could not expand the conflict without courting extinction; and if they fought in a limited way, as we wanted them to, we were sure to win. Why were we sure to win? Because our sophisticated and diversified tactical atomic arsenal would more than cancel out Soviet manpower advantages, while their inferior industry could not compete with ours. Warming to his theme at this point, and exposing in the process the ideological underpinnings of his technical assumptions, Kissinger insisted that the introduction of nuclear weapons on the battlefield would utterly disrupt Soviet reliance on massed manpower. In a limited nuclear war everything depends on leadership, daring, personal initiative, and mechanical aptitude. Since this is where we shine, whereas "a society like that of the Soviet Union, in which everything is done according to plan and by government direction, will have extraordinary difficulty inculcating these qualities," all the advantages will be with us. The grand conclusion of *Nuclear Weapons and Foreign Policy:* "Limited war and the diplomacy appropriate to it provide a means to escape from the sterility of the quest for absolute peace."

The new doctrine seemed like a godsend in many military quarters; it promised to dispose of a number of pesky birds with the one stone. It was by now clear that the banquet speeches of European government heads did not correspond to their genuine appraisals, that the affectionate back-slapping and solemn vows of undying solidarity periodically exchanged between American and European politicians were not unalloyed gold on either side. America, while goading the Europeans to accelerate their military efforts and to submit their forces to an integrated leadership, kept her hands gently pressed around her allies' throats by keeping in her own hands control of the nuclear warhead, and by refusing to share her nuclear technology. Our allies, for their part, pursued a policy of calculated inertia, which made it apparent that the original NATO blueprint for redressing the military imbalance on the continent could not be realized, and that the American military contingents on the continent, sent to stimulate the grand rearmament, had to remain to cement an alliance that kept coming apart.

In this situation, it was inevitable that the American concentration on the nuclear strike would become the model for the NATO planners. If the richest and most powerful ally was relying more on nuclear deterrence and less on ground resistance in order to bring economic and military needs into "realistic focus," the less affluent Europeans reasoned that the same rule applied with even more justification to themselves. Tactical atomic weapons seemed to be the cheap and easy mechanical substitute for socially inconvenient conventional armies, and the theory of limited atomic war the magical solution to dissolve away hitherto intractable difficulties.


II


Military doctrines are supposed to be arrived at dispassionately, impersonally, scientifically—that is the myth. Actually, as in other social matters, political tug-of-war, the sway of public opinion, the pressure of influential people, and just plain chance play their part in deciding the issue. In the postwar age, the technological revolution had become self-propulsive, and the military doctrines inevitably followed the military weapons. The scientists and engineers first came up with the new arsenals, and then the theorists tried to figure out some justification for them.

The appeal of the limited-war doctrine was strong because it seemed to supply an answer for a gigantic military establishment which no longer knew how to use its weaponry, and to reinvigorate an alliance which was unsure of its image. What made it more than an academic exercise, or declaratory public relations, was the prior decision, taken pell-mell, without thought or realization of consequences, to make the Western armies dependent on atomic weapons. Consequently, even if the theory could not withstand examination, the argument was persuasive that the die had already been cast, that the armies could fight no other kind of war in any case, and that we might as well make the best of an irreversible decision.

Here, too, the idea of getting a bigger bang for the buck, of letting the machines do the roughhouse work of mowing down the Red hordes, was seductive. The idea was so much in the air that the decision had been tacitly assumed in many quarters in the West before any of the new weapons were available. In February, 1953, General Sir Richard Gale, commander of the allied Northern Army Group in West Germany, revealed that in anticipation that atomic weapons might become available, the forces under his command were being trained for atomic warfare. In October the first gigantic 85-ton, 280 mm. atomic artillery piece was shipped to Europe, to be followed the next year by maneuverable rockets and missiles, Honest John, Corporal, Matador, and Regulus. In June, 1954, Congressman Sterling Cole, chairman of the Joint Committee on Atomic Energy, declared that "tactical atomic weapons may confront the Red army with an impossible operational dilemma. The conventional NATO defenses are already of such strength that the Soviets could not penetrate them without first massing their ground forces in preparation for a breakthrough. Once the legions of the Red army are so concentrated, they expose themselves to the mortal peril of counterattack by nuclear weapons."

In August SHAPE circulated a plan for reorganizing NATO forces to compensate by atomic power for the reduction of ground forces, and in a subsequent interview, General Alfred Gruenther, the NATO supreme commander, explained, "We have determined that our strategy in the center requires the use of atomic weapons, whether the enemy uses them or not, and we must use atomic bombs to redress the imbalance between their forces and ours." Finally,

Field Marshal Montgomery, the deputy supreme commander, announced in a widely quoted lecture in November: "I want to make it absolutely clear that we at SHAPE are basing all our operational planning on using atomic and thermonuclear weapons in our own defense. With us it is no longer: 'They may possibly be used.' It is very definitely: 'They will be used, if we are attacked.' "

The generals, having been handed the weapons, hastily improvised a strategy to use them. After that, the political leaders assembled in solemn conclave in December, 1954, to authorize the military commanders to do what they had publicly announced they were already doing. Then came the theorists, bringing up the rear, to devise a rationale for the strategy, and to impart to a series of tropistic impulses and light-minded plunges the pretence of foresight and reasonable thought.

Dulles experimented with limited-war ideas or, at least, jargon, in the years following his "massive retaliation" speech, and judging by the article he published in the October, 1957, issue of *Foreign Affairs,* he at this time became a full convert. Heretofore, he explained, we and our allies had to rely on a deterrent strategy based on our massed nuclear power. It was a concept acceptable only as a last alternative, and there was no other. "But the resourcefulness of those who serve our nation in the field of science and weapon engineering now shows that it is possible to alter the character of nuclear weapons. It seems now that their use need not involve vast destruction and widespread harm to humanity. Recent tests point to the possibility of possessing nuclear weapons the destruction and radiation effects of which can be confined substantially to predetermined targets. In the future it may thus be feasible to place less reliance upon deterrence of vast retaliatory power. It may be possible to defend countries by nuclear weapons so mobile, or so placed, as to make military invasion with conventional forces a hazardous attempt."

The new revelation had an even shorter existence than the one it had been designed to supplant. Like a flashing star whose light shines most piercingly upon us when it has already ceased to exist, the limited-war discussion reached its highest point of intensity in the popular press when the proposition was already dead as seriously conceived military policy. One could paint in the privacy of a studio or library near-pastoral scenes of chivalric armies gracefully tossing tiny jeweled atomic bombs and shells at each other, followed by withdrawal movements to permit the umpires to chalk up the results

—but it looked different on the battlefield. What were these precise, discriminate tactical atomic weapons which one could pinpoint on targets? Kissinger opined that weapons could be limited to 500 kilotons. Five-hundred kilotons! Was he serious? It was unnecessary to have any vast military experience to see through the burlesque, the more farcical because it was so portentously offered and so solemnly intended. A 500-kiloton weapon was twenty-five times more devastating than the Hiroshima bomb. How long would anything be limited, or anybody be left, when pineapples like these began to fly around?

Thomas Murray, former Atomic Energy Commissioner, pointed out that there are no really small discriminating weapons. Even a 2-kiloton weapon shot from a Davy Crockett recoilless projector has two hundred times the explosive force of the largest conventional bombs of the Second World War, which were used strategically against cities, not on the battlefield. Four of these tiny shots are equal to the total bombardment which wiped out Hamburg. "To believe," said Lord Tedder, wartime head of the British Air Force, "that there will be tactical atomic weapons which could be used without leading to the use of the ultimate so-called strategic weapon ... would be to live in a fool's paradise." Vice Admiral Brown told the National Press Club in Washington that he had no faith in any so-called controlled use of atomic weapons. "I would not recommend the use of any atomic weapon, no matter how small, when both sides have the power to destroy the world."

This had all been established before the limited-war discussion was taken up by the university and foundation warriors. In the late autumn of 1955, the United States Army and Air Force carried out a joint exercise, called Sage Brush, in Louisiana and neighboring states. After 70 "Hiroshima" bombs were dropped on Louisiana in one day, the umpires ruled that all life "had ceased to exist" in the state. Hanson Baldwin, the *New York Times* military analyst, drew apocalyptic conclusions from the practice battle in which a theoretical total of 275 nuclear weapons, ranging in power from 2 kilotons to more than 40 kilotons had been expended. He wrote: "The biggest lesson of Exercise Sage Brush is that there probably can be no such thing as a limited or purely tactical nuclear war. ... If Sage Brush had been actual instead of simulated, it is safe to say that much of the 12-state area would have been partially destroyed and the surviving inhabitants menaced by radioactivity." Carte Blanche, the war game organized by SHAPE in West Germany, the Lowlands, and northeastern France in June, 1955, also had horrendous results, and although the published figures of the number of simulated deaths and wounded were considered by military commentators as fictions designed to reassure the public, they had the opposite effect of panicking European public opinion.

There were other flaws in the theory aside from the impossibility of drawing a practical distinction between strategic and tactical nuclear war. Upon scrutiny, our supposed advantage in waging this particular kind of war turned to ashes. Our lead in small nuclear weapons was a passing one. The Russians would soon match us bomb for bomb, and shell for shell. (As a matter of fact, whether because they were impressed by some of the boasts and threats of the NATO statesmen about the superior Western battlefield tactics, or whether in the line of the normal improvements which every arms race calls into being, the Russians have since 1953 re-equipped, retrained, and modernized their troops until they have outdistanced the Western contingents in quality and equipment.) It was recognized, too, that atomic war would require larger forces, not smaller ones, since the losses would be massive, and the need for replenishments the heavier. This, too, had been established by the studies and war games that the United States Seventh Army Corps conducted in Europe in 1952-53, although nobody wanted to pay any attention to the conclusions for a while, since they did not fit in with the decisions that were being made.

As for our superiority in leadership, daring, boldness, enterprise, innovation, initiative—who could tell? How much were such courtier assurances worth? There has not yet been a national state whose spokesmen did not inform its people that they were the favorite of the gods. It is a disease to which democracies are particularly prone. There is no need for the American republic to be an exception to this universal rule, but we would confess to a lack of ordinary common sense were we to commit our armies or future on the basis of any warranty as unreliable as that. The very clincher of the case for limited war was now turned against the doctrine when Roger Hilsman voiced the conclusion of the investigation that "there is nothing to indicate that a good big atomic army would not be able to defeat a good little atomic army."

Dean Acheson scorned the doctrine on political grounds, as well. Aside from its military impracticality, he said, "Our allies would see at once that the proposed strategy would consign them to a fate more devastating than would compliance with the demands of the

Soviet Union. The merit of this strategy, they would be told, would lie in its avoidance of 'all-out' nuclear war, but it would seem to be all-out enough for them, even though designed to restrain the major participants from battering each other with hydrogen bombs." It appeared to him to be essentially a proposal for the two great powers to protect their homelands from destruction by agreeing to fight a nuclear war on European territory.

When these implications sank in, the limited nuclear war doctrine lost its glitter. As a matter of fact, it sank so low that its chief architect abandoned his brainchild. One still hears it occasionally put forward, since discredited military doctrines are never abandoned outright. They continue to lurk in the background of the military establishments, much like those outmoded Grecian gods on Mount Olympus, who, though no longer in favor, continued nevertheless to carry on a ghostly existence. Once limited nuclear war had slunk to the background, however, we were again in a maelstrom of confusion as to how these weapons were supposed to be employed. The weapons had given us, thus far, not hegemony or security, but mutual terror and a military vacuum. The nuclear bomb, like a fabled treasure, had cast a curse on all who tried to appropriate it for their own puny purposes. Our theory of war was an eclectic jumble; our strategy lay in the limbo of contradiction.

III

With or without a coherent doctrine, NATO went careening down the nuclear course. The momentum was too great to be easily halted, and in any case, no one knew what else to propose. Dulles assured the Europeans that the atomic field weapons reinstituted the "forward strategy" and enabled them to throw back the aggressor "at the threshold." After numerous studies, NATO adopted in 1957 the MC-70 plan to create a force of 30 combat-ready divisions, rechristened the "shield" (the American nuclear force was the "sword"), which by all but eliminating reserves, and other sleight-of-hand alterations, was claimed to give the West a stronger battle line than the one provided by the Lisbon layout. It is more than doubtful that had the 30-division establishment actually been built, it would have altered the equation of 1953 other than to raise still further the armaments level on both sides of the iron curtain.

Despite the new terminology, NATO ground forces remained

mere accomplices to nuclear deterrence, with no defense functions of their own. If they succeeded in holding up an assault until the big retaliatory forces could be brought to bear, NATO would only be "defending a corpse." Their primary function was, as before, to offer enough opposition to activate a nuclear war. That being the Europeans' not unreasonable estimate of the situation, they saw little advantage to trying any harder to meet the new schedules than they had the old.

Besides, the monetary and strategic calculations that had been employed to secure adoption of the program proved erroneous. Instead of being cheaper, the tactical atomic weapons turned out to be more expensive. The re-equipment of the ground forces within existing budgets restricted the development and production of non-nuclear weapons to the point where NATO was in danger of losing its capacity to fight a conventional war before it gained the capacity to fight an atomic one. Since for England and France NATO forces constituted not a defense force but a ground deterrent supplementing the grand nuclear deterrent, and they thought it was good enough as it stood for that, they continued to make haste very slowly, as they had been doing all along.*

Before it could really get underway, NATO's atomic shield program struck the shoals when the Russians sent their Sputnik into orbit in the fall of 1957. This technological breakthrough dramatized

* At the end of 1960, NATO's shield remained at about half the minimum operational strength projected in 1957. Officially it contained 21 combat-ready divisions. Actually, military observers considered 12 to 16 divisions a more accurate figure, and these were inferior in equipment to the Soviet forces facing them in Central Europe. Forces were somewhat increased in the wake of the Berlin crisis, but most of them came from America, which, according to Hanson Baldwin, "is sending more troops than all the rest of the nations of NATO combined." American strength in Europe was considered close to six divisions, and overall German strength was up to nine divisions. According to Helmut Schmidt, the German Social Democratic military specialist, "The number of combat-ready divisions in Central Europe at the end of 1960 can be said to be the equivalent in fighting power of at best 14 divisions. If within a few years, the German army is fully built up, armed, and trained, the total fighting power of NATO in Central Europe will be on the order of 19 divisions—assuming, that is, that the forces of the other states are not in the meantime further depleted. . . . The alliance will be confronted by 20 war-ready Soviet divisions in East Germany, which in the event of war, could be increased to 40 divisions in less than two weeks, and could later be further increased to 80 divisions. The Polish, Czech, and East German forces are not included in this. In an emergency under present conditions the ratio of military power after about ten days would be about 3 to 1 in favor of the Eastern bloc, and would further and more substantially shift to the Soviet advantage from the eleventh day onwards." (*Defence or Retaliation.*)

Russia's development of an intercontinental missile and awoke the Westerners to the fact that Russia was already building up a stock of intermediate missiles with a range of 1,500 to 1,800 miles, capable of wiping out most bases in the NATO area, as well as razing the cities. Again a crisis of confidence shook NATO, and again the United States was thrust into the position where she had to keep running faster and faster to stay in the same place. The day of nuclear parity was hard upon us, and what one could threaten to do, the other could threaten to do, and what one could devastate, the other could devastate.

The United States, in an atmosphere of crisis, tried to restore the *status quo ante* by negotiating a series of bilateral pacts and setting up intermediate missile bases around the continent. In vain! All the divisive tendencies in the NATO alliance were intensely aggravated when the Russian missiles destroyed America's military advantage and made irrelevant the already dubious assumptions of Western strategy. The European neurosis of ambivalent attitudes and conflicting fears took on a settled character. On the one hand, the Europeans feared that if the moment of truth came, the United States would be unwilling to support a peripheral clash with its thermonuclear might when the consequences could be her own incineration. On the other hand, the Europeans feared that the United States would convert a local battle, whether in Europe or elsewhere, into a world war which would obliterate Europe. The brave declarations of NATO's resolve to turn any military encounter into a nuclear war maximized deterrence while eroding the national will to carry through such a strategy.

The equalization of military power blew into a blaze Europe's long-smoldering discontent with America's overlordship. All the high-sounding speeches about partnership and brotherhood in a grand crusade, all the intricate machinery of multinational NATO staffs, never altered the fact that it was the United States—and the United States alone—that had the power of decision over all nuclear weapons, big, little, and medium-sized. While the Western nations were still bleeding from the effects of the last war, they were grateful to receive American bounty, and were in no position to challenge America's monopolist role. By the late 1950's, when they had recovered their strength and some of their bargaining power, they began to chafe under the unequal arrangement. After the missiles came, they were in open revolt against it.

The ill-fated Suez war rammed home the lesson that there were

only two first-class powers left in the world, and that even France
and England no longer had freedom of action for their more
grandiose global policies. Their humiliation set in motion nationalist
fevers that have not abated to this day. What was the point, the
reasoning went, to become the infantry for the American artillery,
in an American-oriented and American-managed military enterprise? What was in it for them? Once this became a prevailing
thought of the two major European nations, they were resolved
to free themselves, to the extent that they could or dared, from the
loving embrace of the Big Brother overseas.

France, under De Gaulle, went into open revolt against the
NATO system once she was clear of the Algerian war. She has
for all purposes withdrawn her naval forces from NATO command.
Her cooperation with the NATO staff is nominal. She is concentrating on building up her own national nuclear force, and while
this may never amount to very much, it is the military symbol
proclaiming, flaunting, De Gaulle's intent to pursue an independent
foreign policy with pronounced anti-American overtones. France
has set her course to push her national advantage; she refuses to
subordinate her interests to any alleged or real higher interests of
the American-led Western alliance.

The British Tories responded differently. They thought to build
up British national power through the finesse and skill which they
prided themselves they possessed in generous measure. They clung
to the hope that they enjoyed a special relationship with the United
States, and could therefore, by playing it cool, and by making themselves indispensable, win Washington's aid to refurbish their dilapi-
dated nuclear force. Under the Eisenhower-Macmillian agreement
in 1959, Britain agreed to grant this country the use of Holy Loch
as a base for Polaris submarines, and another site for a BMEWS
early warning base. In return, the United States was to deliver the
Skybolt to the Royal Air Force by 1965. This was a solid-fueled air-
to-ground missile designed to carry a half-megaton warhead 1,000
miles, which the British figured on using in their aging fleet of
heavy bombers. But in December, 1962, the United States decided
that it would cost too much to bring Skybolt into production, and
that our growing arsenal of Polaris missiles and Minutemen made
Skybolt redundant—and we unilaterally and peremptorily canceled
the project. The Tories were left high and dry. They had staked the
future of the British nuclear deterrent and of the Royal Air Force
on this weapon, and now the weapon was unavailable.

To meet this new NATO crisis, and give the British a loser's consolation prize, the Kennedy-Macmillan mountain labored mightily at Nassau and brought forth two puny mice. President Kennedy promised to sell Britain a number of Polaris missiles and inertial guidance systems if and when Britain builds her own atomic submarines. This promise enabled the British Tories to claim, for electoral purposes, that England will remain a major nuclear power—a claim that is taken by the informed with a grain of salt. British foreign policy is due to veer sharply. It will take a different direction under the Laborites than De Gaulle's, but it will be no less national-minded and no less indifferent to Washington's Grand Design. As for the NATO multilateral force, as it has evolved since Nassau, what is proposed is a fleet of 25 surface ships each bearing 8 Polaris missiles, manned by mixed nationals, with the United States and Germany bearing the lion's share of the costs.

Aside from Germany, none of the Europeans are really for it for a lot of sound reasons.

The multilateral force suffers from the same deficiency as the NATO partnership. "Assigning" forces to NATO is just legal legerdemain. The forces remain national forces under national direction, and are sent here or withdrawn from there as the individual governments see fit. And whatever the markings on the Polaris or other weapons that we may assign to a NATO force, the decision to use them or not to use them will be made in Washington, and no place else. That there is to be no confusion on this score, the *New York Times* of February 27, 1963, reported that "the American representatives will make it clear that there will be only one finger on the trigger of any nuclear force established by NATO. It will be that of the President of the United States." As a matter of fact, it is reported that Polaris missiles are to be fitted with a radio-lock and will not be able to be fired without a coded radio signal from the United States President or his representative.

Besides, the project is actually a political strategy for the infighting among the Western powers, not of consolidating NATO. The purpose of the fleet is to isolate France and frustrate her intention of becoming an independent nuclear power, to nip any grandiose scheme for a Franco-German entente, and finally, to satisfy Germany's great power ambitions vis-à-vis England and France. NATO strategies have always had a certain unreality about them. But the multilateral force is the worst. No one can make out a claim that it is supposed to serve a meaningful military purpose

alongside the far mightier and better protected United States
Polaris submarine fleet. While the project adds nothing significant
to the military equation, its announcement has not only aroused the
suspicions of the Soviet adversary that by means of this stratagem
Germany may eventually emerge as an independent nuclear power;
it has also set our NATO allies at sixes and sevens. If the multilateral force ever sees the light of day, it will aggravate the West-
European division. The Nassau solution did not resolve, or mitigate,
or even paper over the NATO crisis. It signifies instead that there
is no solution in sight to NATO's slow inglorious decay.

Not that the Russians have had any better luck with their alliance.
Their decision to monopolize the bomb has cracked the bloc on the
other side of the Iron Curtain even more decisively, or, at least, to
the accompaniment of more raucous noises. The air is thick with
quotations from Marx and Lenin that the Russians and Chinese are
hurling at each other's heads. And, no doubt, there are genuine
differences over policy as well as conflicting national interests. But
a good half of the quarrel has little to do with conflicting inter-
pretations of Marx and Lenin, and very much to do about Russia's
determination to be the nuclear sword of its alliance, and consequently the arbiter of its foreign policy. If France with 45 million
people will not stand for this amount of surrender of its sovereignty
to America, it is hardly surprising that China with 700 million
people is determined to repulse Russian pretensions. And by a
symbiotic impulse, the two dissenters have been drawn toward each
other. Just as the Rapallo Treaty of 1922 between *Junker* Germany
and Communist Russia, while not leading to any lasting friendship
between the two outcast nations, helped break up the Versailles
system, so the Franco-Chinese understanding, while not leading to
any entente between the two, will help disintegrate the postwar
lineups.

The analysts have concentrated on this or that detail of America's
proposals, or even tone of presentation, in an attempt to be helpful,
to contribute their little mite to save a faltering alliance. But this
is not a crisis that can be resolved by improved manners or intentions. Nuclearism has created an unsolvable conundrum. If the
United States were to distribute nuclear weapons to its allies, it
would bring Armageddon that much closer, and an alliance that is
slowly disintegrating would violently and rapidly blow apart. If the
United States were to give nuclear weapons to NATO—that
presupposes a politically united Europe which does not exist.

Fifteen nations which have so far been unable to agree on a standard tank are unlikely to agree on united control of a nuclear armory. So this is academic as well, aside from the detail that this country would, by its action, create the very third force that our foreign policy is devised to thwart. The nuclear bomb is just too terrible a weapon for the forging of alliances, as it is as a basis for military strategy. You cannot adjust a jeweled timepiece with a blow torch.

The grand nuclear striking force—in the form of unheard-of nuclear stockpiles, vast fleets of long-range bombers, and growing accumulations of missiles on the ground and beneath the waters, screened by radar antennae and satellite watchmen—is there intact. But what is its function? Both superpowers have frozen each other into paralysis—that much the big bombs have accomplished. They have also smashed up the possibilities for strategy. Strategy has been debased to building more and more weapons—and hoping for the best.

If and when hysteria or paranoia ever dispels the paralysis, and the big push starts, there isn't a general staff in the world that has a notion of what will happen, what kind of war will be fought, how long it will last, and what and who will be left intact after it is over. Liddell Hart, who was one of the early advocates of operational research and predicted many of the developments that governed the Second World War, has thrown up his hands at any attempt at predicting the course of a thermonuclear war. "There is no sense," he has written, "even in planning for such a war. The destruction and chaos would be so great within a few hours that the war could not continue in any organized sense."

But the human mind finds it impossible to grasp a new revolutionary reality in one swoop, and even the experts with access to secret information had to have a number of years before they could stop fighting the Second World War all over again—especially since thermonuclear weapons called into question the ancient profession of arms. As late as 1954 the British White Paper on defense was talking of "broken-backed warfare." As British and Western strategists visualized it, a global war would begin with intense atomic attacks lasting a short time and inflicting great destruction. If the results were indecisive, hostilities would continue with declining intensity, "and a period of broken-backed warfare would follow, during which the opposing sides would seek to recover their strength, carrying on the struggle as best they might." Three years later the British admitted in a new White Paper "that there is at present no means of providing adequate protection for the people of this country against the consequences of an attack with nuclear weapons." Duncan Sandys, the British Defense Minister, made the startling admission, "We have taken a very bold step in deciding not to do the impossible. We decided not to defend the whole country, but to defend only our bomber bases." He then added what sounded like the peroration of a funeral speech: "I must pay tribute to the people of Britain for the readiness with which they have accepted these harsh but inescapable facts" (although there is no record of his countrymen having handed him a mandate of this sort). After the big rockets came, most of the experts dropped the theory of an extended war. They now believe that because of the scale and speed of destruction, a major war will last a very short time and will be decided exclusively with those forces and arms that are around and engaged in the decisive nuclear bombardment. We have thus arrived at the point where the sole value of the horrific nuclear weapons is to frighten both superpowers against using them, for if they are ever to be used, it will be all over for both sides: "The death of civilization as we know it," in the words of Hanson Baldwin; "A Frankenstein to destroy both sides," according to the late General MacArthur. The purpose of building up the military leviathans is to keep them in the freezer. The reason for devouring ever more of the national substance in an increasingly frantic arms race is never to go to war.

We are tied up in a nuclear stalemate and the utter sterilization of strategy. Both sides can annihilate each other, and both sides know it. Our nuclear arsenal is still superior in its total striking power and in the variety of its many trinkets and gadgets. But that is not very reassuring in the face of Russian ability to raze our cities and leave our country a smoldering ruin. Since the arms race has produced a rough sufficiency in the terror balance, it would appear to be the counsel of wisdom to say: Let us call a halt. This is a good time, now that both of us have achieved a rough working parity, to come to a mutually beneficial arrangement. There is little point in spending $50 billion a year on weapons to terrorize each other when we can accomplish the same purpose at a quarter, or a tenth, of that cost.

We can scale down the two nuclear forces proportionally so that each of us keeps enough long-range vehicles to destroy each other's cities if one of us attacks—say, 50 ICBM's with 10-megaton

warheads. This is still a respectable terror force able to kill anywhere from 30 to 100 million people. This ought to be sufficient to
deter the other side from starting any nuclear attack. Under this
rough-and-ready arrangement, both belligerents can still have their
military machines, their generals and admirals, uniforms, saluting,
military marches, training games, just so neither power feels
denuded of its attributes of manhood. It is furthermore all sanctified
by the respectable doctrine of minimum deterrence, finite deterrence,
or countercity strategy. As a matter of fact, were we to offer such
a substantial reduction, we could very likely get agreement from the
other side, since it corresponds to the Russian strategy. With our
abilities to keep tabs on major Russian arms developments by satellite
and aerial photography, the question of policing the agreement is
not intractable.

Or, we don't have to do it with Russian agreement; we can do
it unilaterally. Jerome B. Wiesner, who had been President Kennedy's scientific adviser, wrote in the *Daedalus* Fall, 1960, issue:
"Studies made independently by the United States Army and Navy
have indicated that, even in the absence of agreements limiting
force size and permitting inspection, 200 relatively secure missiles
would provide an adequate deterrent." Well, that's all we need,
isn't it?—an adequate deterrent. Professor Seymour Melman estimated that if we made this kind of reduction, we could cut our
1964 military budget to $9 billion, and save $47 billion.

The trouble with this sensible solution of making the best of a
bad bargain is that it cuts across the arms race and the cold war;
and too many people have become accustomed to both and have
organized their lives and thoughts in accordance with their impera-
tives. Too many vested interests have been committed to both the
cold war and the arms race to vacate the premises voluntarily.
Consequently, the statesmen, who because of chance, social connections, or abilities, headed the governments, rejected such a settlement as clearly unrealistic and impractical and visionary and instead
drew the conclusion that the lesson of the nuclear impasse was to
push the arms race still more relentlessly. The leaders of the American establishment, and the nation with them, were hell-bent on
regaining the supremacy that they possessed a decade earlier—even
though when they had such supremacy, they had been unable to
impose their national design on others.

The practical, statesmanlike policy was to keep running faster and
faster.

CHAPTER 4   Counterforce and the Nuclear Priesthood

BEFORE delving into some of the mysteries of counterforce doctrine and related military metaphysics, it is well to take a look at the newly arisen caste of military intellectuals who came into public prominence in the late fifties, and are playing an important planning role in the Pentagon since the McNamara regime. The cold war had the pernicious effect of militarizing American life for the first time since the founding of the republic. All our previous philanderings had been episodic, and stopped short of permanent housekeeping arrangements: we had our brief fling at *machtpolitik* when the first Roosevelt wielded the "big stick," but after the war with Spain, the military establishment shrank rapidly, and the nation resumed its civilian ways. We built up a formidable military machine during the First World War, but disbanded most of it after the armistice. Now, we are in the grip of something new in our history: a military caste presiding over a permanent establishment, and disposing of unheard-of largesse, which defines national problems in terms of military reality and disqualifies other definitions as unavailable and unrealistic. This is a modification of our traditional social structure, and one which restricts our freedom of choice, and creates a bias for military resolutions.

The larger social impact of the rise of a mammoth military establishment will be discussed later in another connection. What is relevant to note at this point is the unusual cultural renaissance sweeping through circles not hitherto renowned for their intellectual interests. After the Second World War the Pentagon endowed a number of "think factories." In the last decade their influence on the nation's thought became tremendous. There was a veritable efflorescence of creativity. The scene became rich with cultural excitation as the new school of writers began to flood the nation with an ever-rising output of magazine articles, brochures, symposia, books, mass-media interviews, to the point where warmaking and military strategy won ratings as radio and television entertainment fare, and where the military metaphysic became an approved conditioner of public opinion.

Though this new intellectual discipline is promoted by mathematicians, statisticians, physicists, and though its practitioners garnish their writings liberally with the jargons and pyrotechnics of their several crafts and specialties, most of them show a strong addiction to the Aristotelian logic-chopping of medieval schoolmen. The result is a bizarre metaphysic where the offsprings of the syllogism jostle against the latest nomenclatures of the natural and social sciences. The exoticism of the mix runs deep because the devotees of the new cult are not seekers for the Kingdom of God, but are dedicated priests of earthly wars. The distinct tinge of mysticism, and even madness, surrounding the enterprise derives not from the intellectual qualities of its individual pathfinders, but from the nature of the quest.

Despite the differences in the writings, ranging from nuances and verbalisms to tactical and strategic divergencies, the military theorists dwell in the same bleak and surly world of ruthless power struggle, and base their strategy on the common assumption that moral nihilism—and only moral nihilism—rules the councils of history. It is a world that would have been easily recognized by Machiavelli and the *condottieri* of the Italian Renaissance wars. Just as the struggle for power was an amoral chess theorem for Machiavelli, so they have sought to reduce the current struggle of nuclear war to an impersonal mathematical games theory.

Without realizing its symptomatic significance, some of them have instinctively slid back to those nihilistic periods of history to grasp for precedents suitable to our present condition. Thomas Schelling, one of the caste's high priests, an alumnus of the Rand

Corporation and the Defense Studies Center, informed us in *The
Strategy of Conflict:* "Where trust and good faith do not exist
and cannot be made to by our acting as though they did, we may
wish to solicit advice from the underworld, or from ancient des-
potisms. . . . The ancients exchanged hostages, drank wine from
the same glass to demonstrate the absence of poison, met in public
places to inhibit the massacre of one by the other, and even deliberately exchanged spies to facilitate transmittal of authentic information." The balance of terror, it is explained, is simply a
modern version of the ancient institution of an exchange of hostages, except that "today's military technology makes it possible to
have the lives of a potential enemy's women and children within
one's grasp while he keeps those women and children thousands
of miles away."

Thomas Schelling unflinchingly grasped the nettle of this harsh
reality of things with this unterrified conclusion: "There probably
are circumstances under which we might try to launch an all-out
preventive or preemptive strike if there were appreciable hope that
the Russians would be physically incapable of destroying us in
action, and especially if the damage they could do in return could
be held to really modest proportions."

Following up this latter pregnant thought, Albert Wohlstetter
and Herman Kahn went to great lengths to educate the country
in the military realism that it would be perfectly sane for the Russians (and by implication, for us) to start a nuclear war if either
of the belligerents could keep down their own losses to twenty
million while knocking out (or hoping to knock out) the other.
The nature of the unrelievedly nihilistic world in which the nuclear priests reside and perform their mathematical exercises, drives
them, as if pursued by furies, to search for the philosopher's stone,
the magic formula whereby we can outwit and get the drop on
the enemy to shoot him down, while he is unable to do any more
than impose damage of modest proportions—like twenty million
deaths—on us.

Language, we know, is an excellent index of a people's culture.
Just as Freudian slips of the tongue reveal more about a person's
hidden feelings than his conscious rationalizations, so the vocabulary
usages of a people tell more of their folkways than the lucubrations
of official apologists. Hitler's Germany deepened the culture of our
times with such popularizations as storm trooper, *schrecklichkeit,
fuehrerprinzip, judenrein.* The Holy Inquisition gave us *auto da*

*fé.* Czarism contributed *pogrom, nagaika, cossack*. Stalinism imparted to both the traditional Marxist formulae and the democratic catch phrases of the French Enlightenment—democratic centralism, vanguard party, purge, proletarian dictatorship—the sinister connotations of modern totalitarian barbarism. Our military intellectuals, with the aid of Madison Avenue magicians, have made notable contributions to this philological enrichment. The world has been taught such new terms as the "clean bomb," or the "humane bomb," for a projectile that will destroy millions but deposit comparatively little fallout. Another cunning term in the new military jargon is "bonus." If an attack is launched for the purpose of destroying a missile site, and if in the course of this destruction a nearby city with its inhabitants is wiped out, the latter is a "bonus," something thrown in free of charge, so to speak. There is also "doomsday machine," "overkill," "megadeath," "megacorpse," not to mention the strictly trade appellations such as "preattack mobilization base," or "postattack nuclear environment."

The rise of a school of amoral military metaphysics does not stem from its practitioners' moral inferiority to the rest of the population. In a larger sense, it is an unavoidable mirroring of the morality of the nuclear confrontation, and a necessary response to the age of the cold war. History's pendulum has swung back to an epoch like the Renaissance where the struggle for power is denuded of moral habiliments —and even fig leaves. Because of the growing desperation of the international contest, the gladiators are being egged on toward every manner of callousness and nihilism. The military intellectuals have simply been staring too long in Medusa's face; while it has not turned them to stone, it has perverted their judgments and given them too cynical and paranoiac a view of reality.*

* Here is one of the creations that Oskar Morgenstern scared himself and his readers with in *The Question of National Defense:* "It may, for example, soon be possible to introduce secretly into a country chemical agents that would not destroy life but would temporarily destroy the will power of the population, and in particular the leaders of the country. This is neither impossible to imagine, nor difficult to execute in the near future. Perhaps it is already being done at present. Perhaps it would be a good idea to feed tranquilizers to all the participants of international conferences in order to produce agreements. It would be interesting if that were done secretly by one side only. Then the country receiving such treatment might surrender without realizing what it does." This opens up a fascinating world, more vibrant and polychromatic than the pedestrian one in which we dwell.

Another example that shows that the oversuspicious are not always the most judicious is furnished by Oskar Morgenstern's reading of the Russo-Finnish war of 1939. The rest of us had figured that the Russians went in not sufficiently prepared,

Their biggest public role—as well as the cause of their subsequent public discredit—came during the so-called "missile gap" crisis. Russia's achievement of a working parity of terror after she launched her first Sputnik created a real crisis in our military doctrine and perspectives. The attempt to probe for real solutions and alternative policies was incontinently swept aside by a pseudo-scholarly propaganda which channeled all efforts into overcoming what was later admitted to be a nonexistent gap, and resolved the crisis of military outlook with a concocted counterforce theory. By clothing their militaristic fanaticism with the pretense of scientific omniscience, they turned the nation's attention away from the real problems of the nuclear impasse to the synthetic solution of a continuing arms race.

The operational researchers turned the tables on the prevailing opinion that a near stability had been attained in the terror balance. They proceeded to demonstrate, in the manner of medieval theologians, that the balance was precarious, and that unless drastic remediable steps were taken, it was going to become more precarious. They split hairs to prove that our nuclear deterrent was insufficient to deter, or according to some, that it was a credible deterrent at all. What was decisive, they explained, was not how much damage our nuclear carriers could do to the enemy homeland, but how much damage we could impose after he had attacked us and eliminated all or a large part of our nuclear striking capability. Under the new form of reckoning, it developed that we

---

without an adequate understanding of the difficulties of terrain, unalerted to the local circumstances, were consequently thrown back, and finally subdued the Finns at far greater costs in manpower and to their own prestige than the disproportionate sizes of their respective armies warranted. But while the wily Russians took us all in, there is one man they did not succeed in fooling. "Russia does not tell us anything," we learn, "unless it is by virtue of a careful design. . . . Indeed, even when military action occurred in which Russian forces were involved, not even then were their latest weapons or devices—or even their best troops—used. The Russo-Finnish war is a classic case. It produced among the neutral Swedes as well as in Hitler's mind the idea that the Nazi army could cut through Russia 'as a knife through butter.' This was the result of planned, costly deception. This was bluffing on a grand scale and in the classic manner. It paid off."

It certainly did. Russia suffered casualties of twenty million and had over half of its economy ravished. But the argument is broken off too soon. To really get the full savor of this bluffing on a grand scale and in the classic manner, we ought to show how Stalin continued to trick the stupid German armies by prodigally feeding them his manpower and industries until he had the fools at the gates of the Don. Which is about the size of the Stalinist explanation of the war.

were living in a fool's paradise in thinking we had an overkill capability. Not only did we have nothing of the sort, we did not even have enough to properly deter him from making an aggressive lunge at us.

The key concept around which the speculations revolved was "surprise." According to the arguments of the military writers, nuclear weapons hand a preponderant advantage to the aggressor. By pouncing on the enemy without warning, the aggressor is in a position to put out of action the bulk of the opponent's nuclear retaliation system, and thus is in a position to threaten to use the remains of his nuclear force to destroy the enemy society outright unless his dictates are accepted. The aggressor would very likely suffer some retaliation in the course of his aggression to the extent of several million deaths and a proportionate material destruction. But the military intellectuals were convinced that that was an entirely reasonable bargain.

They consequently bombarded the public with the warning that we were in danger of a surprise nuclear attack, not as a generalized danger, but as something clear and present. Albert Wohlstetter, in an article published in the January, 1959, issue of *Foreign Affairs,* and widely referred to by many other operational analysts, was sure that there were a number of quite plausible circumstances when the Russians would be making "sensible strategic choices" which would entail "from their point of view the smaller risk" if they launched a surprise attack on us. Then he made this ominous comment: "Suppose both the United States and the Soviet Union, given the opportunity to administer the opening blow, had the power to destroy each other's retaliatory forces and society. The situation would then be something like the old-fashioned Western gun duel. It would be extraordinarily risky for one side *not* to attempt to destroy the other, or to delay doing so, not only because it can emerge unscathed by striking first but because this is the sole way it can reasonably hope to emerge at all." Klaus Knorr held similarly in his 1959 book, *NATO and American Security,* that "the risk of Soviet surprise attack on the United States may well be substantial, and, indeed, dangerously high." Bernard Brodie stated in *Strategy in the Missile Age* that the advantage in striking first "would be tremendous," so that "even rational men could start a total war." Alastair Buchan wrote in *NATO in the 1960's* of the "enormous advantage now accruing to the man who strikes first, and the degree of surprise that the missile permits that does more than anything else to create the instability of the strategic balance."

The thesis, repeated by many political and military notables, soon found its way into the literature issued by the Democratic party, and became intertwined with the growing hysteria about the "missile gap," which was placing our defenses in jeopardy and leaving us exposed to Russian blackmail. The danger was palpable, the solution was clear, and from the throats of a thousand good men and true issued the deafening shout, "More arms!" The advocates of the different services and doctrines differed on which types of arms and researches they favored, but they were all united in advocating an accelerated arms race in which there was "something for everybody."

Russia's supposed superiority in missile production, the decisive advantage accruing to the aggressor, and the reasonableness of preventive war, were the trinity for rationalizing the arms race. It was this thesis that was employed by the Democratic party in 1959 to justify its demand for a $7 billion increase, and which the Kennedy Administration carried through upon taking office. The missile scare resembled remarkably the periodic armaments scares that swept England, Germany, and France before 1914, generally when military budgets were up for consideration. It followed with uncanny likeness the "bomber gap" scare that preceded it.

There, too, the public outcry achieved its concert pitch two years after it was first realized that the Russians were building a long-range air fleet. It was similarly compounded in unequal amounts of duplicity, ignorance, and hysteria, and stoked with unconscionably exaggerated information and unfounded claims. In 1956 the American people were told that the Russians were building 25 long-range bombers a month. Several years later, when the bomber scare had accomplished its purpose, it was admitted that the Russian long-range bomber force consisted of 150 to a maximum of 200 planes as against our force of 680 B-52's and B-58's (disregarding the obsolescent medium bomber fleets on both sides, the slightly aging British bomber fleet of 180 planes, or the land- and sea-based fighter bombers of the NATO powers).

The missile scare followed the same lunatic course. Two years after the Soviets tested a long-range rocket, the experts outdid themselves in fanciful projections of the enemy turning out missiles like sausages and soon having this country at their mercy—

unless we threw all caution to the winds. After the moneys were duly voted, and we had triumphantly attained the level of a $50 billion peacetime defense budget, it developed that the Soviets had not been manufacturing missiles at anything like the rates that had been suggested to justify the swollen appropriations. Senator Stuart Symington admitted that our estimate of Soviet ICBM's decreased by 96½ per cent between December, 1959, and September, 1961. We had exaggerated the Russian missile threat by thirty times. It now developed that despite her lead and capabilities Russia did not have the four to one, or five to one, lead that had been predicted for 1962; as a matter of fact, she had only built about 50 ICBM's, a number equal to or somewhat below our own.

As summarized by the *New York Times* of November 27, 1961, "The 'missile gap,' like the 'bomber gap' before it, is now being consigned to the limbo of synthetic issues, where it always belonged. . . . The same forces and the same Congressional and journalistic mouthpieces who manufactured an alleged bomber gap in the 1950's sponsored, and indeed invented, the alleged missile gap in the 1960's. Today, judged by the hard-bitten estimates of actual Soviet strength, to which all services apparently subscribe, the 'missile gap' has vanished; the quantitative advantage, if any, is on the side of the United States."

While the factual basis for the arms-race thesis has been shown up as spurious, the argumentative part of it has never been repudiated, and this represents an even greater danger to the country's thinking than any real or imagined "missile gap." For while the latter could do duty for a single appropriation raid, the thesis of "the advantage of the surprise" and "the sanity of preventive war," if accepted as good coin, can justify an expanding arms race ad infinitum. It can be employed repeatedly to panic a distraught people into ill-considered preemptions or arms buildups to ward off imaginary blows.*

* P. M. S. Blackett, the noted British physicist and Nobel prize winner, demolished the proposition in his article in the April, 1961, *Encounter*. He met the military academics on their own chosen ground and demonstrated, by means of various numerical models, that "no country could make use of even a very substantial degree of nuclear superiority by staging a first strike without incurring a high probability of very heavy destruction."

Blackett continued: "Both common sense and the more detailed arguments of abstract military theory alike associate stability with near equality of defence capability." The American analysts were able to reach the opposite conclusion and to

Were the Russian leaders brash enough to take the word of military theologians that in a surprise nuclear strike which destroyed half the population of the United States, they would merely suffer ten million deaths in the retaliatory attack, would anyone not affected by the military metaphysic think that they had made a "sane" decision, when by not striking they would have had no deaths at all? But who can be sure that Russian casualties would be "limited" to ten million deaths, and the attendant destruction? Battles and wars have always been things of risk and uncertainty, and the Russian military commanders would have to be less than intelligent if they counted on their initial blow crippling most of our retaliatory capacity, even as it stood in 1959 or in 1956.

There are the general uncertainties and pitfalls of a surprise attack: target maps might be inaccurate or outdated; some of the warheads could misfire; some of the bombs and missiles might fall wide of their targets; the other side might be warned in time to strike back with preemptive blows; the little-understood dangers of fallout would pose a terrible threat. The location of every long-range bomber and every missile site, and the deployment of all medium-range bombers capable of carrying nuclear warheads, would have to be accurately known. Even if only 50 American bombers escaped the holocaust to deliver 10-megaton bombs to Russia, they could wipe out up to 75 to 100 million people. Even several hundred fighter bombers carrying mere atomic bombs could take a toll of several tens of millions. If only 20 of the ICBM's remained to deliver warheads of 5 and 10 megatons, they could cause 40 million deaths. In the light of these possibilities and probabilities, if our system of the 1950's was insufficient to deter the Rusians from starting a preventive nuclear war against us, and to make the concept of surprise attack unattractive to rational men, then the the whole theory of nuclear deterrence might as well be scrapped, for it cuts across the assumed psychology that governs the generality of rulers and peoples that leads them to cherish their own lives and homelands.

Besides, the concept of a surprise knockout blow is contrary to

---

equate any approaching equality with dangerous instability necessitating a renewed arms buildup on our part by introducing the element of "moral asymmetry" between the contestants. When we have overwhelming arms superiority—that is stable, because our intentions are good. When the Soviets approach equality of arms capability—that is unstable, because they are aggressive.

Russian military doctrine. They don't believe in it. They believe a major war of the future cannot be decided by one or a few swift strokes. Lending veracity to their published theses on this score is the organization of their armed forces. Raymond Garthoff, one of the best informed students of Russian military affairs in this country, came to this conclusion in his 1959 book, *The Soviet Image of Future War:* "Soviet leaders are not poised to unleash their—and our —military power as soon as the theoretical probability of military victory crosses some calibrated balance of 50 per cent, or 70 per cent, or indeed perhaps even 90 per cent. In the Communist view, history cannot be made hostage to the mathematical probability computations of some 'Communivac.' Thus total nuclear war—though not necessarily other limited forms of war—seems ever less likely as a rational tool for the Soviet Union to advance its position."

History affords all sorts of examples of one military power launching a surprise attack upon another one, but two nations never find themselves at war with each other by surprise, even when the attack is made first and the announcement that a state of war exists is made afterwards. As Clausewitz wrote, "War does not spring up quite suddenly." There is invariably a psychological buildup of conflict. There is invariably a mounting political crisis. Of course, it's different in Oskar Morgenstern's book where "a good surprise attack would not take place in the midst of a critical situation. On the contrary, there would first be created a harmonious, peaceful atmosphere with plenty of high level negotiations going on, if Russia really wanted to strike us." But in the real world it is impossible to be that Dostoyevskian, even in the nuclear age, without thrusting one's own society, long before the opponent's, into utter chaos.

In the case of both recent successful military surprises, the Japanese bombing of Pearl Harbor, and the German attack upon Russia, the previous political situation indicated the inevitability, or strong probability, of war between the opposing nations. It was an open secret that war was imminent between this country and Japan after we served our series of demands upon the Celestial Emperor's representatives. Washington did not know precisely where Japan would attack, but they were fairly sure that she would attack. The Japanese caught us completely off guard at Pearl Harbor only because of the stupidity or irresponsible carelessness of our local commanders, not because an attack was unexpected, or came out of the blue. Hitler's break with Stalin was not as well

telegraphed ahead of time, but even in this instance, aside from
direct warnings that Stalin received, the political impasse reached
in the negotiations between the two sides should have alerted Russia to the probability of a war between them—a probability which
had to be viewed as a certainty when Hitler began massing troops
in the Balkans. In other words, in the world where wars are prepared and fought, total surprise is the rare exception. While miscalculation and stupidity can never be ruled out, these contingencies
are problematical and unpredictable. Russia, no more than we, can
count on these in the formulation of strategic plans.


II

Once the momentum of the arms race had carried our military
establishment well past the confines of minimum deterrence, the
military intellectuals felt that this vast and increasing agglomera-
tion of weapons needed the justification of a new doctrine. It was
inherently irrational to continue turning out ever more elaborate
and ever more expensive weapons for the purpose of not using
them, and they feared that the situation might invite proposals
to scale down the magnitude while maintaining the balance, or—
even worse—might lead to demands for comprehensive disarmament. The same imperative to overcome the paralysis of foreign
policy, and to escape from the "sterility of the quest for peace,"
which had propelled Kissinger to his ill-starred theory of limited
nuclear war, now pushed Herman Kahn and his Rand Corporation associates to counterforce theory.

It was abhorrent and intolerable to the military mind to see its
prize weapons condemned to sterility. By one means or another,
they had to be pushed onto the theoretical or actual battlefield.
The grand purpose of counterforce theory was to break the hypnotic
spell of belief that nuclear wars could not be fought and would
not be fought and must not be fought. The purpose in popular-
izing counterforce theory was to mold public opinion that nuclear
wars were not only possible but likely. But if we were smart—if
we followed the advice of the men who knew, built up the equipment, and fought along the right counterforce lines—we would
"prevail." Nuclear war was more terrible than conventional war,
but it was manageable; the difference was a matter of degree, not
kind, provided we, the people, weren't stingy with the war budg-

ets, and were ready to take the necessary risks. The great merit of Herman Kahn's 650-page dissertation *On Thermonuclear War* was that the author unhesitantly blurted out what others had shuddered to admit even to themselves. Because he tried to think through the implications of his colleagues' fugitive proposals and disconnected assumptions, and tie the threads together into a comprehensive system, Kahn's work may be viewed as a climacteric of the military intellectuals' doctrinal labors. He brought the doctrine to its high point of elaboration, generalization, and even mysticism. And by so doing, he also undermined the intellectual part of the enterprise through exposing its irrationality and irresponsibility.

According to general counterforce argument, one of the ways that a major war will start will be by the Soviets launching a nuclear strike at the United States. If we build the right kind of force and make the right kind of preparations, we can force the Russians to direct the initial attack at our nuclear forces and not at our cities. Why? Because the Communists would fear that an attack upon our cities that left our bombers and missiles intact would be answered by an attack on their cities which would vaporize their society. So they would have to fight the kind of war we want them to fight. The war would then go something like this: The Russians deliver their "first strike," attempting to knock out as great a part of our nuclear force as they can. We return the blow with what is left of our nuclear force, hewing strictly to the line of destroying their nuclear capability and nothing else, because according to the metaphysic, were we to attack the Soviet cities, that would leave their nuclear forces intact to clobber us— this time with finality—a second time.

If our retaliatory strike, as it is hoped, reduces the enemy nuclear forces to impotence, then we have got the Russians where we want them. We could threaten to use our remaining nuclear strength to send them and their entire society to Kingdom Come unless they surrendered on our terms, and they would have no alternative except to accede. If, in the process of knocking out the enemy nuclear forces, our own forces were also expended, the war would end in a stalemate; and we would still preserve our society, even if in a more or less damaged form. Since the enemy, as well as we, would have mobile bases in addition to fixed sites and air fields, we would have to hunt these down with our strategic air force planes, while the Soviets would be busy in the

same way over the United States. Our civilian populations would
wait meanwhile in their fallout shelters or underground caverns to
see how things were going to turn out, while our Nike rockets
would try to hunt down the enemy reconnaissance hunters. The
estimates of counterforce theorists oscillate widely from ten million to several tens of millions to over half of our population as
the number of deaths to be anticipated in such a war. They regard twenty million or thirty million or sixty million—depending
on the expert—as an acceptable figure, and are convinced that if
the nation accepts their sundry diagnoses and takes their different
prescriptions, it could survive and rebuild itself.

While this kind of war restores the dynamism of our military
establishment, its defect is that it still leaves the initiative to the
enemy. Since he shows little disposition to try to settle things in
this manner, and has instead shifted the contest to economic and
political infiltrations and to support of insurgent guerrilla movements, he could "nibble us to death" while we were waiting for
the apocalyptic "first strike" to start the grand counterforce war.
Besides, our ability to demolish largely empty Soviet missile pads
and bomber bases did not seem half as fearful a retaliatory threat
a the one posed by our old countercity policy. In an attempt to
bring their theory into closer play with the cold war, the counterforce proponents therefore provided an alternate and operative
model.

This war starts with our side striking first. After the Communists
have perpetrated some dastardly provocation—the unlikely and
arbitrary example of overrunning Europe is usually given, or more
recently, an attack on Berlin—we would evacuate our people from
our large cities to previously prepared blastproof and fireproof underground shelters, and then issue our ultimatum: "Withdraw your
forces from these territories, or stop doing what we don't want
you to do, or else we will attack your nuclear forces. We may also
(in the guise of the implacable Nemesis) obliterate one or several
of your cities to punish you for your wrongdoing." (In the trade
this is known as counterforce plus.) If our ultimatum is not honored, war would then begin by our striking first, and presumably would follow much the same course as in the previous model.

Once we agree to enter the Wagnerian-opera world of the
counterforce theorists, many things are solved. According to the
counterforce school we do not have a vast overkill capacity and
an unnecessarily extensive delivery system; we have barely enough

to get by. It is not time to end the arms race and to try to scale down the two deterrent machines. The arms race has hardly got started, and we are in need of more of everything. It is true that there are some theorists, like Oskar Morgenstern, who are content to keep the arms race going for extramilitary reasons. ("If people were motivated by peaceful purposes alone, many basic discoveries would not be made. The most interesting things in science at present are done only if they are related to war and war preparation. . . . War preparations are necessary in order to justify the deepest human desire for knowledge. . . . Society does not accept the desire for knowledge as legitimate unless it is somehow tied to war.") But such outspoken neo-social Darwinists are in the minority, and the continued pouring of the national substance into arms technology must be justified for the majority on grounds of military necessity and national safety.

For the counterforce model war we need a tremendous number of missiles. (According to Klaus Knorr, the figure ranges from 30,000 to 40,000.) To make the weapons relatively invulnerable to enemy strikes, the missiles will have to be encased in underground holes of reinforced concrete, and the sites provided with elaborate complexes. Our forces will have to be made mobile by widely dispersing the missiles and multiplying their numbers, so that at least several missiles or bombs can be directed against each target, increasing the likelihood of a successful hit. Our reconnaissance and espionage by means of satellites, electronic equipment, and manual means will have to be turned into a major industry since we will have to have at all times a complete, up-to-the-minute map listing the location of every last enemy missile site and airfield. A massive supersonic bomber force equipped with its own missiles and radar equipment will have to be on air and ground alert, ready to take off to ferret out and destroy the mobile enemy sites. Extensive shelter cities will have to be prepared to protect our populations while we are retaliating or issuing ultimatums. And when the enemy responds by building up his weapons, we will have to press harder on the accelerator to keep our lead.

As a seriously conceived prevision of a nuclear war, counterforce is sheer dementia—doctrinairism run amok. That it could be put forward in all solemnity as a national military policy is a sign that the nuclear race is driving people beyond the confines of rationality. It is impossible in industrial societies to separate nuclear forces from populations. Military sites are close to cities, and when weapons are as destructive as nuclear warheads are, even were they to score bull's-eyes on targets, they would vaporize the surrounding areas for miles around and contaminate entire countries and continents.

But why should the enemy, fighting for his life, spare our cities, even if he could? And vice versa? With the proliferation of these weapons, and the uncertainty over the location of mobile and dispersed sites, there is no problem to diverting 10 or 20 per cent of the forces to blow up enemy cities while the main thrust is directed at the known military concentrations. A salvo of high-burst shots across the American continent would reduce a good part of the country to a smoldering ash even while the enemy's main forces aimed to reduce our retaliatory strength. Besides, if we are going to play at the game of unstructured suspicion, why should our enemy not assume that the sophistical strategy of counterforce is not a cunning ruse to hide most of our missiles near the cities while he is diverted to blowing up our empty deserts and prairies? In any case, cities and populations cannot be separated in the world of the living.

Counterforce assumes, with even less justification than the limited-nuclear-war theory, that the devastation of continents and the annihilation of millions can be combined with a perfectly controlled conduct of the war and a precise application of violence to the degree and at the point that the directing staffs decide. To do this it must abstract itself from such realities as the destruction of the communication systems as one of the first casualties in a mutual nuclear bombardment. Even if the two governments, cowering in underground shelters, are still physically in being and continue to pretend that they are directing the destinies of their nations, they will have lost control over much or most of the situation.

They will have no means of knowing how badly we have damaged the enemy. They will not even know the exact extent of our own damage. If one side remembered counterforce in the midst of the panic and tried to warn or threaten the opponent, it would most likely have no way of getting its message into the hands of the counterpart government. If by chance the enemy did hear of the threat, it would have no way of knowing whether the other side was bluffing or could actually make good on it. If it believed the threat and wanted to forestall it, it could probably do nothing about it because its forces no longer would be functioning in any coherent manner and it would have lost direction over them.

The vision of a grand thermonuclear opera directed by a duo of *regisseurs,* with either one in a position to call time out while the damage was being assessed, negotiations resumed, postattack blackmail attempted, and the decision cooly arrived at as to whether we should resume clobbering each other, is the stuff nightmares are made of. There will be no Queensberry interchanges in the midst of the unheard-of chaos, the flooding waves of anguish and embitterment and despair, the collapse of the world around.* Is it seriously proposed in this second half of the twentieth century that a great nation rest its future on a gamble of this kind?

And to what purpose is the whole enterprise? To what purpose are we to set up an armed state which, if the comprehensive programs of the counterforce advocates were realized, would swallow up the larger part of our patrimony and necessitate a totalitarian military regime far more bloodthirsty than the relatively benign model of Khrushchev Sovietism. To what purpose are we to fight a war in which thirty million deaths would be accepted by us as a satisfactory cost? The operational researchers have become so engrossed with the mechanics of nuclear strategy that they have lost sight of its presumed purposes.

At one moment of sobriety Herman Kahn informed us that after a nuclear war "life is going to be stark, elemental, brutal, filthy, and miserable," and that all remaining resources are going to "be commandeered and shared without owner-identity in collective misery (one might say 'disaster socialism')." If "victory" in a nuclear war means the loss of the very social arrangements which we endeavored to defend or secure by fighting that war, then we are worse than an ignorant clan of Kentucky feudists. Surely, we can negotiate a better settlement than "disaster socialism" without subjecting our people to the nuclear horror. Kahn himself thought

* Senator Russell of Georgia does not have a good position on civil rights, but he showed a lot of common sense on counterforce. After listening to weeks of testimony in the Senate Armed Services Committee, he declared on the Senate floor on April 11, 1962: "There have been some estimates and some so-called mathematical computations of the casualties that would result from a nuclear war under various assumptions, including a positive attempt by the adversaries to limit targeting to military installations and facilities. . . . To me these extrapolations are exceedingly unrealistic. They presuppose a war being waged with rational restraint by both sides. I doubt that there could be anything rational in the awful eventuality of nuclear attack. . . . In my opinion, if nuclear war begins, it will be a war of extermination."

so. He said, "I am not denying that so far as the real world is concerned, under almost any reasonable definition of Soviet or U.S. goals, both would gain more if they compromised the ideological conflict than if they fought it out." But this was simply a *bon mot* uttered during a coffee break prior to getting back to the serious work at hand, which was how to fight a nuclear war and "prevail."*

When irrationality becomes a group phenomenon rather than an individual aberration, the explanation for it must be sought in the social environment instead of the psyche of the personality. Since the counterforce theory is not merely the emanation of an extremist academic sect, but dominates the thinking of the Air Force, and has been accepted as official government policy, and since it is asserted by various national spokesmen who, as if they were possessed by unclean spirits, persist in running violently toward the precipice of their own destruction, it must be assumed that the arms race itself has become a source of mental unbalance. Kenneth Boulding has

---

* Herman Kahn was clearly intent, when he published *On Thermonuclear War,* on establishing his reputation as a latter-day Clausewitz. In this he succeeded only too well—in many circles. But apparently he was totally unprepared for, and indeed, genuinely flabbergasted by, the roar of horror and indignation which his book evoked among many, particularly in the intellectual community. He had been so enveloped in a specialized atmosphere for twelve years at the Rand Corporation that the grisly meaning of his charts and models had escaped his full comprehension. When James R. Newman said, in his review appearing in the *Scientific American,* "This is a moral tract on mass murder: how to plan it, how to commit it, how to get away with it, how to justify it," Herman Kahn loudly protested that he had been misunderstood.

Misunderstood or not, a man who has become a public figure of sorts cannot afford in our mass democracy to have a public image of an amoral monster. Herman Kahn abruptly changed his posture. In his appearances on television panel discussions, one saw a mild, benign, philosophical sort of man, eager to probe and examine all aspects of the question. The arrogance of the military martinet, the presumption of the pedant, the collector of obituary notices in the mass had disappeared as if he had never existed.

The Hudson Institute, a new "think factory" that Kahn set up in the summer of 1961, went to great lengths to demonstrate its open-mindedness. An advisory committee was selected that included such diverse figures as Dr. Edward Teller, the father of the H-bomb, Louis B. Sohn, the world-government advocate, and the Reverend A. J. Muste, a peace agitator for unilateral disarmament. The official brochure stated: "While the institute will not seek to be foolishly idealistic, it does believe that the existence of large numbers of readily deliverable H-bombs and an active arms race makes it necessary to devote serious, detailed, informed thought to such things as disarmament and world government."

In his more recent book, *Thinking About the Unthinkable,* published in 1962, Herman Kahn demonstrated that his newly acquired open-mindedness had not yet changed any of his essential views, but they had transformed his manner.

written that unilateral national defense has ceased to be a feasible
social system, and our efforts must therefore be spent not in find-
ing how to operate it more efficiently but how to replace it with
something better. "For this reason, I regard the whole Rand enterprise as fundamentally obsolete." And he concludes that society
must be in "a dangerously pathological condition" when so many
of its best minds are diverted from soluble to insoluble problems.

CHAPTER 5   Counterforce and the Russians

In her pure, immaculate condition, counterforce is too presumptuous and voracious a goddess for any government or treasury to adopt. The military directors, treading their way among three service bureaucracies and as many weapons systems, have had perforce to fit military doctrine to these competing demands. Many, or most, of the sharp distinctions between "limited deterrence" and "counterforce" dissolve in the practices of the military establishment. The subtleties of competing theories disappear with the proliferation of parallel weapons systems, with ICBM's and strategic bomber forces assigned to destroy enemy transportation and communication centers as well as nuclear forces, with submarine Polaris missiles assigned to demolish industrial area and cities, with attack planes from navy carriers set for first- or second-strike targets, with fighter bombers based in Europe or the Far East assigned to close-in targets. The Pentagon target list, which presumably keys our military strategy, includes practically everything that any service has proposed. When the target lists of the different services were integrated several years ago under Secretary of Defense Gates, there was an increase rather than decrease in the number of targets assigned. The reconciliation of competing demands was resolved by the simple expedient of recognizing the validity of almost all of them.

The theory of the "mix," rationalizing the melange of unrelated and sometimes mutually exclusive concepts and strategies, has been gaining in acceptability as the older services have rediscovered roles for themselves in the nuclear age. The Navy has re-emerged as a competitor of the Air Force, with its Polaris submarine fleet and its first nuclear-powered aircraft carrier boasting a four-and-a-half-acre flight deck, four steam catapults which make it possible to launch her planes one every fifteen seconds, and a nuclear plant which enables her to circle the earth many times at high speed without stopping.

The exigencies of the cold war, and the kind of conflicts which they are imposing, push our government in the same direction. While our military establishment has been concentrating preparations for the apocalyptic strike of World War III, it has been involved in peripheral wars and encounters in which the theories of the intellectuals did not come into play, and which resembled the battles and forays, not of World War II, but of World War I. The government has consequently been forced to modify at least its addiction to the big bomb and the big missile, and to go over to some degree to the Soviet theory of balanced military forces.

When General Maxwell Taylor, the apostle of balanced forces, was recalled from the wilderness to head the Joint Chiefs of Staff, he announced his intention to realign our armed forces and military strategy. He explained that in order to meet international crises, we would have to shift from a heavy reliance on nuclear weapons to a more rounded defense. Sounding like one of the Soviet marshals, he declared, "We must be prepared to cope with general atomic war, limited atomic war, conventional warfare, and what I have called parawar. We cannot afford to gear our plans to any single weapons system or to any single dogmatic concept of how the future will develop." Lending weight to General Taylor's remarks was the army reorganization started in 1962, which entailed the addition of more divisions, and the introduction of a new brigade-and-battalion structure capable of fighting both nuclear and non-nuclear kinds of war, as well as the tripling over the next two years of our capacity to transport ground troops by air.

The return to concepts of conventional warfare notwithstanding, the governing momentum of the arms race remains toward nuclear immolation. The military establishment concluded after the missile breakthrough that we must run faster and spend more to recapture the hegemony which we had lost. Once the larger military budgets were voted, and the "missile gap" and the sedulously propagated fears of Russian first strikes could then be dropped, our military spokesmen started to boast that we were getting loaded up with enough military hardware to be able to absorb any punishment the Soviets could mete out to us and, still go on to rip up their homeland root and branch. The counterforce theorists have won their case to the extent of getting some of their specific arms programs accepted, and of impressing leading government officials with their semantics and modes of thought.

On October 21, 1961, our Deputy Secretary of Defense, Roswell Gilpatrick, after elaborating pointedly on our many weapons possessions, announced in a speech: "The destructive power which the United States could bring to bear even after a Soviet surprise attack upon our forces would be as great as—perhaps greater than—the total undamaged force which the enemy can threaten to launch against the United States in the first strike [Counterforce Model Number One]. . . . If forceful interference with our rights and obligations should lead to violent conflict—as it well might—the United States does not intend to be defeated." [Counterforce Model Number Two.] In a speech he gave in Chicago on February 17, 1962, Secretary of Defense McNamara went further than any high civilian official had ever gone in embracing counterforce semantics. He said, "United States nuclear power . . . is able to survive a nuclear surprise attack and strike back with sufficient power to destroy the enemy target system. . . . Our forces can be used in several ways. We may have to retaliate with a single massive attack. Or, we may be able to use our retaliatory forces to limit damage done to ourselves and our allies by knocking out the enemy's bases before he has had time to launch his second salvos. We may seek to terminate a war on favorable terms by using our forces as a bargaining weapon—by threatening further attack. In any case, our large reserve of protected firepower would give an enemy an incentive to avoid our cities and to stop a war. . . . We shall be committed only to a system that gives us the ability to use our forces in a controlled and deliberate way."

Thus we entered the present period of triumphant counterforce with the stress on "controlled response," while proclaiming our vast weapons superiority over the enemy. In his November 28, 1963, speech to the Economic Club of New York, McNamara explained that in the past two years alone we have increased the number of nuclear warheads by 100 per cent and more than doubled the megatonnage in the strategic alert forces. By 1968, according to the current budget figures, we should have 1,770 Atlas, Titan, Minute-man, and Polaris missiles, besides our B-52 and B-58 bomber fleets.

What will this margin of superiority, if maintained, give us? Will it transfigure our diplomacy? Our more qualitative superiority from 1948 to 1954 did not do it. It was not effective in stopping the Communist victory in China in 1950. It was not effective in stopping the Russian invasion of Hungary in 1956 before they had long-range missiles. Our superiority did not keep our clients in power in Laos. It will probably not save our clients in South Vietnam. Military prowess is only a single component of a social-economic-political complex in today's international diplomacy.

Furthermore, as the fifteen-year experience of the arms race testifies, the other fellow is not standing still. When we harden our bases, the opponent will build larger megaton weapons and use penetrating or delayed-action bursts to blow them up. When we disperse them on mobile sites, the opponent will develop area bombardment or interdiction techniques to neutralize them. If it looks as though we are building up a first-strike, preventive-war capacity, he will multiply, harden, and disperse his missiles to foil us again. Even "hard" bases will become "soft" as enemy ICBM accuracy increases. He does not have to match us missile for missile and plane for plane. He just has to keep his technology abreast of the time, and have enough warheads and carriers in the midst of a bombardment to pulverize our main cities. That is sufficient. The fact that we can kill him three times over does not enter into the equation.

The military doctrinaires and fanatics have thrust us into a labor of Sisyphus—an endless arms race, a mystic hunt for a ghostly security that is unattainable in nuclear terror. An arms race does not lead to the eventual Eden of stable deterrence or a position of strength, for it merely raises the threshold of violence without altering the terror balance. Such a race will be finished only when the world has exploded into armed conflict.


II

As the challenger moving up from behind for the championship prize, Russian militarism has tended to imitate the American model. Although it absorbed the technological innovations into its own ideological system, modified them in accordance with its own needs, and momentarily sprang ahead of its rival on several sectors, both its doctrines and weapons systems developed in response to the example of the transatlantic colossus.

For a while, when Malenkov and Khrushchev were fighting for leadership, it appeared that they were uncertain about the conclusive character of nuclear war, and whether something new had actually changed militarism since Frederick Engels had written about it. Malenkov thought so, but with Khrushchev's assumption of the premiership, the official line reverted to the formula that only capitalism would perish in a calamitous war, but communism would survive. It was Russia's version of "prevailance." The Party magazine *Kommunist* explained after Malenkov's dismissal that in propagating the idea of the destruction of civilization, the capitalists were unscrupulously exploiting peoples' desires for peace. "Such a concept blunts the vigilance of the people toward those who in the preparation of atomic war would like to take the peoples by surprise."

The subsequent evolution made clear that there was no real difference in the Soviet appraisal of nuclear war, or even of the public relations appertaining thereto. The controversy had been concocted in pursuance of narrow faction needs. When Khrushchev was safely ensconced in the Kremlin, he said the same thing that Malenkov had said about the effects of nuclear war. In September, 1960, the same *Kommunist* declared that "the working class cannot conceive of the creation of a Communist civilization on the ruins of world centers of culture, on desolated land contaminated with thermonuclear fallout, which would be an inevitable consequence of such a war. For some peoples the question of socialism would in general cease to exist: they would physically vanish from the planet. It is thus clear that a present-day nuclear war in itself can in no way be a factor that would accelerate revolution and bring the victory of socialism closer. On the contrary, it would hurl mankind, the world revolutionary workers' movement, and the cause of the building of socialism and communism back by many decades."

It was an ironical reversal of positions. Now American military intellectuals were insisting that a counterforce nuclear war could be fought in which presumably capitalism would survive; and Major General Talensky, one of Russia's most authoritative military writers, was saying that it was criminal to underestimate the devastation of a nuclear war and was taking the position that though capitalism "will succumb completely" as a result, it was "anti-humane" to advocate it. Talensky further reflected that the growing violence of war was reversing the age-old history of mankind and making war unusable as a means of solving political disputes, "that war as an instrument of policy is outliving itself." (*International Affairs,* October, 1960.)

The efflorescence of Soviet military doctrine began after Stalin's death. Up to that time the necessity to depict the megalomaniacal dictator as "the greatest military genius of modern times" and "the inspirer and organizer of all victories" left little room for creative or even coherent thought. The writers were thoroughly occupied with Byzantine embroideries on the theme of the Great Fatherland War. They had to keep up the aura of infallibility at all costs. This does not mean that the military arts were standing still. In the early 1950's the Soviet Union was credited with an operational fighter strength of 10,000 aircraft, and the Red armies were poised to sweep over Europe in the event of a nuclear attack. And by 1954 the Russians were turning out both long-range bombers and hydrogen bombs. There must have been staff plans in existence for how these new weapons were going to be employed in a war. But judging from the public writings, the decisions seem to have been taken piecemeal and never placed within a conceptual framework. Only when Stalin's iron lid was removed did theoretical military discussions blossom.

The Stalin era was closed with this flat declaration by Admiral Kuznetsov: "The experience of the Great Fatherland War is no longer sufficient." Talensky, at the time editor of the staff theoretical journal *Military Thought,* castigated the habits of sycophancy and hairsplitting. He turned military discussion away from a barren preoccupation with windy sociological speculations and back to analysis of combat. After two years of self-criticism of the inadequacies of military thought during the Stalinist era, the elements of a new strategic concept began to emerge.

The post-Stalin doctrine did not overturn the old one; it attempted rather to incorporate within a consistent fold the new weapons and the tactical and strategic alterations that they imposed. In contrast to Western thought, the Russians continued to emphasize the importance of ground troops and to insist that nuclear weapons, because of their vast destructive power, made larger rather than smaller forces necessary. That this was no mere theoretical projection was clear from the mass army, continually modernized and mechanized, that the Soviets kept in being, with two-thirds of all aircraft assigned to ground support to this day. The Soviet concept was an adaptation of the traditional one that no single weapon is decisive. Zhukov's 1957 declaration that "victory in future war will be achieved only by the combined efforts of all arms of the armed forces and on the basis of their coordinated employment" remains a staple article of Soviet faith.

Like their Western counterparts, the Soviet strategists were disturbed by the problem of surprise, which had been down-graded, when not completely ignored, in the previous Stalinist exegesis. The Red armies of the Second World War disproved—at enormous cost —the elder Moltke's proposition that an initial strategic mistake could not be corrected in the course of that war. But nuclear weapons are so annihilating that a nation on the receiving end of a surprise nuclear strike may theoretically be sufficiently crippled to render ineffective its further military response. All the writers agreed that surprise had grown in importance, and some went so far as to add surprise to the existing deities of the permanently operating factors. Of course, this still remained a literary solution, and did not suggest how the Soviet military establishment expected to meet the contingency.

It is possible that for a while Marshal Rotmistrov and some others began to toy with the idea of a preemptive blow in the same fashion as Western strategists. (The Marshal's article in the Spring, 1955, *Military Thought* stated that in nuclear war surprise was one of the decisive conditions for success.) Preemptive war is defined as war initiated to forestall an imminent enemy attack, as distinct from preventive war, which is initiated to forestall a future attack, or to start a war that is believed to be inevitable, before the enemy grows stronger. It can also be defined the way Bismarck did, as similar to a person deciding to commit suicide because he is afraid of death. H. S. Dinerstein of the Rand Corporation pounced on Rotmistrov's article to accuse the Soviets in the January, 1958, issue of *Foreign Affairs* of having adopted the policy of preemptive war, which naturally was denied.

The difficulty is that the distinction between the two kinds of wars may be a distinction without a difference. How does one side tell in practice whether its opponent is secretly and unobtrusively getting set for a massive nuclear strike? Reports from espionage agents? Often these are no more reliable than gossip picked up at local bistros in Tangiers and Berlin (and very likely, that is their origin in many cases). Suspicious movements of troops and equipment? What if the suspicions are mistaken? We have read how a radar reading can mistake a flight of geese for the approach of enemy aircraft. The sacred geese of ancient Rome, we know, awoke the garrison by their cackling and thus saved the city from the Gauls. But the wild geese of today may be our undoing by throwing radar inspectors into a mistaken panic.

At any rate, the Soviets are no believers in atomic blitzkriegs, or lightning aerial wars. They consider all these theories unscientific and adventuristic. While they concede that such tactics might be effective against militarily weak, demoralized, or disintegrating nations, like Poland in 1939, or France in 1940, they reject the notion that they could be decisive in a struggle with a strong, virile, and militarily prepared country, in which category they count the Soviet Union. In the same article emphasizing the importance of surprise, Rotmistrov carefully specified: "Surprise cannot however yield a conclusive result, cannot bring victory, in a war with a serious and strong enemy."

Up to the end of the fifties, Soviet military doctrine attempted to combine the methods of the Second World War with nuclear weapons and technology. Here was the character of the future war as outlined by Colonel I. Baz in a comprehensive article appearing in the chief Soviet army journal, *Military Herald* in June, 1958: The carnage would be far ghastlier, but there would still be a clear-cut winner and loser. There would be an initial exchange of thermonuclear strikes between the two sides, but devastating though these would be, they would not settle the matter. The vastness of the warrior host that would take the field, far greater than the hundred-odd million mobilized for World War II, and the expanses of the various fronts, covering virtually the entire globe and defended with every conceivable weapon from the commando switchblade to the nuclear bomb, on land, on sea, under the sea, in the air, and through the air—all would ensure that the death grapple would not only be more savage than any that had gone before, but would be of long duration, with no single battle deciding the issue.

With the publication of *Military Strategy* it is clear that the Soviet military posture is increasingly symmetrical to the American one. In the current Russian doctrine, war between the nuclear powers would still be total and global. The initial strategic missile strikes, however, would be crucial. The war would probably be a relatively short one, but the country still had to be ready for a possibly drawn-out conflict. But regardless of the crucial character of the nuclear strikes, the combined efforts of ground forces, air defense, aircraft, and the navy would be necessary to achieve victory. The Soviet establishment must therefore be a balanced one, with strategic rocket and bomber forces, antimissile and air defenses, and massive mobile and mechanized ground forces with supporting aircraft and missiles. There must also be a navy dependent on nuclear-powered submarines.

The Russians give short and scornful shrift to any concept of "controlled response." They emphasize that where the nuclear powers are drawn into battle, the war will be all out. Furthermore, nuclear strikes, so far as they are concerned, will be delivered simultaneously against the Western delivery systems as well as against the main administrative, economic, and transportation centers. The Russians know all about our distinction between counterforce and countercity strategy, but they reject it. They don't believe in it. While they continue to warn, as before, that limited wars can easily escalate into total war, they now make brief mention of the possibility of limited wars, and note that their military establishment must be prepared to wage them. Finally, the idea of preemption has reappeared in their doctrine. If the enemy is set to attack, their forces must be ready to forestall such a blow, they must have the means "of exploding the aggressive designs of the enemy by timely delivery of a crushing blow against him."

Does the Russian doctrine as to war's duration represent a military lag? Most Western analysts tend to the idea of a very short war, after which either both sides, or one side, or no side, will try to dig out of the debris to "prevail," that is, to maintain an existence. But with the introduction of new weapons and defenses there is a lot of uncertainty. In any case, the Soviet military establishment, perhaps for as many wrong reasons as right ones, was (until recently) better conceived and wrought for political purposes than its American counterpart. Its all-round character made it a more flexible instrumentality for buttressing policy than the overspecialized and nuclearly overcommitted American establishment.

After Russia achieved a nuclear capability, she wedded her concept of balanced forces to minimum deterrence. The Soviets built a long-range air force after 1954, but it was not nearly as extensive as we had expected, or as their industrial strength permitted. They built an intercontinental missile force after 1957, but again kept it to a far more modest size than our analysts anticipated. They were content to limit their force to one which could stalemate the nuclear power by imposing on Europe and America unacceptable damage, and they enhanced the credibility of their retaliatory might by their impressive space program. Besides, their ICBM, the T-3, is an unwieldy monster, 110 feet long, about 90 tons in weight, and they probably intended to wait until they had second-generation missiles before going ahead with renewed buildups.

In his January, 1960, speech to the Supreme Soviet, Khrushchev announced a new policy of giving a more central position to the long-range missiles accompanied by a one-third reduction in military man power. The chief motive for the new policy was the same one that animated the Eisenhower Administration in 1953 when it was announced that we were to have a bigger bang for our buck. The Russians wanted to reduce the cost of maintaining a mammoth standing army while building expensive offensive and defensive systems; they wanted, as one commentator remarked, more rubble for the ruble.

Russia's program of reduction survived the U-2 crisis of four months later. But it did not survive the armaments expansion announced by the Kennedy Administration and the renewed rocket-rattling over Berlin. Even had there been no Berlin crisis, the logic of the arms race would have forced the pace. The American turn to solid-fuel missiles requiring short countdowns, to mobile bases on submarines and carriers, to hardened bases underground, was making increasingly obsolete the Soviet system of a handful of fixed above-ground bases with enormous missiles requiring long countdowns and dependent on the secrecy of their location. If the Russians adopted the maxim of our military intellectuals that one must deduce the opponent's policy not from his intentions but from his capabilities, they could have concluded that America was preparing for preventive war. The symbiotic relationship of the arms race led again to the flattery of imitation. The previously announced decrease of Soviet armed forces to two and a half million was cancelled, the military budget was increased, and the Russians were off in a cloud of dust on a course parallel to our own.

In her September, 1961, tests, Russia successfully tried out devices for higher yield-to-weight-ratio warheads; she exploded a new monster terror bomb which could obliterate some of our entire states; and she experimented with space shots which blocked out radio communications and jammed radar installations for several hours over immense areas. She was now in a position to extend the range of her long-distance rockets, since she could reduce the weight of payload and increase the amount of fuel. Their tests demonstrated, according to Hans Bethe, that "the Russians have essentially caught up with our technology."

In the last three years Russia has been building up her fleet of submarines equipped with underwater launching devices similar to those that fire the Polaris, she is building Polaris-type missiles, and she is steadily hardening her long-range rocket bases. The Russians are ahead, as a matter of fact, in the larger strategic weapons; their missiles have greater thrust and can carry larger warheads. The United States has a greater across-the-board development lead in the numbers of her missiles, and she has larger bombing and nuclear-powered submarine fleets and in general a more extensive establishment. Anyhow, it doesn't really matter who has the lead. If we assume that in 1964 our nuclear striking forces are superior to Russia's by a factor of three, or even five or six, Russia still has a parity of saturation, though not of overkill. We both have the wherewithal to do a thoroughgoing job on each other.

In one respect, the Soviets are more fortunate than we are. Their authoritarian system has prevented the Communist bureaucracy from exuding a subcaste of military intellectuals. The Communist party elite has kept the monopoly over ideology, including military ideology. Though the Russians also have their military Moloch, and the high military personnel are an honored section of the elite, they are not an autonomous section, and as was made clear in the removal of Marshal Zhukov, the military officials must pay fealty to the civilian overlords. Moreover, their nationalized and authoritarian system keeps all questions of budget allocations firmly in the hands of the top Communist elite. They are not buffeted, to the same degree that we are, by enormous and powerful interests for specific weapons accumulations. In consequence, the Soviet hierarchs, military and civilian alike, while adopting a weaponry similar to our own, have not succumbed to the lure of counterforce.

Why should they? They are convinced that the tides of history, as helped along by their cadres and supporters, are moving their way. If they do not talk softly while carrying a big stick, they at least talk defensively as the aggrieved party fighting for justice. In a speech delivered at the University of Michigan on June 16, 1962, and heralded by our press as an official and major pronouncement of United States policy, Secretary of Defense McNamara tried to interest the Soviets in the proposition that in the event of war, we both follow a counterforce strategy of fighting each other's military forces while sparing the civilian populations. The reply from the other side was savage. Khrushchev called it "a monstrous proposal" that sought "to legalize nuclear war and thereby the murder of millions upon millions of people"; he lectured McNamara that "nuclear missile war erases the line between the battlefield and the rear"; he excoriated "the grossest of deceptions" and warned that "it is the civilian population that will be the first prey of the weapons of mass annihilation."

We had left ourselves wide open for this kind of reply. It is a warning signal that in a country specializing in public relations, the public-relations sense of knowledgeable and able politicians and administrators has been blunted by too long preoccupation with the outpourings of the military theologians.*

* Actually, the main message of McNamara's speech was directed to our NATO allies. The attempt was to use counterforce as an argument against independent national nuclear systems, since it spoiled everything to have "competing and conflicting strategies." "Relatively weak national nuclear forces with enemy cities as their targets are not likely to be sufficient to perform even the function of deterrence" and instead would be inviting "a preemptive first strike." McNamara insisted that the latest word in strategy made indispensable "a centrally controlled campaign, centrally controlled reserve forces," and an "indivisible target system." As we have seen, our European allies were not impressed either with counterforce as a strategy or with leaving decisions to Uncle Sam.

In his November, 1963, speech to the Economic Club of New York, McNamara suddenly discovered that contrary to all previous assertions and estimates, NATO had more and better equipped combat troops in Europe than did the Soviet bloc. This statistical victory over the Russians was presumably announced to emphasize the possibilities for conventional warfare in Europe as part of America's latest strategy of "controlled response." It also furnished the rationale for the removal of our missile bases from England, Turkey, and Italy, and our increasing reliance on our offshore naval missile forces. "Somewhere," stated C. L. Sulzberger in the December 2, 1963, *New York Times,* "Khrushchev seems to have lost 100 divisions. But our allies aren't convinced—even if they do nothing about their conviction. European experts think Moscow still has 160 front line divisions of which 96 are in Europe. To these can be added 63 from the Moscow Pact. . . . [NATO] is still defended by only 23 fairly badly equipped divisions."

CHAPTER 6    A Cultural Lag

PEOPLE reason that there will not be a new major war because surely no government will be demented enough to start one when the risks are total and eternal. After all, if you lose, you lose everything, and if you win, you only lose. And the same people who say this live in perpetual dread that we are nevertheless on the edge of another catastrophe, and can find no comfort or peace of mind in their own reassurances. Two world wars have swept away the certainties that the threat of unloosing unspeakable horrors is enough to stay the ruler's hands. Who is unaware that identical arguments were bandied about before 1914, and that they proved unavailing against the ambitions and passions of peoples and governments?

But how we have progressed since those days of innocence! The war that was dreaded before 1914 was a European one, and the Cassandras who were aghast at the prospect were thinking of the devastation of a continental culture. Now a conflagration would be universal, and the destruction would be not of populations and cities, but of our entire civilization. Before, when they peeped into the chamber of horrors, the most calamitous of the Jeremiahs invariably drew back in disbelief. No, they said, war under modern conditions is too frightful and destructive, and civilization has moved too far ahead to permit it. Now, we are both less trusting and more inured to such horrors. We have plumbed the depths of man's capacity for cruelty and self-destruction. And mass society has shrunk the individual at the same time that the head-fixing machines of overorganized national states have conditioned their citizenries to a Prussian automatonism.

If it is true that in the present era rulers and ruled dread war more than they desire war, why are they so helpless in disengaging themselves from its steel embrace? For several thousand years wars have been things of calculation. Guile and coldblooded egotistic premeditation enter into all war lusts, fevers, and aggressions—past and present. Clans, tribes, and nations have started wars to become its beneficiaries, never its victims. If such materialistic calculations were made by rude tribal chieftains and illiterate Oriental potentates, certainly they must rule the councils of our leaders who have spawned schools and shoals of investigating committees, evaluation councils, study seminars, operational divisions, planning commissions, and who cannot move a step in simple administrative decision, much less one so momentous as war, without the guiding memoranda, briefing papers, and strategic balance sheets drawn up by a ubiquitous and serried bureaucracy.

Some have deduced too literally from this premise that wars are the result of a simple matter of miscalculation, and that if the author were to point this out to the party or parties in question, they would at once recognize their elementary error in logic or mathematics, and with this recognition, dissolve the danger. Before the First World War writers like Norman Angell sought to demonstrate that war was "the great illusion" because it didn't pay. You could get a higher return by investing the money in good railroad bonds. Curiously enough, also on the eve of the Civil War, a Southerner, H. R. Helper, wrote a book, *The Impending Crisis of the South,* to prove to the slave oligarchy that slavery did not pay.

Using a related method of thought, though based in this case on academic rather than banker's rationalism, an American historiography sought to demonstrate the lack of necessity for the Civil War. It placed the responsibility for the carnage on the extremists of both sides. According to the thesis, if the abolitionists and their followers had not been in the grip of an idealistic illusion that they were Jehovah's chosen instrument to chastise the sinners, and if the fire-eaters had not been obsessed with secession, then reasonable men on both sides could have gotten together and worked out a compromise solution of benefit to both the North and South, which would have saved this nation the consequences of four years of savage warfare, and a heritage of bitterness not yet washed away. Now, all can certainly agree that the South could have secured a better arrangement in 1860 than it was left with after 1865, or even after 1873, and we can apply the same thesis to the First World War. In the light of the results, certainly Germany and England would have been well advised in 1914 to come to terms on colonies, markets, and raw materials. Even a less than equitable agreement would have afforded greater prosperity and power to both contestants than did the sanguinary trial at arms which reduced them to the status of second-rate powers.

Thus far, such preachments have not succeeded in deflecting history from its old course of movement by conflict and violence. The calculation of governments and nations does not follow the procedures of calculating machines. History is made with the human materials that nature provides. This means not only that man's calculations are subject to error, but that he can think only within the social context, and measure with the values, conceptions, passions, prejudices, and self-interests that are current at the time. To the slaveholder of 1860, compromising away slavery was unthinkable. It would have merely invited further Northern arrogance. To the Englishman of 1914, a proposal to voluntarily give up the smallest part of his empire was a counsel of madness or cowardice. Compliance with it would have encouraged Germany to swell her pretensions. In either case, no leader could have retained his following for five minutes after proposing it. No private citizen would have held the good opinion of his neighbors or friends for any longer period of time. Theoretically, at least in a democracy, alternative policies are supposed to be weighed by the government and debated by the public. But in critical moments passions run high and sweep away debate. The opponent of the official line is not held to be in error, but is stamped as a traitor—and he and his opinions are given short shrift.

Ruth Benedict has pointed out how a culture is a more or less integrated configuration displaying a consistent pattern of thought and action. Because of a society's integration, it has limited flexibility. It tends to apotheosize every aspect of its adaptation and tradition, and to view every proposal to change even incidentals as an attack on, and a threat to, its way of life—which is extended to mean the only right way of life. The dominant traits of a society become compulsive. Consequently, even in relatively flexible cultures, which are undergoing continual change, an untenable arrangement has to reach its breaking point before relief is possible. The statesmen can only premeditate coldbloodedly on the basis of the going conceptions and the social dispositions of their societies. They can plan only in accordance with functional rationality, which is never the same thing as idealistic rationality.

It is this functional rationality that is supposed to stay the hands of the nuclear powers. Since neither side has taken sufficient leave of its senses, thus far, at any rate, to adopt the theory of fanatics that it can "prevail" in a thermonuclear exchange, it ought to follow that the balance of terror has ruled out a major war. This balance of terror is a current restatement of the theory of the balance of power, the idea being, "One sword holds another in its sheath." Nations as a rule do not go to war when the odds are spectacularly against them. Hence, if the peaceful states—or more specifically, the states that are satisfied to keep the status quo—confront with overwhelming force the warmongering states—or more specifically, the states that want to upset the status quo—the warmongers will be intimidated into virtue, and the peace will be saved. But the history of balance of power politics shows that it is an unstable and impermanent arrangement.

The proposition has had limited successes in certain brief periods of history when the status quo powers had the upper hand. The balance of power keeps the peace while the balance holds. It never holds for very long, though. Civilized societies are by their nature in the grip of dynamic change, and relative balances between a cluster of sovereign enclaves necessarily and constantly are in a shifting medium. When the mutual relationships have altered sufficiently, the conservative dikes collapse under the accumulated pressures.

Sooner or later one side grows stronger because of new alliances, or because it has grown more rapidly technologically, commercially, industrially, or in population, or because it has accumulated larger gold hoards or more rifles, or because it has hired more mercenaries. Pursuant to what it now considers the new power distribution, this side requests a new deal. This side wants additional territories, or new strategic boundaries, or better outlets to the seas, or extended spheres of influence, or whatever it is that men and nations consider important at the particular time. If its diplomatic requests are not

afforded recognition (and how can they be? Granting them would
irretrievably shift the power balance over to the rival) the two contending powers or blocs have no alternative except to submit their
differences of judgment as to what the true distribution of power
really is to the arbitrament of arms.

In modern history Great Britain has been the most ambitious and
the most successful practitioner of the politics of the balance of
power. The Hundred Years War cured her of ambitions to maintain dependencies in Europe. From Elizabethan times to 1914, the
avoidance of fixed continental entanglements, and the preservation
of a balance between the powers, became the lodestar of her foreign
policy. It was her aim, by adroitly shifting her weight in this or that
direction, never to permit any single power to dominate the continent. When the industrial revolution set her far ahead of the rest
of the pack, she could manipulate the scales while standing aloof
in "splendid isolation." From the Congress of Vienna to 1914, the
policy has been adjudged to have worked satisfactorily, which is
probably right, provided we slice away the twenty-year period from
1850 to 1870, and disregard such trifles as repeated colonial expedi-
tions and punitive wars, the Crimean War, the American Civil War,
the Italian and German wars for unification, the Franco-German
war.

The balance policy did prevent the embroilment of the powers in
a major scramble like the Napoleonic revolution, or the Thirty
Years devastation, but only because Britain was the strongest single
power, with an industrial preponderance and an unchallenged navy.
Her joining any existent alliance, or forming any new coalition, was
sufficient to give that bloc an imperious weight against any possible
combination that could be arrayed against it. But no sooner did
Germany's industrial and military strength begin to equal her own
than the balance was ground to dust, and the system of alliances
turned Europe into two armed camps headed for catastrophic war.
As Lowes Dickinson wrote of the balance of power in *War: Its
Nature, Cause and Cure*, "It means on the one hand, an equality, as
of two sides when an account is balanced, and on the other hand,
an inequality, as when one has a 'balance' to one's credit at the
bank. The balance of power theory professes the former, but pur-
sues the latter. It is thus, in fact, a perpetual effort to get the better
of the balance; and as this effort is prosecuted on both sides, the
ultimate issue is war."

In a preceding age, Edward Gibbon, misled by the indecisive

contests of the European monarchs and the prosperity of a commercial interlude, fatuously concluded that Europe had attained a common level of cultivation so that it could be considered as "one great republic," and though the balance of power would continue to fluctuate, the minor alterations and corrections could not essentially alter the European harmony. The great historian lacked a historical outlook for his own time. Before his death he was to witness the eruption across the channel of a despised mass which had been denied a place in his cultured society of philosophers and kings, and which went on to demolish the nicely constructed edifice of the European association of aristocracies.

After the First World War the United States sought to appropriate the scepter that was once Britain's proud possession, but she was unable to match Britain's majestic standard of the past. Her international inexperience coupled with Europeans' illusions that they were still in possession of their prewar might, impeded the creation of a new world balance in the interwar years. In the Second World War Britain could no longer meet German armed strength, and even British and American power combined were inadequate for the challenge. The two allies had to secure the additional help of Soviet Russia. After the holocaust only two first-class powers remained, the United States and the U.S.S.R., and the hegemony of the first lasted scarcely a decade before it was challenged *de facto* and *de jure*.

Why will the balance of terror between the East and West work any differently this time than it did between England and Germany? Can the cold war be anything more than the prelude to a thermonuclear war? Technology is exploding in an unprecedented way, and the political revolution of our time is daily changing the face of the globe. By the end of the century, or sooner, the present economic, political, and military balance will have shifted so markedly to one or another side, that the leaders of the dominant bloc may decide that they—but not the enemy—will be able to rise like a triumphant phoenix out of the nuclear ashes; or what is more likely, the leaders of the dominant bloc will self-confidently press their advantage until a local contest sucks in the principals to the point where neither side can extricate itself from the fatal sequence of events.

The experience of the past half-century makes this supposition more than likely; and if correct, we are all marching, with national drums rolling, and ideological flags unfurled, down the road to doomsday. There is a difference, however, between 1914 and today; how decisive, remains to be seen, but a difference, nonetheless. The nuclear weapon has introduced a new element into the historical calculus. The thought is that while nuclear warfare has not converted man to goodness or nobility, it has possibly frightened him into sensibility. Because it ensures the destruction of both sides and threatens man's biological existence, it will not, this time, be considered a realistic arm of policy; that where statesmen and soldiers were ready to expend the lives of ten or twenty million of their countrymen in what turned into a mystic quest for a ghostly victory, they will shrink back from responsibilities so onerous, and from contests so purposeless, as those which nuclear wars impose.

The conduct of statesmen and nations since the advent of the nuclear age has been scarcely reassuring, although the present animosities would probably have long since erupted into World War III but for the braking process exercised by the mutual nuclear terror. But unless new ideas are brought into the comity of nations, unless new modalities are devised for civilized discourse, the kind of arms race now in progress will almost inevitably make the decision for war at some point irresistible. Statesmen and nations will turn their backs on nuclear death only if new social arrangements permit that decision. Under present arrangements, military deterrents afford no more than a reprieve.

II

War is the payoff of the military system. It is the foundation and extension of the power distribution in civilization. It has been pushed to the background within the state collectivity by a system of law and authority based upon acceptance or consent; while rarely employed, it remains in being if and when needed to reassert the state's sovereignty. In the power distributions between states, determined by relative economic prowess, technological skill, cultural efficiency, and political sagacity, war has been and remains the *ultima ratio,* the only method thus far devised to test pretension by performance, the military arithmetic by which the power balances can be struck off just as commercial balances are paid up on the day of settlement. On occasion, when an embattled people seek to free themselves from a hated yoke, as in the case of the Jews under the Roman Empire, or the Albanians under the Ottoman Turks, they may strike out blindly without thought of cost or consequence. This is the exception to the rule. As a general proposition, particularly in the clash of organized states, war is a calculated play for advantage, in defense as well as offense, coldbloodedly figured as a gamble for high or supreme stakes.

If it is true that war has been down through the centuries a sanguinary form of political bookkeeping calculated for profit and advantage, and if it has reached the point of no return where it can no longer produce profits or advantage, why does the institution persist? Why, instead of withering away, is it in a golden state of efflorescence? Can it be that only rulers and militarists persist in clinging to this ancient institution, but the common folk are ready to discard it? Even a cursory investigation establishes that that is not so, that while the generality of peoples dread war and do not want war, they are as convinced as their governments that the international system of armament and threat cannot be discarded. Were another war to start, they probably would display even less elation than they did in the last one. They would probably be more grim about it despite the oceans of propaganda that have been spilled over them. But they would go. They would do what their governments told them to do.

Shall we then say that it is simply another manifestation of a cultural lag, that the human mind has not yet been able to invent new social arrangements to conform to the new technology? This is obviously the case. It is a platitude of our times that political thinking is miles behind scientific thinking. But this sweeping theorem, because it is so sweeping, is not very enlightening. When we try to formulate some of the specifics of the cultural lag, we see why it is such a labor of Hercules to shift the time-honored basis of civilization.

Human societies have developed unevenly. The confrontation of disparate cultures, as the Roman with the Gaul, the Spaniard with the Aztec, the British with the Hindu, the European with the American Indian, always led to social convulsion and revolutionary dislocation. This has been true throughout history, but the confrontation of the industrialized West with the underdeveloped world has never been so universally unsettling as in the present revolutionary epoch. At the very time that the system of sovereign, armed, national states has been shown to be unworkable, and where these leading states have after two world wars gathered into opposing war blocs that threaten the survival of civilization, the deprived and exploited peoples of Asia and Africa are reaching out for the very same combination of national sovereignty and industrialization in order to assert their national dignity and to make good their claim for modern living standards.

In years to come, were the trend to continue undeflected, after some of these nations have industrialized, they might acquire nuclear bombs and other formidable military equipment to confront each other with the same threat of annihilation that Russia and the United States fling at each other today. But that is the music of the long future. Right now, and for the epoch ahead, the decision by warfare that has governed for six thousand years remains operative for them. Indonesia can fight Holland, the Vietnamese can outpace the French, Egypt can quarrel with Israel—and the principles of the game are as true as when the Assyrian came down like the wolf on the fold, and when Saul slew his thousand and David his ten thousand.

Many of these wars are between insurgent nationals and powers that own nuclear weapons, as in the case of the Algerians against the French, or the Vietnamese against the French, where Admiral Radford and Secretary of State Dulles were reported to have proposed American intervention and the dropping of atomic bombs; or the North Vietnamese against the Americans. But nuclear weapons have not been used in any of the colonial wars, and most likely, they never will be. The ultimate horror weapon is of uncertain worth against guerrilla insurgency, and the Western nations have concluded that the moral revulsion of mankind would overwhelm anyone that had the temerity to decree that kind of extinction for a people who themselves had no nuclear weapons and could not reply in kind. Even in the limited engagements fought on primitive terrains, the use of the airplane, napalm bombs, and bazookas makes these wars profligate in the destruction of humans. But to use the grisly language of the statisticians, they are no more destructive relative to population and wealth than the forays of antiquity or the Middle Ages. They are manageable.

The main danger that these second-string traditional wars will graduate into up-to-date nuclear wars lies in the possibility that the leaders of the two war blocs, Russia and the United States, will get involved in them; and what started out as a guerrilla battle between an insurgent faction against a colonial power, or between a dissident faction against a feudal or tribal aristocracy, will become metamorphosed first into a covert, and then a full-blown, war between

the major powers. Almost every bush-league war carries this potential, for the two war blocs are in such stiff-necked opposition
that any political shift or social change anywhere in the world, with
no significance in and of itself to either of the behemoths, becomes
an intolerable loss of face which it is worth millions upon millions
of dollars or rubles to prevent or undo. If there is to be a World
War III, this will probably be the shot that sets off the gaieties.

It will not likely start over Berlin. It will not likely start because
some jittery radar inspector mistakes a flock of geese for an enemy
missile attack. It will not likely start because demented generals
blackmail their government into getting in the first nuclear rabbit
punch. It has the best chance of starting by the two sides beginning
to feed arms and advisers to their respective factions in a minor
engagement, and getting sucked in, until neither Big Brother is able
to extricate himself. At this point, the missiles and bombs will elbow
aside the politicians and diplomats; they will do the talking and will
take over the making of decisions.

The danger makes indigent peoples wary of falling into the
clutches of either power bloc. However, it has not made factions so
wary that they want to stop fighting for their causes, or cease bargaining for arms and support from whomever they can. It has not
deterred, and it will not deter, them from having recourse to wars
to overturn hateful social arrangements. Not only is the gap between
life in the world's metropolitan centers and its backward regions
immense, but it has grown intolerable to the natives in the rice
paddies and on the plantations. These people now have spokesmen,
and these spokesmen say that their constituents must be permitted
to partake of the fruits of modern civilization.

It is too superficial a view of the revolution of our times to say
that the Western powers are rapidly divesting themselves of their
colonies, and soon all of them will be represented in the U.N. as
independent nations. There are still colonies in Africa, and there
will be much turmoil and probably bloodshed before the black man
comes into his own. More important, many of the backward countries are run by privileged cliques who remain clients of the industrial powers and who seek to freeze unsatisfactory local dispositions. The economic and technological problems of transforming
these vast, poverty-stricken regions into reasonably prosperous
nations are enormous and will take many decades to solve. The
political problems of clearing the paths for industrialization are
many and thorny. At the same time, the peoples of these vast

stretches of the globe are frenziedly and impatiently reaching out
for what they see as attainable. The interaction of these three forces
guarantees that the revolution will seethe for a long time to come,
and that the winning of political independence will be only the
prelude to intense conflicts between groups, tribes, classes, within
the nation, and between the nations.

Since the political leaders of Africa, Asia, and South America
have not discovered any ultimate principles of settling differences
other than the military one, and show no greater compassion in
managing their affairs than that shown by their erstwhile masters,
the revolution of the underprivileged breeds militarism, and has
not been and will not be free of military activities. But this is not
the main problem of war in our time. It is not the militarism of
Egypt, or of Israel, or Ghana, or India, that is frightening the world,
and it would be unreasonable to demand of the recently colonial
countries that they carry the burden of abolishing the war institution. If anyone is to take the lead in this reversal of an old custom,
it will have to be the powers that for better or for worse are the
political leaders of humanity by virtue of their industrial and
military might. Only if the nuclear powers assume the leadship for
creating a new international order to replace the order of war can
there be any hope that the social revolution sweeping across three
continents and affecting the majority of the world's peoples will
be able to find new instrumentalities for adjudicating its quarrels
and peacefully realizing its purposes.


## III


At the very time that the underdeveloped peoples are moving
heaven and earth to get developed, and in the process upsetting old
balances and unsettling old harmonies, the struggle between Russia
and the West, which has been an undercurrent of history for forty-
five years, has blown up into the major contest of the international
community. Although Soviet Russia was an impoverished and
isolated state in the twenties and was preoccupied with its own
industrialization plans and internal bloodlettings in the thirties,
it became the second industrial power and the leader of a rival war
bloc to the West in the fifties. Where Communists once consisted
of ragged and irregular bands of subversives to be dealt with by
the police and the law courts of the West, Soviet Russia now stands

at the head of a retinue of states pressing home a cold war against the opposite camp.

With two leviathans thrashing about for world influence and opposing concepts of social organization, the area of world convulsion is complete. There is no island in the distant oceans free of the spreading storm. There is no outpost sufficiently off the beaten track to escape the attention of the movers and shakers. The natives of Bali are handed Russian equipment to join in the Indonesian fight against the Dutch; Greenland is fitted out with radar screens to supply the West with warning signals of enemy missile flights; and tiny Iceland, close to the Arctic Circle, with no railroads and no army, has found itself a member of NATO and the possessor of a sizable Communist opposition, at one and the same time.

There is a school that holds that the world cannot go off the war standard while the ideological battle rages between East and West, that it is vain to imagine that the war system can be dispensed with until the world goes all Communist or all capitalist, or when an interaction of the two leads possibly to the distillation of some third system. The difficulty with waiting for a more propitious occasion to launch a grand peace effort is that the more propitious occasion may never come. The view, in any case, is unhistorical. It idealizes, by implication, the past story of mankind. Some of the fiercest wars of annihilation, in the ancient world as well as the modern, were between nations of similar social cultures. Rome and Carthage were both based on slavery, and Rome copied the Carthaginian system of latifundia after it razed Carthage to the ground. In the First World War, Germany, France, and England were socially very much alike, and Russia and Austria-Hungary were socially very much alike, and they all fought to the death to wipe out their cultural blood relations. In the Second World War, the fear that Nazi Germany would gain hegemony over Europe was sufficient to mute social animosities and bring England and the United States into an alliance with Communist Russia. It is an illusion to think that conflicts between states are removed, or even necessarily mitigated, when they adopt similar institutions, or adhere to the same religious or philosophical systems, or organize their economies along parallel lines.

Were the question of Sovietism whisked out of existence today by some touch of a magic wand, the world would not become transfigured into a community of states cherishing one another in Christian brotherhood. Instead, conflicts that are now held in check by the overriding requirements of the cold war would burst, once this imperative was removed, into a flower garden of hatred and evil. There would be new war lineups. The contestants would display a fervor no less intense than the passions of today on behalf of entirely new ideological expressions. In the light of the sanguinary history of mankind, and the rich variety of crusades for which man has proven capable of bashing in the brains of his kind, the most that one can say about ideological wars is that, like civil wars, they tend to be fought more tenaciously and more passionately than the regulation conflicts between states. Whether this old rule is still worth anything in the mechanized ferocity of war in our own age is problematical. The distinction has certainly been narrowed at the least.

The thought that the war system can end only if and when the whole world has adopted one common social system is a throwback to the nineteenth century notion of universal and fixed stages in history. According to this idea, humanity passed from barbarism to slavery, to feudalism, to capitalism, and would eventually move on to the next stage of social organization. Marx and Engels made use of the schema to predict the coming triumph of communism. They saw it first conquering in the advanced industrial countries of Europe; then the backward areas would follow suit by repeating the evolution that the advanced countries had pioneered. The generalization of the stages of social evolution had its uses, and helped writers from Saint Simon to Spencer to reorient social thought. That does not mean that there was ever one universal system throughout the world; and things today are working out more unpredictably and chaotically than could have been fore-shadowed in the Marxian handbooks. The Communist revolution started in Russia and proceeded to China. The Western governments rallied their peoples in opposition to this new order by extending social benefits to produce a welfare-state modification of the old capitalism. Most of the emergent colonial nations have set up state systems which have borrowed from both of the major opponents.

Instead of greater uniformity, there is greater diversity. Instead of an evening-out of wealth and cultural attainment, there is as much unevenness as there has ever been. It is possible that in centuries to come technology will have forced through a standardization that history has heretofore never witnessed. But the epoch of national revolution, symbolizing the strivings of two billion people to over-

A CULTURAL LAG                                             123

come the neglect of past millennia, is bound to be the epoch of plurality, of startling disparity, of a variety of permutations and computations on the essential themes of national states dedicated to industrialization and material enrichment. The backward peoples will necessarily produce novel mutations because they graft onto every variety of traditional and tribal society the end products of three hundred years of Western science and technology. Where the airplane is brought in and the juju remains, you cannot get Adam Smith or Karl Marx pure. The instability of the times, and the clash of two antipathetic world powers, is part of the explanation for the cultural lag in continuing an unworkable militarism. Isn't that a roundabout and lengthy way of saying that man has not learned to relate his institutions to the demands of his technology?

Why is man, who was such a success in primordial times in adapting to natural changes, such an inadequate adapter to social changes? The very accumulation of cultural tradition, which accounts for his ability to create his world of cities and machinery, sets up vested interests which bar the way to further change and which can only be subdued by conflict, by misery, by hysteria, by the large expenditure of social energy. Social change can never proceed with the simplicity and directness of redesigning a machine or repairing a building. It is secured only in agony.

The war establishment is a case in point. It originates in the social needs of organized states; but once set up, it lives a life of its own. It follows the law of bureaucracy. Every bureaucracy has a tendency to proliferate, to extend its influence, to augment its power, to create a continuing need for its services, to make itself indispensable as the administrator of the state's business. The military bureaucracy is in an especially privileged position to exact respect for its corporate claims because it oversees a department of the state's affairs which has jurisdiction over questions of life and death. If the military department mismanages its business, it may mean the overturn of the regime and the loss of a people's independence. The military can make use of its strategic indispensability to enlarge the demand for its services by embroiling the nation in the war that it is supposed to avoid.

The late Joseph Schumpeter, in discussing the Egyptian militarism at the time of the New Empire, wrote: "Created by wars that required it, the machine now created the wars it required." That is militarism's innate tendency, like the tendency of capital to maximize profits, whether always realized or not. Born out of the antagonisms of sovereign states, the military works instinctively to perpetuate these antagonisms in order to justify its own existence. Sociology is well acquainted with the phenomenon where a group is dedicated to making its predictions come true.


IV

Since, under modern conditions, the war machine does not consist of fighting men who furnish their own lances and bucklers, but is dominated by supply ministries and arms contractors, some of the popular antagonism to war has been centered on its organizers and those who supply them with the sinews of combat. In the pacifist reaction of the twenties and thirties that followed the First World War, there was a great outcry against the munition makers. There was a general feeling that they were responsible for artificially whipping up patriotic hysteria against other countries in order to sell their wares, and that they used money and propaganda to thwart and defeat all peace-making and disarmament efforts. The theme found ready acceptance among the civil servants of the League of Nations. In 1921 a commission that had been appointed to inquire into the private manufacture of arms issued a report with these findings: (1) that military arms firms were active in fomenting war scares, and in persuading their own countries to adopt warlike policies; (2) that they systematically attempted to bribe government officials both at home and abroad; (3) that they disseminated false reports concerning the military programs of other countries in order to stimulate armament expenditure; (4) that they sought to mold public opinion by purchasing control of newspapers in their own and foreign countries; (5) that they organized international armament rings through which the arms race was pushed by playing off one country against another; (6) that they set up international trusts which increased the price of armaments to governments.

Before many years had passed, every schoolboy who was at all interested in social events could recite the litany: how in the South African war the Boers shot British soldiers with British rifles; how in the Dardanelles campaign Australian and British troops were mown down by British guns; how the munition makers upheld their bloody fraternity above the fury of the trenches when the French high command refrained from shelling the Briey basin, which supplied Germany with much of its ore, in return for which the Germans desisted from bombarding Dombasle in Meurthe-et-Moselle, where equally large scale operations were supplying the French. It was common knowledge that highly placed ministers, generals, and journalists had accepted bribes from arms manufacturers, that the agents of these firms were trying to discredit all peace efforts, and that cabinet ministers, members of parliament, and men of the cloth enjoyed an ample representation on the lists of stock owners of the leading arms corporations. Krupp, Thyssen, Vickers-Armstrong, Schneider-Creusot, Skoda, Bethlehem Steel, all became infamous household names, members of the Secret International, who sat on each other's boards of directors and carried on the vulture game with neither scruple nor conscience against their own peoples.

The atmosphere was thick with moral indignation. An article entitled "Arms and the Man" appeared in the March, 1934, issue of Henry Luce's *Fortune,* and which today might be rejected by the *Nation* as being too shrill and ideologically extreme. The caption under the title read: "A primer on Europe's armament makers; their mines, their smelters, their banks, their holding companies, their ability to supply everything you need for a war from cannons to the *casus belli;* their axioms, which are (a) prolong war, (b) disturb peace." The article's conclusion: "Without a shadow of doubt there is at the moment in Europe a huge and subversive force that lies behind the arming and counterarming of nations."

At its extreme, the attack on the munition makers proceeded from the view that it was this international gang of financial highbinders and their allies that was responsible for inciting otherwise peaceable nations to war so they could sell arms and make blood money. That is the way Lord Welby explained to the British public the obstacle to better international understanding. "We are in the hands," he said, "of an organization of crooks. They are politicians, generals, manufacturers of armaments, and journalists. All of them are anxious for unlimited expenditures, and go on inventing scares to terrify the public and to terrify Ministers of the Crown." George Bernard Shaw pinpointed the rebellious mood of the interwar pacifism when he had Undershaft, the arms king, explain it in *Major Barbara:* "The Government of your country! I am the Government of your country, I and Lazarus. Do you suppose that you and half a dozen amateurs like you, sitting in a row in that

foolish gabble shop, govern Undershaft and Lazarus? No, my
friend, you will do what pays us. You will make war when it suits
us and keep peace when it doesn't. . . . When I want anything to
keep my dividends up, you will discover that my want is a national
need. When other people want something to keep my dividends
down, you will call out the police and military. And in return you
shall have the support of my newspapers, and the delight of imagining that you are a great statesman."

This agitation against the munition makers and their blood
profits was drowned out by the propaganda accompanying the
second round of the great war. The final echoes of the interwar
sentiments and of the Nye Senatorial investigations were heard in
President Roosevelt's proposals after Pearl Harbor for limitation of
profits and for "equality of sacrifice." But they hardly left a ripple
in the frenzy of clearing the decks for unlimited war production.
The line of least resistance was to allow the industrialists to organize
the supply lines in accordance with their own preferences. The conservative mood of the fifties, which emphasized the unity and common interests of the nation, finished the job of discarding the ideas
of the thirties. In the excitations and fears engendered by the cold
war, it became a form of naive and unkempt village radicalism to
harp on the profits of military contractors, and to suggest that a
vested interest was being created for war and against peace.

There is no doubt that the old outcry against the munition makers
was based on a crudity and an oversimplification. The facts cited
were generally correct; however, as a sociology, the thesis lacked
depth and proportion. That is why the favorite remedies, ranging
from supervision and licensing of private arms manufacturers to
nationalization of the arms firms, were on the superficial side. The
League of Nations' devotees ignored the difficulty in a modern
industrial society of differentiating between military and conventional production and research. They slurred over the reality that
the "munitions trust" was not a distinct villain but interwoven
with the rest of the industrial establishment. They exaggerated the
independent role of the military contractors in government policy-
making. If anything, the views of the twenties have more applica-
bility to today's military industry in this country than they had for
the European situation of the time.

Were the arms manufacturers plying a trade that cuts across the
ideas of the bulk of the nation and maintaining themselves exclusively by bribing legislators and buying up newspapers and public

media channels, the nation would have long since found spokesmen and created the means to overturn this unwanted thralldom. The arms manufacturers have done all these things, and probably are continuing to do them at the present time. Their activities, conditioned by their professional interests, exercise an inordinate influence on the nation's foreign policy and military trend. But they are not moving against the grain. All this is permitted by public opinion because the nation is unconvinced that there exists a workable system to replace the system of violence. The munition makers could not have prospered, or even survived, before the First World War, after the First World War, and now during the cold war, except for the towering fact that the national state is a slave to war habit. The nation, like the narcotic addict, may despise and hate the junk peddler, may stage an occasional revolt against his greed, his exactions, his conspiracies, but so long as it carries the monkey on its back, it cannot do without him.

When a nation is committed to the military logic, the nation understands that it must have the military tools. When its economy is organized on lines of private endeavor and profit, its military hardware is produced under the same arrangements by which it procures its television sets and cigarette lighters. In Soviet Russia, where all industry has been nationalized, and where the League of Nations ideal of abolishing the private manufacture of arms has been realized with a vengeance, there are no military contractors who set afoot campaigns to sway the public and the Congress into purchasing their particular airplanes or gadgets. There are no accommodating corporations to employ military personnel in highly paid posts when they retire from the armed forces. Nevertheless, the national commitment to the military logic has produced a no less formidable military establishment which, through different institutional forms and appropriate social styles, also exerts a massive influence on national policy. The Russian military staff, integrated into the generalized Communist Party elite, may have less independent institutional strength than its American counterpart. Even in the United States, however, the military coteries, powerful as they have become, and buttressed by the wealth of the private contractors, are socially and ideologically part of the generalized power elite. They push forward their respective claims in a friendly milieu. Their representatives are not *arrivistes* or bootleggers in the world of status and power; they are honored members of the top-level fraternity.

All the same, it is to be wondered at that the thesis of the interwar years has been so muted in the cold war decades. Theodore Roszak of Stanford University writes: "Once among the most disreputable of businesses, the weapons industry has since the end of World War II acquired a new and exciting identity, one which has managed to court the favor of the intellectual community as well as the admiration of the general public." This is to be accounted for by the same conservative mood which has transformed the "economic royalists" of the thirties into *Fortune*'s glamor figures of the fifties, and where Matthew Josephson's *Robber Barons* have been displaced by foundation-financed hagiologies.

For there is no need to accuse the arms manufacturers, or the general staffs, or both, of being the secret architects of the current arms race to realize that this vast and profitable power complex, subsisting on war preparations and the animosities between nations, has a vested interest in the cold war, and a tendency to use its growing power for its perpetuation. This operates impersonally, like a Parkinson law of bureaucracy, without any reference to the private preferences of generals and corporation executives, and it has no bearing and is not affected by their possibly exemplary conduct toward home and family. The left hand of private morality never wants to know what the right hand of public morality is doing.

If the public outcry against the "merchants of death" were to have any correlation with the size of the military establishments, then the clamor ought to be piercing enough to drown every competing voice and plea. The breakneck arms race preceding the First World War, and the growing military establishments, which horrified and frightened a generation of socialists and pacifists, were modest affairs compared to those of our own day. Hohenzollern Germany was considered at the time to have the most formidable military machine in the world, and after the Agadir incident she had been rapidly increasing her military budgets. In 1913 her government spent what was then thought of as the enormous sum of half a billion dollars, larger than the military budget of either France, England, or Russia. This enormous sum represented about 4 per cent of her national income, a third of the American expeditures of recent years relative to our national income, especially if we take into account American military aid around the world.

Since this country has today from ten to twelve times more actual production than the Germany of 1913, it means that after making due allowance for the money inflation, the Pentagon has at its disposal thirty dollars for every dollar that was at the disposal of the Kaiser's generals and admirals. If the military party was able to dominate the Germany of 1914 and engrave the *Junker kultur* on the nation's brow, our own military party has thirty times the resources to dominate the United States and impose its military metaphysic on the national mind. It might be said that the German militarists were under the influence of social Darwinism and reveled in the glories of conquest, whereas our own militarists are firmly attached to freedom's cause and the Sermon on the Mount, and continue to press for more weapons and larger budgets only to safeguard the precious heritage of democracy from godless marauders outside our gates. But a glance at the American military establishment is not reassuring.

## V

The war lord has been traditionally the potential foe of civilian rule, and his potential enmity has repeatedly burst into overt hostility. His entire training and experience led him to cut the Gordian knot of social conflicts and complexities with the sword. The military environment of peremptory command and unquestioning obedience has made him contemptuous of and impatient with the debates and cavils of politicians and civil servants. In the state organization, where the military has been assigned the monopoly of organized violence, the war lord has time and again tried to use this monopoly against the civilian governments he was sworn to protect. When the American and French revolutions brought in the era of popular rule and democratic process, they aggravated the tension between the civilian and the war lord. Democratic government now harbored within its own bosom an institution organized on a diametrically opposite concept of authoritarianism, an institution, moreover, which had the ability in potential of overthrowing all other institutions and setting itself up as a usurping sovereignty.

The history of democracy in its insurgent phase has consequently been a history of intense suspicion of the military establishment, of keeping the military bottled up, of fashioning every possible safeguard to prevent the war lords from throwing their weight about, of keeping them within the narrow confines of their prescribed duties and professional responsibilities, of surrounding the military bureaucracy with every conceivable civilian control, of enthroning in society the industrial and administrative rather than the martial virtues. Democracy might have realized its antimilitary aims had society evolved in the way that Cobden and Spencer projected. But when capitalism and industrialism perfected instead the series of sovereign states competing for privilege and colliding in war, the military arm inevitably grew larger and more muscular, and the military ethic repeatedly crowded out the civilian ethic.

The modern military establishment, as it was perfected in the European states since the French Revolution, exhibited everywhere two notorious and congenital traits. The first was an organic predilection for reactionary wellsprings of society, an identification with the aristocratic and privileged, a preference for authoritarian political circles, ideologies, and spokesmen. In the democracies no less than in the dictatorships, the officers' castes remained the preserve and source of spoils for the sons of the upper classes. It made little difference when recruits of humbler origin were permitted into their ranks; the aristocratic tradition was so fierce and unyielding that any populist or egalitarian notions that the young officer may have harbored when entering the military academy disappeared like drops of water in contact with a hot iron. The tradesman's or functionary's son, rather than softening the Tory character of the establishment he entered, was more likely to assume the postures and mimic the pretensions of the most extreme in order to establish his own right to belong to the snobbish and superior warrior caste.

The second reflex of the military establishment has been toward the creation of its own sovereignty within the sovereignty of the state. The war lords are inclined to brook no interference in the running of their domain while exhibiting a voracious ambition to extend their own jurisdiction. The drive is inherent in the military organization and has been mitigated only when confronted with countervailing power. The military establishment is helpless without the backing of government which supplies it with weapons, manpower, scientific technique. But once supplied with these accoutrements and appurtenances, the war lords emerge as a major power bloc within society, and they soon learn, if they have not already known it, that society operates by the competing pressures of power blocs. From servants of society who have been generously accorded rank, the war lords begin to see themselves as lord high protectors and benefactors of society, but for whose exceptional skills and martial qualities their country would fall prey to the aggressions of the outsider. As soon as the military establishment has grown important enough, civilian control becomes something that is not to be accepted in good or bad grace, but something to be outwitted and evaded.

In the course of their business dealings and official contacts, staff officers learn that civilian government is a porous institution. They are able to buy and subvert journalists and legislators. They are able to make alliances with business and professional interests for the realization of common goals and mutual benefits. When this stage is reached, generals and admirals become military politicians, and the military establishment an unofficial partner, junior, senior, or equal, as the case may be, of civilian government.

As a consequence there is within the generalized government establishment a division which is an obdurate foe of political liberalism, an assertive power pushing its own parochial interests and ambitions. Where the government is autocratic, as in the case of the Kaiser's Germany, the arrogance of the military caste, which in the notorious Zabern affair proved too embarrassing for the prewar Reichstag, is masked by its full integration into the larger social caste of the ruling nobility. In France, where the government was a democracy, the Dreyfus crisis brought into the open the conflict of an army dominated by nobility and clericals, who ran their private empire with little more than nominal attention to the constitutional formalities and the formal government charged with the running of the state and responsible by popular suffrage to the electorate. When in this instance the military was caught in an outright crime, it showed its power by taking the entire nation to the brink of civil war. Even in England, the most stable of the European democracies, the military crowd successfully blackmailed Parliament in 1914 in the Irish controversy when the officers threatened to resign en masse if the government enforced its grant of home rule for Ireland. It was a showdown which would have left lasting scars had England not been shortly hurled into the World War and the test of strength dissolved in the total mobilization.

In unstable societies, or those that hit the shoals of civil crises, the military tries to become the arbiter. It makes and unmakes governments; at times it tries to seize the reins of power for itself. The Latin American governments have been notorious victims of numberless interventions and coup d'etats on the part of military caudillos and juntas. The Balkan countries, after they freed themselves from Turkish overlordship, were dominated by military adventurers and cliques. The same thing goes on today in the Near East, in Pakistan, Thailand, Burma. The military played the identical game in Western Europe whenever any of the countries were rent by social difficulties. In Germany the general staff was behind the unsuccessful Kapp *putsch* of 1920 and was the organizing genius of later alliances with industrial and banking groups to undermine the Weimar regime. In France, after the defeat in 1940, the aged marshals joined in making Pétain the trustee in bankruptcy. The officer corps threatened the coup d'etat by which it succeeded in cracking the Fourth Republic and imposing De Gaulle as a semidictator in 1958. Three years later it tried to dictate terms again to its own recalcitrant appointee, and to the nation, whose servant it was supposed to be. That fears are not absent that under some critical circumstances it can happen here is evidenced by the popularity of *Seven Days in May*—both the novel and the movie—wherein American military leaders are fictionally depicted attempting to usurp the government because they are disgruntled over our making a disarmament agreement with Russia.

THE United States has been very fortunate in the first one hundred and sixty years of her history. One of the important explanations for the strength and continuity of our constitutional government has been the absence, until recent years, of a big military establishment. This does not mean that the American people have been pacifistic, either in character or in personal philosophy. The sagas of carving out a country by exterminating the aborigine populations, of extending the frontiers by naked imposition, of practicing the crudest form of laissez faire in raw pioneering environments, have made for a popular tradition of violence. We have been partial to military heroes from George Washington to Dwight Eisenhower. We have also had a long line of political generals from George B. McClellan and Leonard Wood to Douglas MacArthur. But what was always missing to give institutional strength to the ambitions of individuals, and to breathe the reality of material substance to the dreams of military cabals, was a substantial military corporation which could become the subject as well as the object of national politics.

A tiny regular army, whose companies were scattered at posts along frontiers and forts, supplemented by locally managed state militias led by non-professional officers and rounded out by volunteers, was sufficient for the innumerable skirmishes with the Indians and to fight the border wars. With the turn of the last century, a modern navy and its complements of marines was all that was needed to patrol the waters of the Caribbean and South Atlantic and to subjugate the Banana Republics. The officers of the Order of Cincinnati, formed after the Revolutionary War, could conspire to set up a militarist monarchy; and General Pershing and his entourage could intrigue after the First World War to set up a European type of military machine; but so long as the country was protected by its two oceans, and had no major enemy to contend with, no important segments of American society could see the need for an immense parasitical organization. The crusades of the militarists dissolved as regularly with the coming of peace as night mists with the approach of the sun.

On two occasions the country seemed to be heading for the European military system: after the Spanish-American War, and later, after the First World War. It was saved from the ordeal both times because of the same logic that had saved England in her epoch of naval supremacy. The period of Theodore Roosevelt tub-thumping passed away with no further military legacy than a sizable navy. The huge military establishment set up in the First World War was disbanded because the nation concluded from the experience that its favorable geographical position and industrial prowess protected the position. We could always find allies to ward off initial blows, while our mills and factories enabled us to train and equip the mass forces to deliver in good time the knockout stroke. We supported a big navy, to be sure, but the civil power used to find it easier to control its navies than its armies. Whether because of their larger component of capital equipment to manpower, or for other reasons, navies in Western Europe never had the same ability as armies to interfere in government matters.

While organized militarism remained small, dispersed, and decentralized, the military bureaucracy dealt with Congress and the Executive as a supplicant, not as a power bloc. The civilian President was commander in chief of the armed forces in fact as well as in name. The professional soldiers graduating from West Point and Annapolis had social standing in the salons and households of the powerful, but they were a political nullity. As in the case of members of lesser branches of socially prominent families whose genealogical trees are impeccable but whose worldly circumstances are straitened, their individual members might be absorbed into the power elites, and their military positions used for their prestige value, whether for adorning the board of directors of an insurance company or running for the Presidency; it was the elites of politics and business who did the picking, the deciding, and the absorbing. The war lords were as unwarlike in their dealings with the civilian powers as prize fighters are with their managers. Civilian government had a firm hold on the controls. The values of the political hustings and the business marketplace were the values animating national policies and determining international relations.

Then, in the 1950's, for the first time in her history, the United States succumbed to the fate that she narrowly avoided in 1900 and in 1919. The consolidation of a gargantuan military enclave placed another government division alongside the traditional legislative, executive, and judicial departments. This addition of a full-blown military establishment is bound to upset the historical constitutional balance of government, disarrange the checks and balances of the past, and shift effective power to the administrative bureaucracies any time the military allies itself with another power bloc.

The military dynamic is the more persuasive because the entrance of the war lords on the political scene coincides with the main drift of our society. The rise of the military establishment is not due to the machinations of the military lobbyists. Its origin is not in the ambitions of officers in alliance with high industrialists. It is not a product of a departmental intrigue in using public funds to scare the public and the Congress into granting peacetime conscription for which there was no technical need. All these occurred and were done, and the military propagandists used every stratagem of public relations to fasten a war bureaucracy upon the nation. But militarists had mounted similar campaigns in the past—the histories are full of them—with no more than marginal effects. The post-World War II crusade succeeded where the previous ones failed, and succeeded beyond the dreams of its architects, because it blended with the political climate, because it coincided with the political logic of national policy.

This country came out of the war with the burden of Western capitalism on its shoulders. It was thrust into a struggle with an opponent military power of the first magnitude. The revolution in military technology had reduced our geographical defenses and made obsolete our older strategy of keeping the sea lanes clear with the Navy while relying on industrial strength to mass-produce our fighting forces in the midst of war. Nuclear technology made it necessary to bring a military force into being, and the politics of the cold war called for an extensive military establishment. The lobbyists

and public relations experts simply eased the way, and worked up
the slogans and rationales to push the good work along. The
militarization of the country took place not in spite of the wishes
of the legislators and the public but in response to their wishes.

Now that it is here, the question is whether the military establishment will not conquer the United States long before it has an
opportunity to try to conquer the enemy abroad. That such projects
are not beyond the imagination of military establishments, even in
up-to-date democracies, is shown by the recent French experiences.
President Eisenhower, in his much quoted farewell address, pointed
out that the combination—new for this country—of a permanent
armaments industry and an immense military establishment con-
stitutes a threat to the "very structure of our society," and that
"the potential for the disastrous rise of misplaced power exists and
will persist." Harrison Brown and James Real wrote in *Community
of Fear,*

> A small but not negligible fraction of the $40 billion defense
> budget [now $50 billion] is invested judiciously each year in
> a well-conceived program of public and Congressional relations.
> As a result, the military lobby is now the strongest lobby in
> Washington. Were the State Department to negotiate success-
> fully an arms control agreement with the Soviet Union and were
> the armed services united in their opposition to the agreement,
> the agreement would almost certainly be defeated by the Senate.
> There is little doubt that the armed services exert more control
> over Congress than that body exerts over the Defense Department.
> Indeed, the military elite is clearly in a position to assume actual
> political command over the United States striking forces if there
> are serious signs of "weakness" in United States foreign relations.

The threat is both more immediate and less dramatic than the
quotations suggest. Unlike France, this country is too well integrated
politically to be confronted with an internal war between its civil
and military authorities or, in the foreseeable future, with an outright attempt of a military camarilla to shoulder aside the constitutional system. But neither does the threat of a militarization of
American life lie in the future. It is happening. The drift is
evolutionary and consequently more insidious. For the past fifteen
years the military establishment has been expanding. It has perfected
a power bloc which includes the armaments manufacturers, armies

of local and national political figures, and innumerable cliques of influence in agencies of government. It has set up "think factories" which are flooding the nation with their cheap and vulgar mass-produced output. It has reached out to influence the universities and educational institutions, and has channeled the efforts of tens of thousands of scientists, engineers, technicians, and administrators to the construction of war weapons and the promulgation of a military ideology.

There is little danger of the nation waking up one morning to discover that a general riding a white horse and brandishing a saber has ordered Congress to disperse, and that troops directed by the Pentagon have occupied television stations, air terminals, telegraph offices, and the main government buildings. But there is a clear and present danger that almost imperceptibly the entire nation has fallen under the sway of the military mystique, that the national ideology has become a military ideology, that political reality is now understood only as military reality. While the constitutional system superficially continues to operate without change, behind the constitutional facade power has shifted to a new complex in which the war lords set the tone and define the issues. Considering that the Pentagon empire is only twenty years old, and that the present establishment was only founded in the postwar years, we have to conclude that the pace of growth is frenetic, and that with our American know-how, we may achieve a Prussianization in far less time than it took the original Prussians to do it.

II

There are sure gauges by which to check the importance of an institution or official in a bureaucratic society. The place of an official in the power hierarchy can be ascertained nine times out of ten by the size and location of his office, the thickness of the carpeting, the quality of the furnishings. The importance of a department or institution can be judged by how much funds it is able to extract from the treasury. When Walter Rathenau, head of the German electric industry, organized a raw materials division in 1914 for the war ministry, it was clear to him that war had become a matter of mass production, and he wanted to proceed accordingly. But it was not yet clear to the old desk men at the war ministry, and he was given a small room at the back of the building, and a single secretary. By 1918 the division spread over several blocks of buildings, almost overwhelming the rest of the war office. The American military establishment is in a similar expansion, and the end is not in sight.

The visible symbol of the military state within the national state is the Pentagon. This is a concrete and limestone maze that covers 34 acres on the Virginia side of the Potomac River and is surrounded by an additional 200 acres of lawns and terraces. It is the largest office building in the world. The United States Capitol could fit comfortably into any one of its five segments. The five rings of buildings are connected by 17½ miles of corridor passing through a five-acre pentagonal court in the center. It has the largest exchange switchboard anywhere, staffed by 200 people, with 45,000 telephones connected by 175,000 miles of cable, handling 280,000 calls a day. There are 2,100 intercoms, and the communication system permits four-party conversations between people as far apart as Washington, Tokyo, Berlin, and London. On the premises are located a bank, a drugstore, medical and dental clinics, a ticket agency, three kitchens, two restaurants, six cafeterias, nine beverage bars, and an outside snack bar. The grounds are patrolled by 170 security officers, and there is a daytime population of 30,000.

The sprawling bureaucracy housed in this enormous fortress, in comparison to which all other staff headquarters of the past or present appear cramped and provincial, controls an empire that elicits the respectful attention of any of the heads of our leading corporations. The Cordiner Report of several years ago set a valuation of $160 billion on the property owned by the Defense Department, "by any yardstick of measurement, the world's largest organization." This wealth includes weapons arsenals, air bases, naval stations, army reservations, in all, more than thirty-two million acres of land in the United States, and another two and a half million acres abroad. The total is larger than the combined area of Rhode Island, Delaware, Connecticut, New Jersey, Massachusetts, Maryland, Vermont, and New Hampshire.

The military establishment qualifies for the top echelon by virtue of the biggest office and the most impressive wall-to-wall carpeting. It also passes the test with flying colors by its ability to get the most out of the public treasury. In the years of the Eisenhower Administration, about three-fifths of the entire federal budget went for major military spending, and a larger fraction if military subsidies to clients are included. In these eight years the military was able to dispose of $350 billion on direct expenditures. Under President Kennedy, military spending was pushed up another notch; four-fifths of all federal purchases of goods and services were going for defense. If President Johnson's highly publicized cuts in defense spending are actually validated, the military budget will continue to hover around the $50 billion mark for the rest of the decade, and will continue to devour more than half of the total federal budget.

Even in this country of big money and big organizations, these figures are gigantic. The assets of the military are three times the combined assets of United States Steel, American Telephone and Telegraph, Metropolitan Life Insurance, General Motors, and Standard Oil Company of New Jersey. Its paid personnel is three times as large as that of these corporations. Of a grand total of five million federal employees, more than three and a half million are working for the Defense Department: two and a half million in the armed forces, one million civilian workers. The civilian payroll alone is $11 billion a year, equal to one and a half times the combined payrolls of the iron and steel industry and of all other basic metal producers, and equal to twice the payroll of the automobile industry. The annual military budget is larger than the annual net income of all the corporations in the country.

The activities of such a gargantuan industry are bound to affect our fortunes in a drastic way. In his farewell address Eisenhower said, "The total influence—economic, political, even spiritual—is felt in every city, every state, every house, every office of the federal government." One of the important influences is economic. Many enterprises and many people have become dependent on the military establishment and have a vested interest in a continual arms race. The powerful hold over some communities is apparent when an attempt is made, not to cut down the total spending, but merely to shift from one weapon to another. A proposal to shut down a plant in one location while opening another one in another location produces anguished howls and ferocious pressures from the people adversely affected. Congressmen shout and threaten. The local chambers of commerce bombard Washington officials with letters and cablegrams. Labor union leaders raise their voices in protest. The whole community is mobilized into a mass lobby to save the war work for their own.

Major battles in Congress over weapons systems have nothing to do with technical judgments. They are concealed struggles to save contracts and jobs for political allies and constituents. Every day's headline carries news of state and local officials mounting campaigns to funnel more defense contracts into their territories. A congressional bloc from New York clashes with a similar bloc from California. Eight Midwestern states discuss the formation of an offensive-defensive alliance to get more war business. Leverett Saltonstall, the senior Senator from Massachusetts, a Boston Brahmin and member of one of the old-line aristocratic New England families, issued a leaflet in 1960 to alert his constituents that "Saltonstall's seniority in the Senate means jobs for Massachusetts" and that military spending in the state rose from $246 million in 1954 to $1 billion in 1960. The late President's youngest brother, Edward Kennedy, ran for the Senate from Massachusetts in 1962 on the slogan, "He can do more for Massachusetts." After getting elected, he apparently made good on his promise when he wangled a $50 million National Aeronautics and Space Administration center for the Boston area. As Representative J. L. Whitten of the Defense Appropriations subcommittee summed it up: "Just about every district, and every state, and every labor union, and every store owner is getting a cut out of present expenditures in the name of 'defense.'"

Pork-barrel legislation has a long and well-established history. The most elevated of the nation's solons have never disdained from preempting their shares, and the most high-toned families have cheerfully grabbed at the lucrative contracts. In the turn from pork to patriotism, millions in public funds have mushroomed into billions, and arms patriotism has more lethal consequences than run-of-the-mill boondoggling. The changing outlook that it has brought into being was poignantly brought out during a tragic accident that took the lives of two mechanics at a Nike missile base in New Jersey in 1958. The widow of one of the men explained why her husband had requested a transfer from repairing automobiles to working on Nikes. "We thought there would be more security in missiles because they seemed to be the coming thing." The same idea was explained in *Fortune*'s profile of General Dynamics Corporation printed that same year: "The unique group of men who run Dynamics are only incidentally in rivalry with other United States manufacturers, with many of whom they actually act in concert. Their chief competitor is the U.S.S.R. . . . The core of General Dynamics' corporate philosophy is the conviction that national defense is a more or less permanent business."

Comfort is taken from the argument that large though the sums are that are spent for military purposes, they add up to only 10 per cent of our national product, and that no more than a tenth of the labor force is engaged in this work. In other words, despite the commotion, the military tail is not wagging the civilian dog. But the 10 per cent statistic is deceptive. The 10 per cent immediately becomes 12 per cent if figured in relation to the national income, which is possibly a more accurate way of computing it. It becomes larger still if to the direct arms budget is added the arms aid sent abroad, of which most of the funds are spent on weapons produced in this country. If we then adjust the total figure to the investment multiplier to determine the various and obscure derivative economic activities generated, created, dreamed-up, sustained, and occasioned by the military industry, we have to conclude that possibly a fifth of present economic activity is dependent on the arms race.

Moreover, certain pivotal industries like aircraft and missiles are totally militarized, a number like shipbuilding, radio, and communications are largely militarized. Most of the munitions plants have been specifically designed for military manufacture and cannot be converted to civilian production. Many localities would cease to exist if the plants in their environs lost their war contracts. In a major metropolis like Los Angeles, it is estimated that almost half the jobs are dependent on war work. The stock market is heavily involved in the militarization of the nation and has reacted with exaggerated sensitivity to any downward oscillations in the levels of military extravagance. On any analysis, the military sector is an economic colossus.

Whether this Frankenstein can be unloaded without causing an economic breakdown is a separate question which will be considered separately. But there is no escaping the conclusion that the business enterprise of the United States can now be designated as a war-propelled economy, and that a significant section of the people have become emotionally and economically tied to the military establishment.

III

The social scene is changing in response to this impulse. In 1961, for instance, $21 billion in contracts was ladled out on procurement, and three corporations each latched on to more than a billion dollars, while two more got almost a billion dollars apiece. The top ten corporations were the beneficiaries of over $7½ billion; the top hundred corporations divided among themselves three-quarters of the entire procurement fund. The prime contractors paid out parts of these unbelievable sums to many subcontracting companies. But it was the small group of prime contractors that controlled these monies, that held the whiphand over the subcontractors, and that often bought in or otherwise secured a financial or executive voice in the affairs of their suppliers.

The system whereby the government siphons off immense amounts of purchasing power through taxation, to channel them to a few major firms, centralizes the aggregates of corporate wealth. An immense industrial empire has mushroomed whose sole customer is the government, and whose operations are risk-free. Instead of the customary marketing problems of business enterprises, handled through advertising, packaging, competitive attractiveness, the munitions makers are thrust into an intricate public-relations game where their sales departments operate as little State Departments. The arms contractors maintain emissaries at relevant bureaus and departments of government. They have lobbyists who participate in power high-jinks and intrigues in legislative halls. They keep professional staffs on their payrolls who follow closely the politics of the Pentagon, the White House, and of Capitol Hill, and who are charged with the task of drawing up elaborate programs in the pursuit of the firm's "international relations." Their traffickings with military brass, journalists, public officials, resemble more the transactions of a sovereign power than the huckstering of businessmen in the marketplace.

There is another reason why the relations of the arms manufacturers to the government do not follow the precepts of Adam Smith. The government is the sole customer of the armaments companies, but the armaments companies are monopolistic suppliers to the government. The monopoly is more complete than in the civilian economy. There, a buyer has the choice of half a dozen automobiles even if the price and quality are roughly the same in all cases. He has the choice of half a dozen different makes of tires. A manufacturer can buy his steel from half a dozen producers. In some instances, buyers or wholesalers can restrain the prime producers by importing goods from abroad. The nature of weapons technology precludes even this much free play.

Arms are no longer purchased in separate units; they are integrated into arms systems. These are exceedingly intricate engineering affairs whose manufacture requires the coordinated efforts of

planners, designers, theorists, experimenters, scientists, and technicians, and the investment of unbelievable amounts of capital. The
arms race has its own dynamic: each weapon calls into being a
counterweapon, which in turn makes necessary an answering weapon. Where in the past history of warfare arms changed over long
periods of time, the development pace has now gotten out of hand.
A revolution takes place every five years. The result is that the battle
weapons are beyond the ken of the military personnel. Decision
has passed into the hands of the technicians. The arms contractors
are no longer handed blueprints of weapons that the Defense Department wants them to manufacture. Instead, the contractors maintain huge staffs to follow the technological evolution of the arms
race, and to create, conceive, and elaborate the new weapons systems
which the race imposes. They have assumed the function of convincing the general staff and procurement officials of what new
weapons they ought to have. The staffs of scientific advisers attached
to the military services are generally also in the employ of the arms
corporations and research contractors. The scientists have to stay in
intimate touch with the work of the private laboratories and research
departments if they are to keep their bearings in the ceaseless tread-
mill of arms technology. The consequence of the operation is an
integration of the military establishment and the armaments firms,
the creation of a power complex with identical aims and with a common viewpoint. Into these hands has fallen the *de facto* leadership
of military policy.

Where such immense sums of money change hands, and where
90 per cent of the contracts are awarded without competitive bid-
ding, it can be taken for granted that there will be collusion, that
smart operators will attempt, and often succeed, in lining their
pockets, and that some unconscionable profits will be made. Indeed,
it might be argued from one point of view that private profit-
making is one of the few rational aspects of a somewhat irrational
enterprise. The Hebert investigating committee listed in 1960 more
than fourteen hundred retired officers from the rank of major up
who were employed by the hundred top munition concerns. Vice
Admiral Hyman Rickover testified that pressure had been repeatedly put on him by retired officers on the hunt for contracts. At his
famous court-martial, growing out of his charges that the Defense
Department is riddled with lobbyists, Colonel John Nickerson testified that the armaments firms "put pressure on Secretary Wilson
through the joint chiefs of staff, through Congress, and through

contacts by representatives of the aircraft industry with all levels of the Pentagon." If he described the mood of the officialdom correctly, the high-ranking officers are all thinking of getting cushy jobs with the arms firms when they retire from the services.

The fact that one event follows in direct sequence after a previous one is no proof, as every college student of logic is aware, that the first is the cause of the second. So it may be that the activities of General Joseph McNarney and Rear Admiral Lloyd Harrison had no relation to their subsequent employment. Nevertheless, it is worth recalling, for whatever it is worth, that General McNarney led the Air Force cohorts in the successful 1950 battle with the Navy for the B-36 bomber. This resulted in the spending of additional huge amounts for a plane that was then already obsolete and quickly became a white elephant. Then, early in 1952, upon his retirement, he picked up a telephone on a tip from Senator Stuart Symington, who had previously been Secretary of the Air Force, according to his testimony before the Hebert committee, dialed a number in Indio, California, and immediately went on the payroll of the planemaker who happened to be the manufacturer of the B-36. He not only got a job, but what would be generally considered a good job. He became president of Convair at $75,000 a year, and he told the Hebert committee that in the four years since his retirement he had drawn $324,500 in salary and expenses in addition to his regular Air Force pension of $16,000 a year.

The career of Rear Admiral Harrison was no less remarkable. The Navy had awarded to McDonnell Aircraft and to Westinghouse the contracts to build the F3H jet fighter. Eleven of the planes subsequently crashed in test flights. But the Admiral insisted that the contracts be continued because the contractors had good records of performance. The Navy followed his advice for an outlay of $302 million—later admitted to be a total waste. In September, 1955, Rear Admiral Harrison, upon retirement, took a job as Vice President of McDonnell. Congress investigated and decided that the Admiral was guilty of nothing more than an "honest mistake"—not for taking the job, but for recommending the continuance of the F3H program. *Business Week* generalized the situation as a law of armaments-business mechanics: "In business circles, the word has gone out: Get yourself a general. What branch of government spends the most money? The military. Who, even more than a five-percenter, is an expert on red tape? A general or admiral. So make him Chairman of the Board."

The Hebert committee also unearthed some unusually creative efforts on the part of the Martin Company. This war contractor initiated a program of flying down active and retired high-ranking officers to the Bahaman island of Eleuthera for swank parties and entertainments. Among the joyous spirits were some who within thirty days were to appear before the Appropriations Committee to support contracts which included parcels for the Martin Company. The Martin people and the other contractors were not pioneering. The older military establishments of Europe had long ago perfected these arts of collusion. Krupp had a regular policy of employing ex-officers with access to their former colleagues in the war ministry. All ranking officers and those with any special connections with government bureaus or officials were extravagantly feted at the Villa Hügel at Essen. Ehrhardt, Krupp's competitor, complained—a clear case of sour grapes—that "Krupp employs hundreds of officers on leave or inactive, at a high salary, for doing nothing very much. To some families, Krupp's was a great sinecure, providing jobs for the nephews and poor relations of officials who have great influence in the army." Considering the number of scandals in Germany arising out of what was by comparison a bush-league military syndicate, the United States apparatus is relatively free of nepotism. Of course, the Kaiser's Germany was harassed by a Socialist opposition which presumably was more zealous in unearthing this sort of thing than are most of our legislators; so it may be that the differences in ethical standards between the two establishments are not profound.

At any rate, the wastes and overcharges in what is an enterprise of waste and parasitism are the least of the matter. The social problem derives from the dynamic of the establishment, not the abuses incidental to it. The subversion of a civilian economy into a war-propelled economy breeds collusive arrangements between the military and armaments managers as inevitably as the rise of the trusts in the nineties produced rail rebates, fixed prices, and market monopolies.

## IV

The economic shift is accompanied by a political shift that is no less decisive for the society. The military establishment has come up not only as another power bloc, but as a power bloc with some of the attributes of sovereignty. When its special interests and commitments clash with those of the duly constituted authorities, it does not hesitate to pit its strength against that of others. It does not hesitate to use its considerable resources to manipulate the public and browbeat officials.

Such tactics are not novel. They have been employed in the past, and continue to be employed in the present, by other power blocs. But there is a qualitative difference between the two. Where private corporations use their resources to pressure legislators or to influence public opinion, they are not in a position to write limitless drafts on the public treasury to finance their institutional crusades, and they do not carry the authority of public servants sworn to uphold the national welfare. The war lords have the best of two worlds. They are voted astronomical sums out of the public treasury, which has made them so independent as to be able to dictate to their benefactors; they are the trusted guardians of the nation's security, and can use their authority to pursue professional aims. And having made the best of both worlds, they have fortified their institution to the point where they can deal on terms of near equality with the constitutional power.

The concept of an American garrison state was visualized by some of the farsighted statesmen in the midst of the Second World War. Business leaders like Frank Knox, James Forrestal, and Charles E. Wilson, who became intimately connected with the military in the course of the war, saw how the national mobilization had sent a stagnant economy booming as eight years of New Deal palliations had not been able to do. They saw how the business interests had, in alliance with the military, rewon a position of honor and trust that had seemed irrevocably lost during the turmoils of Roosevelt's first two terms. It appeared to them that what was called for was to consolidate the system worked out during the war into a permanent feature of American society.

In an address to the Army Ordnance Association delivered in January, 1944, Charles E. Wilson sketched out the bold dimensions of a military-business-government alliance in "a permanent war economy," based on a continuous preparedness program. We would never stop preparing. Donald Nelson, the wartime head of the War Production Board, took alarm at what looked to him like Prussianization projects. In his book *Arsenal of Democracy,* where he reviewed his wartime experiences, he warned that "the question of military control will confront us not only in war but in peace. The lesson taught by these recent war years is clear: our whole economic and social system will be in peril if it is controlled by the military men."

In the cold-war climate the Charles E. Wilson horticulture was able to flourish while Donald Nelson's shriveled and fell away. The military managers came tearing out of the war determined that their domicile would not again be neglected as it had been in the Harding-Coolidge era, that they would not again be forced to live through the dreary antimilitarist days, begging hat in hand for small appropriations, defending themselves against accusations of warmongering. This time there was going to be no return to the anemic interim when there was little hope to move up in the scale of promotions, and where officers were forced to live in genteel poverty in military encampments.

The war lords took advantage of the disbandment of the swollen wartime forces to confront the nation with a crisis. They moved their heavy guns into position to give the Congress and the people the taste of a campaign the likes of which the country had never experienced. Disaster unbelievable faced the nation, according to the statements, proclamations, warnings, speeches, lectures, analyses, broadcast unceasingly by military and friendly spokesmen of high repute, unless the manpower of the country was placed at the disposal of the military by the passage of a universal military training law.

The Harness committee investigated in 1947 this avalanche of military propaganda and said it was pernicious because it took a cynical advantage of the people. "It is the authority and the supposed objectivity of government which leads people to accept without question the words released by government officials and agencies. ... An individual might be wary and critical of material coming from a 'special interest group.' He knows such groups have an axe to grind, but he will consider it as gospel truth if the government says the identical thing, because he thinks government officials are impartial." The report concluded that "the war department, its personnel, and civilian employees have gone beyond the limits of their proper duty of providing factual information to the people and the Congress, and have engaged in propaganda supported by taxpayers' money to influence legislation now pending before Congress." And the report added, the use of such funds "is unlawful."

The military did not worry very much about the Harness committee accusation, and as subsequent events were to demonstrate, it had no reason to. When Congress flatly rejected the Pentagon plan

in late 1947, the war lords went into a new offensive with all stops
pulled out. The huge officers' corps and professional staff was converted into a propaganda cadre. "The Pentagon line," according to
Colonel William H. Neblett, who wrote an exposé of the campaign
in *Pentagon Politics,* "was that we were living in a state of unde-
clared emergency; that war with Russia was just around the corner;
and that the safety of the nation was dependent upon a speedy re-
building of the lower ranks of army, navy, and air with the Pentagon form of universal military training."

The contest, such as it was, between the military and civilian
powers, ended the following year with a total victory for the military. Congress adopted peacetime conscription in exactly the form
in which it had been drafted by the Pentagon. A small contingent
of House members filed a minority dissent to the favorable report
of the Armed Services Committee, in which they said, "The considerable degree of hysteria prevalent today is in a large measure
due to the propaganda efforts of the Armed Services themselves.
. . . The Army is spending large amounts of the taxpayers' money
to obtain a permanent system of conscription. . . . The Army has
acted as if it is the policy-making body of the nation. . . . Congress
cannot permit itself to become the rubber stamp of a willful group
of officers who want to Prussianize this nation. . . ." But the military
managers could afford to ignore such bleatings from the sidelines.
They had not only gotten what they were after; they were too
strongly entrenched to be discomfited by the protests of dissident
Congressmen.

In subsequent years, whenever the military has been thwarted in
its wishes, it has regularly gone over the head of its constitutional
commander in chief. It does not simply appeal the decision; it em-
broils the public in war scares and horror propaganda, it wheels its
powerful allies into place to thrust Congress into controversy. A
profound illustration of this was the so-called "missile gap" debate
that started in Eisenhower's last year in office and continued to rock
the country and Congress until the Democratic opponent in the
Presidential election alchemized the catch phrase into votes and the
Strategic Air Command got part of its bombers airborne.

Some of the crusades of the military are intramural. It is not
always a united military authority against a united civilian authority.
Often, it is one of the services and its allies against another service
and its allies. The country has trembled to more than one of these
battles of the titans. One of them took place in 1949 when the Navy

and the Air Force squared off. It was the carrier fleet versus the B-36 in what the air publicity men derisively dubbed "the revolt of the admirals." More recently, the country has been treated to a spectacular missile war between the Army and the Air Force. In this particular struggle that started in 1959, the Air Force was staking its honor and reputation on the Bomarc antiaircraft missile, with its contractor, the Boeing Corporation, marshaling every available scrap of political and financial support. In the other corner was the Army holding aloft the Nike-Hercules, with its contractor, Western Electric, mounting the nationwide campaign. Amidst the din and panic, who could tell which was better, or whether either one was any good? Currently, a bitter undercover battle is going on between the manned bomber officers under General Curtis LeMay and the Air Force Systems Command under General Bernard Schriever. The fight has already rocked Congress in the controversy over the RS-70 bomber, and the bomber officers and manufacturers will undoubtedly be heard from again in no uncertain terms.

When these colossi go into a fight, it is no private matter. Before many passes are made on either side, a good number of the country's legislators, armaments kings, establishment experts and kibitzers, news publicists and advertising men, are lined up in solid array giving their all for their respective teams. Woe to the simpleton who would attempt to make a decision on technical judgment!

## V

There is a widespread notion that this picture of the military establishment is now a thing of the past; that when President Kennedy appointed McNamara as his Secretary of Defense, the strong man had been found at last who would ride herd on the generals and admirals and firmly restore Pentagon power to civilian hands. This is a profound misconception of what is taking place.

The current reorganization of the Pentagon is something that had been planned for the past decade and a half. Important establishment figures in business, finance, and government recognized that the structure of the American military complex was chaotic. Even during the Second World War the existence of separate feudal kingdoms, each headed by its own group of samurai, each a law unto itself, proved extremely wasteful, and left the commander in chief helpless in formulating strategy on a number of occasions.

Once we had entered the nuclear age of warfare, the existing military establishment became an anachronism.

The attempt to centralize control was fiercely resisted by the military cliques aided and abetted by their allies. Each had a vested interest to defend. Beyond that, there was a great fear in both Congress and the nation that by centralizing authority in the hands of one person, we would be recreating a replica of the German General Staff which treated with all governments as a sovereign power; for whereas governments come and go, the military is continuous. Far better, many reasoned, to have waste, to have disorganization, to have internecine rivalries, than to create a military Moloch beyond the reach of the civilian authority.

The unification act of 1947, passed over great opposition, was a makeshift arrangement. It set up three departments, Army, Navy and Air. The chairman of the Joint Chiefs of Staff was not the superior of his department chiefs; his role was to be more of an office manager than an executive. The authority and duties of the Secretary of Defense were not too clearly defined. He was at first regarded primarily as a coordinator. Even this mild centralization was fought tooth and nail by the military princes. The unceasing administrative struggles and intrigues are supposed to have finally broken James V. Forrestal, the first Secretary of Defense, and to have led to his taking his own life.

There was a succession of big business and political figures in the office in the next decade—Louis H. Johnson, General Marshall, Robert A. Lovett, Charles E. Wilson, Thomas S. Gates. Every one of them took a few feeble steps to carry out the work that Forrestal had bequeathed them. While this or that aspect of administration was tightened up or coordinated, in the end all of them fell victim to the powerfully entrenched military caste which was determined to run things in its own way. As Theodore H. White wrote in a *Look* magazine article, "By the end of the Eisenhower Administration, control of American strategy lay not in the hands of civilian leadership, but in the hands of the uniformed chiefs of staff."

There was overwhelming logic, however, for a rationalization and centralization of the military establishment, and increasing numbers of influential people favored it. The military chieftains could consequently delay the inevitable reorganization; they could not prevent it. When a strong President entered the White House, and picked a hard-boiled executive to carry through Forrestal's unfinished work, it was as inevitable that the military bureaucracy would be rearranged as that feudal fortresses several centuries earlier would fall under the fire power of artillery. The dominant executive power of our government is doing administratively what it has been unable to attain by legislative action.

McNamara has moved two teams of advisers into the Pentagon to help him get the job done. There is the top echelon Ivy League crowd which is a direct descendant of the wartime Ivy League team of Lovett, McCloy, Patterson, and Forrestal. This is a tightly knit social and political coterie of lawyers, bankers, administrators, public figures, all graduates of the best prep schools and universities, all moving in the same power and social circles. These distinguished alumni of the worlds of business and public affairs have manned the civilian secretary posts and offices, and they furnish thrust and depth to McNamara's administrative revolution. The other team are the "Whiz Kids," the alumni of the "think factories," the foundations, the universities—scientists, academic analysts, professionals, who are called upon to draw up studies, position papers, strategic and weapons analyses, long-range plans, to bring the expertise of the academic world and the laboratory into the councils of decision-making.

Naturally, there has been wailing and gnashing of teeth. The older generation of generals and admirals, who are retired or bypassed in top decisions, feel that no good will come of all this newfangled computer programming, and stir up their congressional and business colleagues to fervent and indignant protests. Not that the generals and admirals are ignorant backwoodsmen who reject the use of sophisticated methods. They took the initiative in setting up the "think factories." Neither are they socially antagonistic to the Ivy Leaguers. Off duty, they hobnob with them. They are crying to high heaven at the injustice and ineffectiveness of the shift in power at the top—the fact that Ivy Leaguers and military intellectuals are being drawn into and merged with the military establishment. They are objecting that the military community is no longer the only source from which military leaders are drawn. They are bitter because initiative has passed—to an extent, at any rate—into the hands of this new caste of military bureaucrats.

The McNamara revolution shows that it is irrelevant to think of the military establishment in terms of military or civilian control. The military bureaucracy has not been displaced or overthrown; it has been broadened with new forces and it is being modernized and rationalized. The McNamara revolution is not a victory for civilian values versus military values; it is a victory—a very modest, restricted victory—for business administration versus parochial administration. Nor should the extent of centralization be exaggerated. In our present society, where military cliques are allied with powerful groups in industry and Congress, it is not possible to ignore special interests completely, or to any great extent. Beneath the facade of a centrally managed and directed organization, parochial groups are reorganizing to assert their special interests through modified forms of intrigue and guerrilla warfare.

The internal bickering and division have never interfered in the past with the military chieftains functioning as a single power bloc whenever their institutional interests were called into question. The arrogance which permitted their several factions to carry their internal quarrels to the public reflected not internal weakness but self-confidence that the power position of the military was unchallengeable. The McNamara centralization has only increased the intrinsic strength of the institution. Jerry Greene, the military writer, described McNamara as a "civilian on horseback" who had mounted the horse from the offside while Congress had concentrated on preventing the rise to the saddle of a "general on horseback." This is overdramatizing it and overpersonalizing it; but the thought is correct.

CHAPTER 8   Militarization of American Life

THERE is a trend in our mass society that works to decrease the specific caste differences between the military bureaucrat, the industrial bureaucrat, and the science bureaucrat. The older military caste coming out of West Point or Annapolis before the world wars was absorbed in the closed world of the military hierarchy. The officer was isolated from other influences of American life. The special relation of the military to the civilian society made him dependent emotionally and economically upon his own restricted substitute society. This specialized military society was ruled by a priestly code of unquestioning and stereotyped submission to the chain of command, a rigid hierarchical order of precedence and status, and a specific outline of conduct appropriate to each social subdivision. Because the military was not allowed to participate in the political and economic worlds, it turned in on itself, and in compensation for its sectarian existence, apotheosized the martial virtues. It developed contempt for civilian habits and procedures; it showed distinct predilections for authoritarian, corporative, over-simplified, and violent solutions for any and all social difficulties, in domestic and international relations.

These traits have carried over to the postwar world through the military's closed educational system and authoritarian organization. But the caste is in a new situation and subject to unusual influences. First, the closed-in world of the past has broken down. In the course of expansion, two things have happened to the military establishment. Tens of thousands of officers are now important men of affairs, in close communion with leaders in every walk of life, trained to deal on equal terms with the best minds in industry, politics, and education. They enjoy recognition and standing among all the elites rather than just in their own cloistered retreats. Second, the evolution of warmaking has converted the military leadership into what is basically an organization and office bureaucracy. The men in the Pentagon are engaged in the kind of activities that the managers of industry or the administrators of government bureaus are engaged in. They make use of the same symbols. They employ the same equipment. They work with the same techniques. They think in the same terms. They consult with the same kinds of advisers. They mix in the same social circles. They look at the world through the same spectacles.

The bureaucratization of mass society has overtaken the military, and the bureaucratization tends to produce a roughly standardized product, particularly in the managerial circles. That is why the top executive of one of the automobile companies, with no elaborate preparation, can become a highly successful manager of the war establishment, and why generals and admirals can step in as top brass in industry. Besides their Pentagon connections that are of inestimable value to the private corporations, some of these retired officers are probably able to earn their fabulous salaries on the basis of performance to no less a degree than their fellow executives who graduated from the Harvard School of Business.

The militarization of American life and the power shift to the military establishment are not the results of a conspiracy. The American people did not build up a monster military organism in response to the machinations of militarists, but in response to the needs and fears of the state. After the decision to build it was made, the institution necessarily extended from the Pentagon to civilian agencies, to munitions manufacturers, to universities, to newspaper editors, to Madison Avenue hucksters.

Once created, the military establishment became autonomous. It intrigued to perpetuate itself; it sought to convince society of its indispensability for all time to come; it endeavored to free itself from outside controls; it began to impose its own views of reality on everybody else; it bent other institutions to its specialized purposes. To the extent that militarization proceeds in our life, to that extent grows the preeminence of the military and of the war lords—whatever their previous vocation—inside the military establishment. When a state is prepared for war, the professional is bound to shoulder aside the amateur, the dedicated priest is sure to lead the lay parishioner. The fact that many others think the same way as the war lords only reinforces the latter's authority and control.

Despite its bureaucratic bulge and sprawling influence, the military establishment is formally under the control of the civilian power, and remains subject to it to a greater or lesser degree. As yet, civilian authorities have not been abased to where they can function only at the sufferance of the military. But the balance of power continues to shift toward the military, and unless countervailing pressures come into play, the military has a manifest destiny to permeate the other institutions. In his last interview as President, given the day after his farewell address, Eisenhower spoke of "an almost insidious penetration of our own minds that the only thing this country is engaged in is weaponry and missiles." The military penetration of our minds is the counterpart, both as effect and cause, of the military's penetration of the economy and its infiltration of government.

## II

When we consider some of the horrendous developments within the scientific and intellectual communities it is clear that progress in this respect has not been negligible. It was once traditional in our commerce-oriented society for our university graduates to choose a civilian career. The intellectual technicians found haven in the newspapers, mass media, and government civil services; and in recent years, numbers of them have entered the huckstering professions. The scientists and engineers went to work in industry, and a minority in government agencies. The lawyers and doctors went into private practice. The teachers entered the public school and university systems. Moreover, because of the country's founding tradition, there was little sympathetic relation between the military and the academic community. When army officers would come down to land-grant colleges in the twenties to oversee ROTC programs, college authorities accorded them the honors and courtesies due government officials, but their reception by others was frigid. We were a civilian society, and our elites had their minds fixed on civilian occupations and affairs.

The rise of the military has overturned this world as ruthlessly as the arrangements of a family are revolutionized when it discovers oil on its hitherto unwanted bottom lands. By commanding enormous sums of money for research, and affording careers to veritable armies of scientists and technicians, the military has sucked into its orbit great sections of the professional world who in the past had other interests. The trend in American research and development is indicative of what is happening. In 1940, the last year before our entrance into the war, the government financed $100 million for research and development out of a total of about half a billion dollars spent, with the bulk of the entire fund going for civilian purposes. In the decade of the 1950's, a total of $80 billion was spent on research and development, excluding expenditures for plant and equipment; this is four times more than was spent in the previous decade which included a world war. The government was the main contributor of the funds, and the bulk of these went for military purposes. Of the $16 billion assigned to research and development for 1962, the government financed more than two-thirds —a larger sum of money, according to Jerome B. Wiesner, than it spent "in the entire interval from the American Revolution through and including World War II"—and at least 80 per cent of the grand total was in the military column. This is symptomatic of how the nation's best brains and energies are being allocated and directed.

The effect has been to crowd other interests, passions, and investigations to the rear, and to engross the intellectual elite in warmaking, war technology, war philosophy, war strategy, war psychology, war sociology, war politics. A major segment of the country's best scientific minds is engrossed in military work, and much of the intellectual community is being pulled into this central circle of activity. That is where the excitement, the prestige, the high pay is—and the opportunity for the ambitious to crash into the dazzling world of power. Where Congress, in the grip of traditional laissez-faire memories and pressures, obdurately resists efforts to vote federal funds for education lest they interfere with eleemosynary efforts of private parties or encroach on the rights of the states or weaken the moral fiber of the people, it evinces no similar fears or qualms about the military dispensing astronomical sums of money which exercise a gravitational pull on the country's higher educational institutions.

There is scarcely a leading university that has not been drawn into the military vortex. According to the Director of the Survey of Federal Programs in Higher Education, in 1958–1959 the California Institute of Technology received 84 per cent of its total budget from government research grants; the Massachusetts Institute of Technology received 78 per cent; Johns Hopkins University, 67 per cent; the University of Chicago, 61 per cent; Princeton University, 55 per cent; the University of California, 54 per cent; Columbia and Cornell, about a third; Harvard, Yale, Tufts, Michigan, and Duke, about a fifth. The Massachusetts Institute of Technology enjoyed an even more remarkable distinction: it made forty-eighth place in the list of the first hundred prime military contractors. Although the golden shower may have ended monetary droughts for many a university president and bursar and is probably the beneficent origin of splendid new buildings and shiny equipment on the campuses, it has also led to the militarization of higher education. Plato and Shakespeare are studied as before, but in an atmosphere increasingly surcharged by militaristic exaltation.

That the war lords are not easy taskmasters, or apostles of free, untrammeled inquiry, was illustrated by an incident in the spring of 1961 when the Army decided to disband the Operations Research Office at Johns Hopkins University because there had developed, according to its head, Dr. Ellis A. Johnson, ethical differences between the Army and the University. It was not that Dr. Johnson was a social rebel; he held to the line that it was "the university's responsibility not to touch on decisions," but he believed that within those decisions the university should do "good research and not manipulate the conclusions brought about by scientific inquiry," whereas the Army leaders had sought to maintain "strict control in detail." The staff of scientists and other personnel of the Operations Research Office was apparently not deemed inefficient, for it made up the nucleus—minus Dr. Johnson—of a new organization, the Research Analysis Corporation, that the Army set up in the image of the Rand Corporation, and which presumably will know how to work up conclusions that will find greater favor with the Army's heads. Similar incidents occurred between the Navy and the Operations Evaluation Group at M.I.T., and even between the Air Force and the Rand Corporation. The Atomic Energy Commission and Harvard disputed for a year over the operation of the Cambridge

Electron Accelerator. According to the University, many of the
AEC demands constituted "a serious abridgement of academic
freedom."

Besides the scientific and technical laboratories of the universities,
the Pentagon also operates its own immense "think factories."
Many of these originated in the universities, such as Johns Hopkins'
Applied Physics Laboratory for the Navy, and the aforementioned
Operations Research Office for the Army. The Massachusetts
Institute of Technology established the Operations Evaluation
Group for the Navy, the Lincoln Laboratories for all the services,
and the Mitre Corporation for the Air Force. The proliferation of
institutions has been so rapid, and the competition for scientists
so keen, that in 1956 a number of the universities banded together
to form a holding corporation, called Institute for Defense Analysis,
to advise the military in the matter of personnel, procedures, and
campus know-how. Other "think factories" started as research outlets of the arms contractors and were then taken over by the military
establishment. Such was the modest origin of the Rand Corporation,
which at first was part of the Douglas Aircraft Company. Another
Air Force cerebral supplier is the Aerospace Corporation which
started as a division of Thompson Ramo Wooldridge.

These "non-profits," as they are known among the *cognoscenti,*
were set up as independent corporations which contract out their
services to the military in order to escape from the civil service
pay scales of the government. They offer salaries competitive with
the highest levels of private industry. While the director of the
National Bureau of Standards receives $19,000 a year, his counter-
part in the "non-profits" receives $40,000, and may in some cases
earn as much as $75,000. The man who in civil service receives
$11,000 can command a starting salary of $15,000 in the government
subsidiary and make more than the Secretary of Defense's $25,000
after he has accumulated sufficient seniority. An incidental result
has been to drain the long-established government agencies, like
the National Bureau of Standards and the Naval Research
Laboratory, of their qualified personnel. The "non-profits" also
enable the military to glamorize its technical adjuncts as non-partisan
educational faculties, "universities without a student body," where
"innovators work in an atmosphere of freedom which encourages
creativity"—to quote one of the handouts. The reports of the brain
trusters get respectful attention from the public and the Congress,
which would not be accorded to declarations of the military's

technical advisers. All the same, the "non-profits" are creations of the military, and subsist on Pentagon funds as surely as if they were directly on its payroll.

Besides its own brain-trust outfits, the Pentagon also supports an assortment of private "think factories," sometimes underwriting as much as three-quarters of their total incomes. Thus, with the proper amount of initiative, push, and know-how, any struggling little enterprise with access to a computer and a few professors can turn itself into a million-dollar enterprise. The Stanford Research Institute, for example, has expanded since 1946 from a staff of three to a staff of 2,000 doing a $25 million business in a new million-dollar building just off the Stanford University campus. The United Research Incorporated was set up in 1947 within the Harvard School of Business. Eleven years later it decided to become a full-blown private-enterprise profit organization. It has a staff of a hundred, and in addition, about forty high-powered part-time consultants, mostly from Harvard and M.I.T. These private independents merely take care of the overflow and the unusual. The steady brain work of weaponry is handled by the problem-analysis shops that are directly attached to the plants of the military contractors. Some of these enterprises, such as those of Douglas and Boeing, are located right in the plant. Other companies set up their analysts in what are called "campuses."

The analyst in private industry often combines two disciplines in various proportions: the mathematical sciences and salesmanship. It is his job to set up and conduct briefings in the Pentagon offices in order to educate the high military along constructive lines. The brass have to be sold on new weapons systems, in which the analyst's product just happens to integrate better than a weapon made by any other company. Boeing improved on the procedure by issuing a handout prepared by its analysts which provides a rounded concept of the proper balance of weapons needed by the military establishment in which Boeing products naturally figure prominently. Thus the analyst in the employ of a profit-seeking (and, generally, a profit-making) contractor has stepped into the breach to assume the role of adviser of, and liaison between, the Pentagon war strategists and his own company's engineers and designers.

The people working on university projects, at the non-profit "think factories," and at the contractors' "think shops" work closely with one another. They are not only engaged in the same line of work, but inevitably there takes place an exchange of men and

ideas. The more prominent practitioners regularly commute between Washington, the universities, the "think factories," and the
contractors' "campuses." For professional reasons they have to keep
track of each other's projects and activities and to keep their fingers
on the political and technical pulse of the Pentagon. What has been
created, in effect, is a para-military subcaste of scientists, scholars,
and researchers submerged in the militarist environment, and in the
employ of the military. These are no laboratory recluses, but men
who move with assurance from the "think factories" to the Pentagon, from the White House to Capitol Hill, as advisers to the war
lords and politicos.

The military technicians are not confining themselves to whisper-
ing into the ears of rulers and feeding the planning committees with
reports and studies. They are also assuming the mantles of national
prophets. This is probably taking place in strict accordance with
the market laws of supply and demand. The military establishment,
once it became a power bloc with a future, hungered for a broader
ideology to justify and inspire its function, and the academics were
the people who, by training and vocation, were equipped to fashion
an ideology. In response to the demand, the "think factories" began
adding social scientists to their staffs of mathematicians and physicists, and some of the more adaptable of the latter, who like Herman
Kahn had been trained in the physical sciences, branched out into
geopolitics and international strategy. When the "think factories"
began to deal with ideas as well as weapons, when, in other words,
the academics became ideologists as well as technicians, they took
on the new function of manipulating public opinion on behalf of
the military point of view.

In their capable hands, the military argument is lifted out of the
narrow roadbed of crude propaganda and converted into a national
ideology. The bare and uncouth logic of military propaganda is
enriched with historical background, given depth by sociological
guidance, refined by allusions to philosophy and the arts, elevated to
heights of science by games theories and statistical exercises, and
finally provided with a jargon sufficiently professional to buttress
claims to infallibility. The paid and unpaid propagandists of the
military establishment can now surround their catch phrases with
the profundities of a national philosophy; the purveyors of public
news can support their slogans with depth analyses drawn from
"our way of life"; the lecturers on the platforms can sustain their

polemics with the authority of military planners, who have been drawn from university faculties. In hundreds of conferences, symposia, and round-table discussions appear members of the paramilitary caste to urge the military logic. In the publishers' lists there appear more and more titles written by members of the intellectual community attached to the military.

The academic community of university and foundation people, not directly taken in tow by the military, finds itself pulled into its sphere of influence by the sheer centripetal force of its energizing center; they are caught in the grip of an intellectual pressure, and have no alternative but to participate in discussions where the rules of the game have been set by others. The content and flavor of public discussion are influenced in the same way, because in a country where numerous diverse interests cut across each other and blur each other, the military is the best organized and most persistent, single-minded, and hard-driving faction. When the military rationale is accepted by both government and nation as the realistic definition of international politics, the boldest apostles of the preachment inevitably make the greatest impact.

## III

In the summer of 1961 a controversy arose out of two incidents involving Major General Edwin A. Walker and Senator William Fulbright, and it seemed as if the country was headed for a head-on clash between the military and civil powers. But the *cause célèbre* blew away, leaving the social drift unchanged. It demonstrated that the social drift is propelled by institutions too well intrenched to be disturbed by fortuitous episodes. The first incident arose when the *Overseas Weekly* ran an exposé about General Walker—a much-decorated veteran of World War II and the Korean War, and then in command of the Twenty-Fourth Infantry Division in West Germany—reporting that he was heavily propagandizing his troops along John Birch Society lines. He had described Harry Truman, Dean Acheson, and Mrs. Eleanor Roosevelt as "definitely pink," and Edward R. Murrow, Walter Lippmann, and Eric Sevareid as "confirmed Communists." He had also tried to instruct his troops on how to vote in the 1960 congressional elections. The disclosure produced a public storm, so that the Army had to administer a reprimand. Almost at once Walker became the hero of right-wing

Congressmen and of the conservative press, who tried to whip up a campaign against the White House for pillorying an outstanding patriot because of his opposition to communism.

The other incident, of an even more serious nature, had its origin in a sensational letter sent by Senator Fulbright to Secretary of Defense McNamara. The military had been authorized by a 1958 directive of the National Security Council to propagandize the nation. Fulbright now called to the Secretary's attention that the military's brand of education had been aggressively rightist, that the seminars it conducted throughout the country under military auspices made use of "extremely radical right-wing speakers and materials," and that the theme ranging through all the programs was that the main danger to this country was internal Communist infiltration. "Past and current international difficulties are often attributed to this, or ascribed to 'softness,' 'sellouts,' 'appeasements,' etc. . . . This view of the Communist menace renders foreign aid, cultural exchanges, disarmament negotiations, and other international programs as extremely wasteful, if not actually subversive. . . . There are many indications that the philosophy of the programs is representative of a substantial element of military thought, and has great appeal to the military mind."

Fulbright concluded that the 1958 directive had committed "a basic error." He urged that military activities be brought "under effective civilian control" and that a board of civilian educators develop a more satisfactory program of instruction at the National War College. Later, on the Senate floor, Fulbright explained that his memorandum to the Secretary of Defense "was based on my strong belief in the principle of military subordination to civilian control. There has been a strong tradition in this country that it is not the function of the military to educate the public on political issues. . . . Their function is to carry out policies formulated by officials who are responsible to the electorate."

Fulbright joined the issue clearly, and the issue was dramatized by the concurrence of the Walker case and the histrionics of conservative Congressmen. But neither the Pentagon nor the White House chieftains had originated the two incidents, and both backed away from any contest. General Walker destroyed his effectiveness for his backers when he admitted to membership in the John Birch Society, and then resigned from the Army in a huff in order to stand for office in the Texas gubernatorial election. That ended the Walker *cause célèbre*. The Fulbright attack was largely ignored by the newspapers, and petered out in a farcical debate whether the Defense Department could or could not censor the (generally ghost-written) speeches of the high brass—a debate originated by the right-wing legislators, and which military men made clear they had little interest in. The Secretary of Defense reduced some of the anarchy in the Pentagon procedures and better aligned Pentagon political activities with the White House—and that was the upshot of the Fulbright memorandum.

Every military state throughout history has lacked flexibility. It is like a warrior accoutered in heavy armor who can move along only stereotyped lines. It is committed to one line of action, and if that line of action becomes inexpedient, then woe to the nation!—for it is incapable of change. The fundamental danger to our country is that in becoming militarized, we are committing ourselves irrevocably to a military solution*—when a military solution is no longer obtainable. The ancillary danger is that the military establishment, by the sheer dynamic of its organization and thrust, may grip the country with an irrational and obscurantist mystique, as the French military did during the Dreyfus affair, or as Hitler did in his tenure, so that rational thinking becomes impossible, and all deviations from the national directive as formulated by the establishment become synonymous with treason.

The advantage of democratic government over personal dictatorship is that it tends to provide a popular corrective to one-sided rigidities emanating from government, and the flexibility to alter course when a line of action proves unviable or disastrous. But if democracy succumbs to the military logic, who is to introduce the correctives? The intellectual leaders, who might conceivably formulate new policies, are not attracted to non-existent political oppositions. They are either being submerged in the military establishment, or are succumbing to the dominant military slant of

---

* The basic text, prepared by the Foreign Policy Research Institute under the sponsorship of the National War College and the Joint Chiefs of Staff, *A Forward Strategy for America,* by Strausz-Hupe, Kintner, and Possony, states, "The priority objective of any American grand strategy is, by a broad margin, the preservation and enhancement of our political system rather than the maintenance of peace. . . . Our policy must be based on the premise that we cannot tolerate the survival of a political system which has the growing capability and the ruthless will to destroy us. We have no choice but to adopt a Catonic strategy." (A Catonic strategy refers not to something derived from games theory, but to Cato of the ancient world, who would rise in the Roman Senate to proclaim in season and out that "Carthage must be destroyed.")

our times. When we want to formulate a policy on disarmament, we turn the matter over to the military technicians.

Dr. Jerome B. Wiesner, President Kennedy's adviser on scientific matters, told a conference of leaders in business and the professions at Arden House in June, 1960, that "most of the people involved in arms limitation planning are people with military responsibilities or military backgrounds, and who know all the things that are wrong with our present military posture, and consequently view the possibility of limiting the military system still further with considerable concern." Dr. Wiesner said he was typical of the kind of people who are in charge of working on arms limitation: "I've been billed as an expert on arms control, and I think I'm an example of what's wrong with the American posture in this field. . . . My background is primarily one of military technology. . . . I came out of college at the time that World War II was beginning, and soon went to the radiation laboratory of M.I.T. where I worked on radar problems, and later went to Los Alamos and worked on atomic weapons. . . . I've worked on air defense, I was a member of the Von Neumann group that began our large-scale missile effort, and I've worked on many other military problems. I came to an arms control problem with all the biases and prejudices of someone who has been working very hard on military weapons—and, unfortunately, most of the people who work on arms control come to the problem from this same background."

The Fall, 1960, issue of *Daedalus,* devoted completely to the question of arms control, is an even more remarkable demonstration of the extent to which the intellectual elite has absorbed the military ideology. *Daedalus* is the quarterly of the American Academy of Arts and Sciences, an organization that has 1,800 members and presumably represents a cross-section of thought and opinion of America's educators, scientists, artists, and literary lights. It would be logical to suppose that such a body, in looking into a crucial question of this nature, would try to cut through the casuistries of diplomats and governments and consider the problem in its full breadth free of the immediate compulsions and pressures that beset all military and government bureaucracies. Instead (aside from a few isolated and honorable exceptions) the compendium is loaded with military assumption and conventional patriotism. Our scholars see themselves not as the guardians of the cultural heritage, or the conscience of humanity, but as the intellectual arm of the national establishment, charged with the duty of providing intellectual fodder to the men in power.

The question is: if the salt of democracy has lost its savor, with what shall it be salted? If we are dependent on military technicians and establishment bureaucrats for alternative policies to reverse the drift to war, will we get them?

CHAPTER 9 Disarmament and Depression

HAS American society become so inextricably fused into a war economy that if the political and strategic conflict that called the arms race into being were to disappear, we could not dismantle the military establishment without thrusting the country into a major economic crisis? A lot of people think so. In an address delivered in 1960 to a group of businessmen, T. Coleman Andrews, former Commissioner of the Internal Revenue Service, said, "If the Soviets should present a sincere and reliable proposal for peace, it would throw us into an industrial tailspin the like of which we have never dreamed." That fears of this nature run through the business community must be assumed from the sharp break on the New York Stock Exchange on August 10, 1959, attributed by the *New York Times* to "peace jitters" arising from the projected exchange of visits between Eisenhower and Khrushchev.

The effect of disarmament on our economy has been subjected to scrutiny and study by a number of American economists and social scientists; a United Nations panel of noted scholars from East, West, and neutral countries has issued a report; our Arms Control and Disarmament Agency has published a panel study—and the consensus of opinion is that if necessary measures are taken, there should be no insuperable problem to converting the war industries to civilian production. This is highly reassuring—

until we read the papers and reports line by line. Then we realize that nothing has really been settled at all. By another route, we have come to the familiar dilemmas of Keynesian economics: the planners can tell what measures have to be taken to avoid depression, but only the governments can decide what measures will be adopted; and the decision of governments depends on the political and social distribution of power within society.

The Communist state is in a superior position in this respect. Since its economy is centrally planned and directed, the business of maintaining effective demand is more of an engineering and allocations problem. With the adoption in recent years of the Khrushchev line of revisionist Marxism, Soviet spokesmen have been assuring the capitalist countries that they can comfortably disarm without fear of economic damage. Whether the advice is given tongue-in-cheek, or stems from a legitimate conversion, it is more sanguine than the opinions of a number of highly placed Americans. If we assume anything analogous to the current political mood, conversion to a civilian economy would trust to the laws of the marketplace. There probably would be emergency grants and tax credits voted to munitions makers in order to ease the transference of operations to other lines, and unemployment and retraining allowances to workers thrown out of their old jobs. The basic changeover would consist of massive cuts of excise taxes, corporation taxes, and personal income taxes, to permit private investment and consumer demand to expand the civilian economy and create new jobs for those lost with the reduction of the weapons sector.

There is widespread skepticism that private enterprise could expand the civilian economy to the extent of the loss. A. S. Goldberger of Stanford University pointed out in a careful study of the problem that the military establishment converts almost instantaneously a dollar of tax receipts into a dollar for current demand. Whatever its other virtues or faults may be, it is a first-class spending machine. An increase in income because of tax reduction does not make the same demand on current production: the individual is likely to spend only a part of his extra dollar; with the rest, he may increase his bank account, or buy more life insurance, or pay off a debt. Investment will probably respond sluggishly as well. "Even with profits after taxes running high, vast expansion of plant and equipment would be unlikely in the face of excess capacity and substantial unemployment." Using past experience as a guide, Goldberger figured that net capital formation might increase by fifty cents for every dollar increase in profits. His over-all conclusion: "Private demand should not be expected to rise to the opportunity created by an abandonment of the national defense program."

Disarmament planners try to overcome this difficulty by one or another variety of public spending. They say in effect, "Don't let us reduce taxes at all, or don't let us reduce them very much; let us use these moneys for pressing needs at home and abroad." The Quaker committee on national legislation proposed that the Government spend $200 billion on a ten-year program for aid to underdeveloped countries, public health, hospital buildings and medical research, natural resources, roads, waterways, old age benefits, child welfare and social security, school buildings, better salaries for teachers, scholarships and research, new housing, slum clearance, urban renewal, civilian space research—and allocated only $30 billion of the amount to tax reductions. The National Planning Association drew up a model five-year budget of $330 billion for public works. In his book, *The Peace Race,* published in 1962, Seymour Melman proposed an integrated program to enlarge the public sector. Going on the proposition that private firms have been unable in the last ten years to provide full employment to the growing labor force, and would probably be unable to absorb the additional workers displaced from military work, he sketched out a far-reaching reorganization based on accelerating the rate of economic growth. This was to be accomplished by enlarging the internal market through the rehabilitation of our own underdeveloped regions and the improvement of living standards of the very poor; by massive public expenditures for education, health, water improvements, public transportation, and housing; and by using war industrial capability to tool up the underdeveloped world. In more general terms, the report issued by the United Nations also anticipated that disarmament would lead to faster economic growth, greatly expanded aid from the advanced to the backward countries, improvements in levels of living, and increased leisure.

II

These are inspiring projects—but they have a catch in them. They are all doomed to remain paper projects unless and until there are big changes in political thinking. The war economy has a diabolical comfortableness about it that slowly submerges almost every part of the population in a euphoric stupor. Where the strong brews of patriotism and national honor keep the man in the street reconciled to high taxes and enormous financial outlays for military spending, he would resist, with all the righteous indignation bred of years of mass media conditioning, comparable government spending for "bleeding-heart causes" and "egghead welfare boon-doggling."

Missiles, planes, and bombs mean jobs; schoolhouses, scholarships, and hospitals mean only more taxes and bureaucracy. Conservative circles have lifted this Tory metaphysic to the status of a national philosophy because they think the business community is safe with big military spending and would be unsafe with big civilian spending. The beauty of the military system is that it is the kind of sheer waste which dovetails perfectly with the rest of the economy; the hardware and gadgets that come out of the laboratories and plants compete with no civilian products, do not interfere with the private corporation's patent rights, and do not accumulate the kind of inventories that retard continued production. When the munitions do not get used in war, they quickly become obsolete, and are junked, or sold at knockdown prices, or given away to our clients. There are no surpluses, and the demand is inexhaustible.

Civilian government spending is another story. Public housing competes with private housing and interferes with the money-making plans of real estate interests. Public power competes with private power and sets up rate yardsticks which are anathema to the profits schedules of the utilities corporations. It was because of these considerations that so many of the WPA projects during the New Deal had to be farfetched boondoggles. The interests that attacked the planners for bureaucratic incompetence stood guard against the introduction of projects that might hint of intruding into the jurisdictions that private enterprises had marked out as their exclusive preserves.

Public works also produce divergent social consequences. A public program exudes and enlarges a supervisory government bureaucracy. While corporation executives feel a kinship of outlook and fraternity with the military bureaucracy, they have a haunting anticipatory fear that a civilian bureaucracy will turn hostile to their interests and will pave the way for government ownership or centralized planning. They love the public works military bureaucracy, and they hate the public works civilian bureaucracy. This congeries of attitudes, habits, and assumptions goes deep—so deep that there can be no realistic talk of introducing expensive civilian government enterprises in lieu of armaments without a revamping of social values. What is being proposed through the various Keynesian schemes, consciously by some, without realization of its full implications by others, is an innovation as drastic as was Roosevelt's New Deal in relation to the America of Coolidge and Hoover, but less evanescent, more structural, more institutional. The problem consequently is not one of economics or engineering but of politics. Politics will have to clear the path before economics and engineering can come into play.

Emile Benoit of Columbia University, who has carved out a niche for himself as an expert on the economics of disarmament and is the chief author of the disarmament agency's panel report, is so well cognizant of the social and political animus that his model calls for disarmament to be spaced out over a period of twelve years—"and that estimate is optimistic." At the end of the twelve-year period, military spending would still run at $10 billion a year, and military personnel would still stand at half a million. He proceeds further to pile assumption on assumption. He assumes that there will be a $7 billion annual increase in government spending for space and atomic energy. He assumes that there will be another $7 billion annual increase to finance the work of a World Peace Authority inspectorate. Even all this would not take us out of the woods, for an initial over-all reduction in government spending of $5 billion would likely lead through its multiplier effects "to a fairly serious downward spiral." So, we are back to the problem of government service programs, and that is the big "x" in the equation. "When it comes to deciding what particular substitute programs should be adopted, the values of the electorate, rather than any narrowly economic criteria must be decisive. There are all sorts of 'needs' in our society, but the choice of priorities is essentially a moral and political decision."

In an earlier paper, where Benoit was not inhibited by the government auspices of publication, he displayed even greater nervousness about the whole matter. He wrote, "It is frequently argued that there is no real problem, and no need for concern, since there are plenty of constructive uses for defense savings, and since the severity of prospective cutbacks may be less, or no worse, than those to which we rather easily adjusted after World War II and after Korea. The conclusions of this paper are rather less reassuring. They suggest that it would be unwise to dismiss too readily the lingering foreboding with which so many practical people—in government as well as in labor and management—regard the possible impact of disarmament. Such fears, even if unfounded in theory, may turn out to have considerable validity in practice, since certain attitudes or institutional obstacles may prevent or delay the adjustment which, on paper, could make a more or less painless transition possible."

So there we are. After consulting all the learned physicians and surgeons of the land, we discover that there is no pill or colored water to cure us of our disease. It is up to us. If we stop smoking, drinking, swearing, and consorting with wild women, and go back to a less hectic existence and arrange our affairs in more generous style, we may pull out of it. If we don't, our chances are not bright.

CHAPTER 10   An Ambivalent Trend

In *War as an Instrument of National Policy,* James T. Shotwell examined the pacifist mood of the postwar twenties and concluded that "the movement for international peace owes its validity, which is real, to the fact that a new civilization has arisen which rests upon the interdependence of nations. . . . It is because the world has turned that corner in history when civilized societies need peace for their continued existence, and find the instrument of war no longer pertinent."

Unfortunately, Shotwell's thesis was somewhat compromised when the world was torn apart by another holocaust. But under discussion are not instantaneous transformations. It takes societies long periods of time and laborious heavings to adjust their thinking and social dispositions to new necessities. In a world where the war system has prevailed for six thousand years a pacifist mood can grow dominant only when society discovers that war has become an unusable instrument, and the human mind casts about for new ways to survive and live. The notion that war could be done away with, that it was not another act of God, was accepted three hundred years ago only by isolated dreamers like Sully and William Penn. Their few seeds sprouted into an article of faith of the entire intellectual avant-garde around Europe with the Enlightenment. The faith was pushed far back in the iron decades of imperialism and *machtpolitik*. But can there be any question that in recent generations the faith has welled up more forcibly, and over greater stretches of the globe?

The movement for peace has passed from the moralist to the statesman. The hopes of isolated eccentric sects have been taken up by social groups of size and influence. The moral trend is not disqualified because the proponents of peace do not seem to have any profound influence on the policies of princes and states, and because a peace movement no less impressive, and probably far better organized, went down ignominiously before the roar of the guns in 1914. This is an attempt to isolate an elusive matter of attitude on the part of peoples, which may be a ponderous and unsmooth response to the changed cultural circumstances of man's being, and which may in time cut its way through to political realization. It is significant that the peace ideology has now conquered as the rationale of what is proper and desirable. Even if much of the government talk is lip service, it is nonetheless true that it is the tribute that vice is now compelled to pay to virtue. Peace has swept all forms and varieties of social Darwinism off the boards, so much so, that every new military appropriation and the manufacture of every new infernal engine of destruction must be justified on the sole ground that it will help preserve the peace.

If it is true that the continuation of the war system represents a cultural lag, it is also true that there are manifestations that may overcome that lag. There is the rise of a public opinion against war. This is a unique creation of the twentieth century; there has never been anything like it in any of the past centuries or millennia. Up to the present era, peoples groaned under the burden of war; they cursed and complained; but the notion of political opposition to it, the notion that you could pressure governments to do away with it, never entered into the calculation. The remarkable Greeks, who anticipated everything, anticipated this also during their fratricidal Peloponnesian wars. But the peace factions of Aristophanes' time were a passing political association that drew the narrowly empirical conclusion that the particular war was not getting anywhere, and that it was time to close it. To oppose war as an institution can be done only by those who have a vision of a different order of human organization—and that is a product of our own century.

The military solution is further compromised in our age because of the spread of nationalism. What was operative for only a small portion in Western Europe following the French Revolution and the wars of national unification, now governs the whole world. In the previous centuries, imperialist powers had the assurance that once they conquered a backward region or overturned an enemy dynasty, they would have no problem in pacifying their subjects. The people used to accept the rule of the new masters as uncomplainingly as they had accepted the rule of their old ones. Now nationality comes to the fore and upsets the game. The new generations refuse to submit. They do not accept the decision. They continue their resistance behind the lines by all means available to them. That is what has produced the impotence of superior military power in Indonesia or Algeria and has inhibited the United States from mounting a full-scale invasion of Cuba. Military forces continue to be deployed, but their efficacy is becoming more limited all the time.

Judging from past experience it is doubtful that the public opinion against war, standing alone and lacking other ingredients, can subdue the violent currents of history. In the decade leading up to the First World War, the extensive Socialist and pacifist opposition was helpless to affect the arms race, and when war was declared, it succumbed to the nationalist wave. In the period between wars there was the Oxford Pledge group in England, and in the time immediately preceding World War II, the America First and pacifist groups in this country. That there was considerable resistance and reluctance here to becoming embroiled in the war can be gathered from the wariness and guile with which Roosevelt moved into the fray. All the same, the peace mood only affected the public relations techniques and propaganda themes of governments; it did not stop war.

In the nuclear age no opinion is more universally expressed than abhorrence of war. One can truthfully speak of a world public opinion, for this opposition can be heard in Moscow as well as in Washington, on the streets of New Delhi and Karachi as well as of London, Rome, and Bonn. It is first on the agenda of popular preoccupation. But this well-nigh universal public opinion is so interwoven with national habits and associations that it is all too often turned to the advantage of the war system. The opposition to war manifests itself as a philosophic principle, as a moral imperative abstracted from the society's social arrangements and its government's politics. As soon as the generalized opposition is confronted with the practical problems of politics into which it divides, the universal condemnation breaks down along national lines. It then finds release in a burst of fury against the opponent across the border whose conduct is presumably responsible for the war tensions. The opposition to war turns into opposition to the nation which is allegedly threatening the peace, but for whose evil machinations humanity would now be living in a state of fraternal bliss. The guilty nation invariably turns out to be identical with the official enemy.

The universal public opinion against war thereupon splits into a series of chauvinisms anxious to punish and subdue the transgressor against the peace. That is why the peace feeling, running deep and across boundaries, does nothing to bind up the wounds of animosity between nations. The bellicose policies of states run on one level; the fear and abhorrence of war on another level; and there appears to be hardly a connection between the two. The President may watch a women's peace demonstration from the windows of the White House and announce that he got the message. He may even send out a five-gallon urn of hot coffee to refresh a group of student antiwar demonstrators. But neither of these friendly gestures has any significance in the world of affairs. The United States immediately thereafter resumes nuclear testing, and the rheostat of the arms race is given another upward twist.

In Russia the peace mood of the people is exceedingly strong. Every correspondent, every visitor, remarks upon it. The memories of the last devastation remain vivid and keep green the fears of a new apocalypse. That does not change government policy, however. Russia has to match the foe gun for gun, just as the United States has to match the foe gun for gun. And the very populaces that are against war feel that it is only proper that their own country not leave itself open to the evil designs of its enemy across the border.

Yet it would be a mistake to write off the opinions of mankind and to declare them of no consequence in the calculations of history on account of their proved impotence to reverse the engines of two world wars and the current preparations for a third. In a question of this magnitude, of changing a people's deeply rooted habits and assumptions, the kind of practicality that is of use in investing money on the stock exchange or winning an election campaign can miss entirely the tangled threads and elusive trends that are weaving the pattern of the future. That the man in the street is often shallow and stupid and bewildered is undeniable.

That, more often than not, he does not reconcile his contradictory convictions, prejudices, complaints, and demands is a matter of record. That his drives and desires can be and are manipulated by men in power, both ancient and modern history affirms. But history also affirms that these drives and desires, when they combine to make up a *zeitgeist* of an epoch, can sometimes metamorphose into a social power.

A constant in the congeries of impulses that have gripped humanity in our century has been the impulse for an ordering of the human organization that goes beyond the national state. The drive has taken a variety of forms, of scores of projects, and of several international organizations. All of them, much as they vary in intent, outlook, and detail, have this much in common: they reflect the mass idea of transcending nineteenth century nationalism, and they rest on the belief that some kind of universal establishment is necessary if mankind is to save itself from a fratricidal warfare that has become intolerable.

The felt need has produced another theory of the stages of mankind. Just as the polis led to the cosmopolis, and the medieval particularist provinces evolved into the modern nation, so the modern nation has a manifest destiny to move to the world state or world federation. Where violence was monopolized by the local princelings or feudal barons, the national state gradually took over jurisdiction with "the King's Peace," and the monopoly over internal violence was then extended to a monopoly over external violence as well. Where differences were once fought out in never-ending clashes of arms, they are now settled within the nation through civil and legal arrangements in which the employment of violence is reduced to largely symbolic forms. Is it not then to be concluded that humanity is being impelled to the next stage of integration where the national states are due to set up a world supervisory and coordinating mechanism in order to adjudicate their quarrels and reconcile their conflicting claims?

## II

There are a number of related schools of thought that believe the logic of the case for world government is so irresistible that once it is properly explained, it will root out misunderstandings, dissolve prejudices, annul contrary preconceptions, and lead ineluctibly to the promised land. The representatives of these associated tendencies see in the present and in the history of the past forty years the slow, groping steps of an evolutionary development heading inevitably for universalism.

Sir Frederick Eggleston, who attended both the 1919 peace conference and the founding United Nations conference as a member of the Australian delegation, is a representative figure of this mode of thought. Eggleston has written:

> Social organization starts in families, kinship groups, and is gradually extended to larger communities, but it works well only when people know each other, share the ideas they follow, and trust their fellows. So what history shows us is a series of groups gradually extending in scope and growing in order and strength of organization. In these groups conflict is very much diminished, if not eliminated, but the groups stand up against one another without any wide ties of union. Furthermore, in the modern world, no community is entirely self-sufficient. It has to get some of the materials for the existence and prosperity of its members from outside, and thus international competition supervenes, and this itself produces conflict. In fact, it is the main cause of war. If what I have said so far is sound, what is indicated as the means of eliminating international conflict is international organization, the continuation of the process which has been going on since the dawn of history, of extending the area of order and organization until it covers the whole world. I think the human mind has recognized this, and during the last fifty years, civilization has been engaged in working out an international organization.

This is a powerful idea, and it is understandable that it has found adherents all over the world. Its groups of supporters read like a who's who of scholars, social scientists, and diplomats. Neither is it surprising, considering the recalcitrance of the material which they have to handle and the rebuffs which they have to absorb, that the world government theorists have divided and subdivided into factions and subschools. Some believe that world government cannot be attained unless we have first established an international law as the foundation for the universalization of national power. They see in the Declaration of Universal Human Rights, in the convention outlawing genocide, in the United Nations Charter, and in the International Court, the initial provisions which in time will grow into an effective body of accepted law to which all peoples and nations will adhere. They view the manifestations of the past half-century as the early stage of the emergence of a common law of mankind.

An ancillary subschool holds that a system of world planning will have to be perfected which will see the growth of an international body of civil servants and technical experts who think in terms of human welfare instead of national loyalties, and who will make use of the scientific knowledge of our age to wipe out the hunger, disease, and maladjustments which are at the basis of so many of the conflicts between nations and classes. They, in turn, see in the humanitarian and technical divisions of the United Nations, the Food and Agricultural Organization, the Economic Commissions, UNESCO, the World Health Organization, and the World Bank the prototypes of an international body which, as time goes on, will bind the people together in a social and economic community, and make inevitable the creation of a political authority. Others, like the United World Federalists, believe that the United Nations suffers from fatal structural defects that prevent it from carrying out the functions of a world government. They therefore call for a basic constitutional reorganization. For them, the creation of an international legislature and police force has to take precedence, since only an organization so armed with power can ensure the creation of a universal community and a world law.

But there is little profit in concerning ourselves with technique until we have defined the problem. Is there any indication that the praiseworthy rationale for some variety of world government or association is in line with the movement of social evolution?

In the world of affairs, law and politics have always been intertwined. Law can exist only in a social framework; society can be organized only on the effective need for community; and community has always rested on a bedrock of power. Law can never soar beyond the orbit of its social and political context. International law has up to now been such a tenuous and ill-defined idea not because of its faulty elaboration by international jurists, but because the international morality which it has sought to define has been ephemeral and unstable. There has never been an effective international law because there has never been an effective international community.

What we have to determine is the historical trend: are we moving toward world law, or are we thrashing about aimlessly, unable to transcend the military law of civilization? For the formalists, the answer is clear. We are at the threshold of the new dawn. C. W. Jenks in *The Common Law of Mankind* sees progress all along the line. True, there have been some setbacks, like the collapse of the League of Nations, two world wars, and the present cold war, but if we compare the present situation with that of 1914, we will have no doubt that we are on the way. In 1914 war was legal; now it is illegal. In 1914 there was no instrumentality to make international law; now we have such an instrumentality. In 1914 there was no permanent international judicature; now we have one. In 1914 there was no secular arm to enforce international law; now the secular arm enforces it in places like Korea and Suez. Unfortunately, this type of listing mistakes the promise for the realization, the appearance for the reality. It ignores the tragic experience of the League of Nations, an experience that demonstrated that the political leaders were more successful in creating an international rhetoric than an international community.

It is all the more obligatory to relate critically the legalisms to the practices because the forty-year span since the end of World War I has introduced unheard-of hypocrisy in international relations. Some of it is not new. The rhetorical pretensions of statesmen have always been superior to their actions. Brutal or despicable conduct enfolded in the noble vestments of sanctimonious oratory is the staple of all written history, and can probably be traced back to the medicine men. A statement repeated many times is the remark that Waleski, a French Foreign Minister, made to Bismarck, that it is the business of a diplomat to cloak the interests of his country in the language of universal justice.

But the technique of converting the mean and tawdry pursuits of national states into the rhetoric of idealistic concern has been standardized and perfected into an international system in our own day. What was a trickle of craft-built goods has become a surge of mass production. This is not because statesmen are less honorable today than they were in past ages, and not because people are more gullible than they used to be. It is not because public morals are weaker than in times gone by. It is because of the yawning discrepancy between acceptable ideology and constrained behavior. All must now give obeisance to peace, to international cooperation, to the uplift of deprived peoples. While the accepted ideal has soared to heights unknown to the ancient Greeks or the eighteenth century monarchs, the motion of politics is still driven by age-old egotistic compulsions.

Hence, the growing gap between language and the activities it purports to describe.

A century ago the war ministry was called the war ministry, and no official felt the need to apologize for its existence. Today we have bigger war ministries than our grandfathers dreamed of, but we no longer call them war ministries. They are now defense departments. Soon they will be known as peace departments. The powers used to call themselves powers. That is an anachronism today. The proper designation is the "developed" countries. Churchill, true to his nineteenth century upbringing, wrote a draft for the projected world organization preamble, in which he launched the new organization under the aegis of the "Associated Powers," but Roosevelt, who had a keener ear for the rhythms of mass democracy, corrected the draft to read, "United Nations." Churchill's designation was more accurate, but Roosevelt's was superior in catering to the mood of the times. Dismayed by the outpouring of empty rhetoric during the League debates, Churchill wrote in 1932: "I cannot recall any time when the gap between the kind of words which statesmen used and what was actually happening in many countries was so great as it is now."

E. H. Carr, in examining this phenomenon during the interwar years, remarked that where practice is least ethical, theory becomes most utopian. Utopia necessarily tends to predominate over reality in international law to an extent unparalleled in other branches of jurisprudence because of the primitive state of international conduct—a tendency exaggerated in a period when anarchy and uproar is prevalent in the practice of nations. But there is more to it than this. It is not just an attempt of the intellectual conscience to compensate in theory for the irrationality of practice. The theorists and international jurists are only a segment of an intellectual caste, all of whom—statesmen, civil servants, journalists, foundation bureaucrats—have been sucked into a whirlpool of moralistic pretense and make-believe. This charade, in which the participants act out stereotype roles, has been thrust on all of them because of the conflict between a popular urge for a new international morality that will save mankind from war, and the deep currents of history which are at the same time carrying peoples along toward unrestrained militarism. Where thought is so contradictory, language becomes opaque and slippery, and rhetoric and conduct only meet occasionally, if at all.

The system of an international double-bookkeeping debases the mental process. The frivolous juggling of the real and the unreal lowers public sensibility to the point where the opinion-makers no less than their audience find it hard to fix the demarcating lines between the true and the pretended aims of public policy. The babel of confusion makes the public mind hospitable to obscurantism and hysteria. It makes it difficult to deal rationally with international conflicts. It debases the literature and thought and reduces the social scientists to propagandists for power cliques.

That is why this is one sphere where it is necessary to be always on guard against self-deception, against getting caught in quagmires of legalist pettifoggery, to test declaration against performance, and to take nothing for granted. The question of whether we are in the early stages of a developing international polity, or in the late stages of the self-destruction of civilization, is a question that can only be answered, if at all, by critical consideration—undefiled by catch phrases of the moment—of the pertinent experience.

CHAPTER 11    Failure of the League of Nations

THE first major experiment in building an international polity
ended, as we know, in ignominious failure. The dichotomy between
statesmen's professions and behavior was an intolerable one, and
produced for a while a public cynicism about all claims to the
higher morality. The League of Nations was supposed to embody
the legal framework for a new international community based on
reason instead of force, on the rule of law instead of the rule of
brute strength. But in the descent from the Olympian heights of
abstract homily to the mundane world of international diplomacy,
the world order that the League was entrusted to uphold was
the world order set up by the victorious Allies. This bore slight
resemblance to the promised land fit for heroes to live in. The
settlements of the First World War were in the long line of tradition where the victors disarmed the vanquished, snatched territories, and exacted tribute. Unlike the bad old days, however, this
was only the first stage of a master project whose conclusion was
to realize the new equitable society where the victors would likewise disarm and share their bounty with their erstwhile foes. But
the second and succeeding stages of the enterprise never got
launched. The League was mired in the Versailles system.

The disarmament negotiations were illustrative of the futility of a system which attempted to superimpose an international morality on the politics of national aggrandizement. Disarmament was at the heart of the League experiment, for the entire rhetoric of international amity rested on the promise to do away with the prewar armed camp. German armament, it will be recalled, was stripped down to police levels by the Versailles treaty, and Allied military inspectors, whose personnel numbered at one time as many as two thousand, roamed about the country to see that the provisions were respected. The Germans were assured, however, that this one-sided disarmament was not intended for the victor's advantage, but according to the Versailles treaty, "to render possible the initiation of a general limitation of the armaments of all nations." This promise of high purpose was then written into Article 8 of the League Covenant, which declared "that the maintenance of peace required the reduction of national armaments to the lowest point consistent with national safety."

The League Council appointed a Temporary Mixed Commission of civilian and military representatives to draw up appropriate proposals, and it was twelve years before the League finally called a general disarmament conference. When it did call the conference in 1932, it was not because the various experts had at last reached some reasonable agreements, or boiled down their researches to workable proposals, but that German pressure and the mounting scandal forced the League supervisors to make a gesture, however meaningless, in the direction of disarmament.

From the first, the representatives on the various commissions split into two schools of thought: those who thought that disarmament would increase security; and those who thought that an increase in security must precede disarmament. Although France was armed to the teeth, was policing its disarmed rival, and stood at the head of a military bloc of Central and East European states, neither this position of continental hegemony, nor its supposed protection by a covenant wherein the nations pledged "not to resort to war," sufficed to assuage her fears for her security. At every opportunity her representatives and those of her allies pressed the theory that additional measures would have to be taken to ensure their security before disarmament could be practically discussed. From 1923 to 1925 the diplomats labored mightily to transform the vague commitments under Articles 10 and 16 into a definitive and automatic system of collective sanctions against any war aggressor. The high

point of the search came with the Locarno treaty, when England
agreed to guarantee the Franco-German frontiers against aggression
by either party, and after the signing of the treaty Germany was
invited to join the League. At last Europe was thought to have
broken through the ring of war hostilities, and Austen Chamberlain
described the treaty as "the real dividing-line between the years of
war and the years of peace."

The League Council thereupon appointed a Preparatory Commission for the Disarmament Conference, and in addition to the
League constituents, the United States and the Soviet Union were
invited, and agreed to become members. When the commission got
down to serious discussions in the spring of 1927, the members revealed such a wide disparity of opinions as to leave no loophole for
agreement. The German delegation wanted a specific numerical
limitation of every important category of armament such as had
been imposed on her. The French delegation wanted to reduce
armaments by limiting budgetary expenditure, which happened to
be the only form of limitation which had not been imposed hitherto
on Germany. The British and American delegations thought any
limitation of military material impractical. And so it went on
every question that was taken up.

When the Preparatory Commission resumed its meetings in the
fall, it produced nothing new, except that its sessions were en-
livened by the appearance of Litvinov, the Soviet delegate, who
made a plea for complete and universal disarmament. Every delegate present assumed it was nothing more than a brazen propaganda
play. Litvinov's proposal was resoundingly voted down, and for the
next three years talk of disarmament receded into the background.

When the United States called a special conference to extend the
naval agreement that had been made in 1921, France and Italy de-
clined to attend. In the meeting reduced to the United States,
Britain, and Japan, the latter was able to sit back and watch the
two Westerners tear up the conference with their squabble. The
British insisted that they needed a minimum of seventy cruisers,
owing to the long lines of empire communications—a number con-
siderably in excess of those it already had or was building. But they
thought it would be a good idea to reduce the size of capital ships,
the category in which, by chance, the United States happened to be
interested. The failure of the 1927 naval conference brought out the
nationalist and militarist thinking processes and motivations of the
powers. Not that a success at the conference would have had any

consequence for disarmament. Three years later, the three powers came to a limited understanding to extend to cruisers the 5:5:3 ratio that had been established in 1921 for capital ships; and it was only the preliminary for the total breakdown of the League balances.

The powers were not thinking in these conferences of establishing a new *ultima ratio* for international disagreement. Their sole concern was whether they might not regulate armaments to get the same power balance results more cheaply—and even that was never assayed with very much conviction. The much-touted arms limitation agreement of the 1930 conference in London was set at a figure that represented for both the United States and Britain the building of additional ships, rather than a reduction of the existing number.

By 1930 Germany was in the throes of a full-blown crisis. The Nazis increased the number of their Reichstag seats from 12 to 107, the Social Democrats were forced out of the ministry, and the nation was getting set to strike off the disabilities of the Versailles settlement. When France, the following year, forced Germany to abandon her economic union with Austria, the pressure to allow Germany to rearm became explosive, and the long-awaited disarmament conference was at long last summoned for February 2, 1932. The discussions at the conference were as unedifying and discouraging as those that had taken place in the commissions. Whenever any delegate would propose some concrete measure for disarmament, the French delegation could be relied on to remind the conference that additional guarantees for French security were required before her support could be expected. The adroit British suggested that arms be limited by abolishing those weapons lending themselves to offensive rather than defensive warfare. This proposal received widespread and enthusiastic support. When, however, the question was referred to three commissions consisting of army, navy, and air experts, it became apparent that no one agreed with anyone else on which weapons were offensive and which were defensive. The conference was back at dead center.

After Hitler became chancellor and it was imperative to come to an agreement with Germany with no further delay, the French came up with the plan to divide the disarmament convention into two stages—a classic formula for stalling. The first stage is accepted as the real proposal. The stages to follow are, at best, problematical. In this case, in the first stage, to last four years, a system of international supervision and control was to be set up over armaments.

Arms limitation proper was to begin only in the second stage. On October 14, Sir John Simon formally endorsed the French proposal on behalf of the British government. Within a few hours, Germany announced her withdrawal from the disarmament conference. She was making good her threat that either the other powers had to disarm, or they had to recognize Germany's right to rearm.

It was the end of an era of liberalistic illusion and of disarmament chatter. It was the beginning of a new arms race and the beginning of the end of the League of Nations.

## II

The breakdown of the League was productive of a voluminous literature to account for the causes of the failure. Much of it consisted of laments in the void that had men and nations acted differently, things would have turned out more happily. If only section 2 of Article 16 had been tightened to squeeze out the ambiguity surrounding sanctions, then Japan would never have dared to invade Manchuria. If only England had followed through on her commitments, then Italy would have retreated from her adventure in Ethiopia. If only France had not been so shortsighted in her military arrogance, then Germany would never have been driven into the arms of freebooters and militarists. If only England and France had united to stop the reoccupation of the Rhineland, then Europe would have been spared the necessity for another bloodbath.

Philip Noel-Baker's exploration for the failure in *The Arms Race,* wherein history is atomized into its factual tidbits, is a classic of this genre: "The League Disarmament Conference was not doomed to futility from the start. It failed, indeed; but if Sir John Simon had succeeded in persuading the British cabinet to accept President Hoover's proposals of June, 1932; if Mr. Stanley Baldwin had beaten Lord Londonderry more swiftly and decisively in the long-drawn cabinet struggle about the abolition of the bomber; if Sir Anthony Eden's belated Draft Convention of March, 1933, had been put forward a year earlier, it might have had a rapid and notable success."

This type of criticism was all beside the point because it abstracted itself from the salient realities. The victorious nations that had joined to set up an international association had not altered their way of looking at things and conducting relations. They had not set any example in their behavior, even toward each other, of being animated by superior fraternal impulses, and of having discarded the cold calculations of national advantage and exclusiveness. They had not introduced any new superior principles of social organization or international brotherhood. They had simply identified their own national cause and interest with the cause and interest of humanity, much as dominant groups within the nation have identified their own privileges with the interests of the entire nation. And in the same way that conservatives within the nation would belabor and excoriate those who sought to upset the legal arrangements of the day as subverters of the national weal, the victorious powers tried to read out of international society those who would flout the will of their legal constructions.

Two things followed. The League was turned into an instrument of the dominant victorious powers intent upon preserving the status quo. And international morality, as expounded by Allied statesmen and savants, was equated to support of the institutionalism designed to prop up the existing arrangements, while international immorality was made synonymous with efforts to change these arrangements. Now, no status quo is that holy, and the status quo that saw the light of day in 1919 was less satisfactory than the one that had set the European powers at each other's throats in 1914. The international morality of the League was consequently never convincing to large numbers of nations, and opinion in favor of the League was never, even in the halcyon days, international in scope. When the international balances shifted and dissatisfied powers felt strong enough to demand changes, the imposing but synthetic structure of the League fell apart.

It is a mistake to look at it as a contest in which the forces of virtue were ranged on one side, and the forces of wickedness on the other. It is easy to slide into such an interpretation, because the Allied powers were the well-to-do democracies who afforded their own peoples relatively generous civil arrangements and living standards, while the revisionist powers were dictatorships who abused their own peoples, and at whose center stood a Germany headed by as wicked and bloodthirsty a regime as history has known. But an internationalism resting on nothing better than a holy alliance dedicated to holding the world inert would be inequitable, impractical, and reactionary, regardless of the types of peoples or states that were challenging the status quo. An internationalism animated by no passion other than the obstinate maintenance of an existent state of things would doom mankind to provincialism and stagnation. It would putrefy in its own juices of futility and purposelessness and would finally disintegrate entirely under the blows of rebellious forces carrying a larger vision of life. One of the profoundest criticisms of Machiavelli was made by Treitschke who wrote that the "terrible thing" about Machiavelli's teaching was "not the immorality of the methods he recommends, but the lack of content of the state, which exists only in order to exist."

When the channels for constitutional change are effectively blocked off, the revolutionary impulses sometimes become encompassed within retrograde or psychotic movements. This does not validate the existing arrangements, or justify the resistance to change. "A state without the means of some change is without the means of its own conservation," goes the aphorism of Edmund Burke. An international association which could provide nothing more substantial than an Article 19 by which the assembly could "advise"—provided it could muster a unanimous vote—the reconsideration of treaties "which have become inapplicable," was not equipped to survive in a revolutionary decade. It is doubtful that it could have survived in a Victorian era.

As soon as the status quo came under effective challenge, the League machinery, designed to frighten off aggressors, was shown to be made of tinsel and paste. This became the special point of departure of critics who were enamored of the legal mechanics of international organization, and who concluded that the cause for the breakdown was that the League was not equipped with punitive teeth. The remedy, it appeared to them, was the adoption of stronger rules to make sure that the international community would come down remorselessly on any would-be aggressor. As in so many experiences, the breakdown of a policy is invariably attributed by some not to the inherent faults of the policy, but to the failure of pursuing it with sufficient vigor. Unfortunately for the critics, collective security, both as rationale and strategy, was too bankrupt to be saved by boldness of spirit.

Collective security presupposed a supranational morality where none existed. It assumed that the military forces of the several national states were apolitical mechanisms which could be employed as other than emanations of these same states. Hence, the spinning of the spurious analogy with the policeman on the beat, who without partisanship or favor, cracks down on all law violators and keeps the peace. However, in carrying out his constabulary duties, the policeman is sustained by a municipal law and courts which are more or less accepted by the public opinion of the entire community. He is also a member of a specialized caste to which has been assigned the monopoly of violence.

Things were not equally well situated with the international community. The only organs of violence at the League's disposal were the military establishments of the powers. When the major powers were united in their purposes, they could, with a high show of international morality, crack down on a small nation that sought to forcibly extend its borders, or revise shipping rights around its waters. In other words, collective security, whatever its intrinsic morality or justice, could work effectively to overawe the minor powers when they were not allied with powerful patrons. The wars which the world feared, however, were the clash of the lions, not the clash of the mice. When the major powers broke ranks, who was to police the policemen? Every nation, with the signs of an approaching storm, made such dispositions as would best protect its own egotistic interests. Collective security then became another name for a major war. Collective security was effective so long as the need for it remained inconsequential. The moment it confronted a three-alarm fire, the system broke down.

Where, because of a special concatenation of circumstances, a majority of the armed powers would be willing to go to war with a revisionist power, the resultant conflict would still have no factual resemblance to a Dick Tracy constable righteously dragging off a criminal miscreant to jail. For, as E. H. Carr said, in *The Twenty Years' Crisis,*

> It is one of the fallacies of the theory of collective security that war can be waged for the specific and disinterested purpose of "resisting aggression." Had the League of Nations in the autumn of 1935, under the leadership of Great Britain, embarked on "military sanctions" against Italy, it would have been impossible to restrict the campaign to the expulsion of Italian troops from Abyssinia. Operations would in all probability have led to the occupation of Italy's East African colonies by Great Britain and France, of Trieste, Fiume, and Albania by Yugoslavia, and the islands of the Dodecanese by Greece or Turkey or both; and war aims would have been announced, precluding on various specious grounds, the restoration of these territories to Italy.

The mechanical defects of the League were not defects of legal draftsmanship; they were reflections of the reluctance of the national states to give up their jungle habits. In the circumstances, the League became the captive of the prevailing international immorality, and the Wilsonian rhetoric, a servile adornment of it. In adding up the dolorous balance at the end of the thirties, some of the historians of the period ascribed the debacle to human stupidity, others to human wickedness. Both traits were in fulsome evidence, to be sure. But there was no indication that leaders and peoples were more stupid or more wicked in the thirties than at any other period of history. In those epochs when they appear to be, it generally follows that the routine of history has been shattered, and the traditional leaders of the traditional societies are unable to devise new concepts for the new exigencies. The League was a sorry testimonial to the futility of trying to construct an international morality on a foundation of competing militarist states, with no loyalties greater than their national sovereignties, and no ambitions more exalted than their traditional vanities.

THE interwar years witnessed another grandiose attempt to create an internationalism on totally different principles—that of the Communist Third International. Where the League of Nations was based on the preservation of the status quo, the Communist International was based on its subversion and overthrow. Where the League of Nations sought to bolster middle class society, the Communist International was dedicated to splitting this society wide open and reassembling the particles into a socialist community. The two organizations existed on such different levels of society and discourse as to never be formally introduced to one another. Throughout the twenties they were engaged in a bitter cold war. It is difficult in our time, when the Western world is dominated by conservative moods, and when attitudes toward the Russian revolution have been conditioned by the savageries of Stalinism, to re-create the spirit of evangelical fervor and apocalyptic faith that swept over great sections of the European labor movements and the intellectual avant-garde in the wake of the Bolshevik revolution. When Marx and Engels wrote in 1848 that the specter of communism was haunting Europe, they were talking about a prediction rather than a fact; seventy years later, Woodrow Wilson, Lloyd George, Clemenceau, and the Kaiser's generals were in real terror of that specter, and the League's activities were conducted in its frightening shadow.

When the Bolshevik authorities under Lenin threw the entire responsibility for the murderous war on the representatives of all the capitalist governments and announced that they were withdrawing from and would have nothing further to do with the criminal fray, when they published and repudiated the Czar's secret treaties with the Allies and called for a new era of open and honest relations between peoples, and a just and democratic peace without indemnities and annexations—they unleashed a movement of ardent sympathy and hope which threatened to leave the traditional middle class leaders of the West shorn of their moral and temporal authority. Masses of humanity surged toward the New Jerusalem which had magically appeared out of the bloody froth of the war of nations. In an attempt to steal the Bolshevik thunder and to retain the moral authority for the organization of the peace in Allied hands, Wilson hastened to proclaim his Fourteen Points in which he felt constrained to assert that "the treatment accorded Russia by her sister nations in the months to come will be the acid test of their good will." On a number of occasions during the grueling months of the Versailles negotiations, he told correspondents and friends that they were in a desperate race with the Bolsheviks. Europe was being subjected to a spiritual pull between East and West.

The moral power of Communism came from its successful recreation of the vision of internationalism. The Socialist movement of the Second International had succumbed to the nationalist fumes, but that was explained by the Russian prophets as a betrayal by the Socialist leaders of the true and unassailable faith. With a purified corps of leaders devoted to the cause and immune to the lures of middle class public opinion and careers, a rational reorganization of society was within easy reach. The proof of their vision was unassailable: the Bolsheviks had realized it. They had shown that by revolutionary intelligence and resoluteness, the Marxists could take state power and start to reorganize society along socialist lines. What they had done, others could do. True, the party of Lenin presided over a country that was no model of material plenty or social harmony. The Russia that the Communists inherited from the Czar was poor and barbarous, and its people were largely illiterate. The job of ruination, well on the way with the Great War, was completed in the three and a half years of civil war which followed. After the Allies set up their *cordon sanitaire,* the Russians were in the grip of famine. As Lenin confessed to the 1920 Congress of the Communist International, "When we introduced the dictatorship, the workers began to starve more than before and their conditions became even worse." Then he generalized the specific instance into a universal: "The victory of the workers cannot be achieved without sacrifice, without a temporary deterioration of their conditions." The revolutionary Soviet republic could offer nothing to the West materially. The shining future that it promised was underwritten by the revolutionary élan of her leaders and the fervor of her ranks. For a time, that was sufficient.

The Communist International was launched as the Mohammedan wing of the Marxian faith. It was going to bring the word of God by fire and sword. The unbelievers, the infidels, the unclean, were many and ever active, and they had to be discredited and dispersed. The hosts of righteousness had to be indoctrinated and readied before the mighty foe could be overthrown and the brotherhood of man realized. The Bolsheviks believed they were the Lord's Chosen, because the era that their generation had been placed in was the era of the final settling of accounts between capitalism and socialism. The Russian revolution was not an isolated phenomenon outside the main currents of Western civilization. On the contrary, it was the opening gun of a Europe-wide revolution which had been long heralded by the founding fathers and was now about to usher in the next stage of human society.

This was not the typical sociological forecast where a formula could cover a trend for the next fifty years; this was a matter of literally the next year or two. Zinoviev, the Comintern's original president, prophesied in the first issue of the official publication that within a single year all Europe would be a Soviet republic and would already be forgetting that there had ever been a fight about it. At the Second Congress meeting in the summer of 1920, Zinoviev had to confess that the millennium had not yet come, but assured the delegates there was nothing to worry about. "Perhaps we have been carried away; probably, in reality, it will need not one year but two or three years before all Europe is one Soviet republic."

Whether it took two years or three was obviously of little moment considering the prize to be won—a prize that was no less dazzling than the second coming of Christ. For after the wars and commotions and the days of vengeance that would first come to pass, the Kingdom of God would be at hand. The proletarian revolution would free the productive forces of all countries from the tentacles of the outlived national states; the dead hand of rapacious capitalist exploiters would be removed from the metropolitan centers as well as from the colonies; and the peoples would join in economic collaboration and social solidarity to enjoy the fruit of their labor and virtue.

That being the operating perspective, it followed that every Communist party had to reorganize itself into a Leninist type of combat party. Obviously, the traditional prewar Socialist party directed by parliamentarians, literateurs, and trade union functionaries was as useless for the job of mounting the barricades of the final class struggle as diplomats in evening clothes would be for trench warfare. What was required was an association of selfless and dedicated revolutionaries, worshipping at no other shrines but the shrine of the Communist revolution, and impervious to the calls of all other duties but the duty of carrying out one's tasks and instructions. The cadres had to be steeled in the ideology and the tradition of the revolutionary elite. They had to be ruthless in exterminating all deviations, heresies, and treacheries, because the enemy was clever and merciless, and could be counted upon to take advantage of any disunity, weaknesses, or vacillations. The cadres had to be bound together by an iron discipline, because only with the precision of a military division could they hope to storm the heights of bourgeois power and to impose the proletarian dictatorship after the victory.

Discipline could no longer be just national discipline like that practiced by the German Social Democratic party in the days before the Great War. That might have sufficed in an earlier stage; now national discipline was an anachronism. By leapfrogging over national boundaries to tie together diverse economies, and by creating the world market, imperialism had made obsolete the customary national boundaries. International socialism had to follow suit by creating a world party of revolution, with an international discipline, a central world staff, and the subordination of parochial national viewpoints to the overriding needs of the world movement. As Trotsky explained it, "By joining the ranks of the Third International, an organization of a given country not only becomes subordinate to the common, vigilant, and exacting leadership, but itself acquires the right to activity participate in the leadership of all other sections of the Communist International."

With this in mind, the Russian leaders pushed through at the

1920 Congress the famous twenty-one conditions to divide the
Leninist sheep from the reformist and centrist goats. The line of
split was driven relentlessly through the labor movements of the
entire world, and thereafter any one who wanted to be associated
with the Moscow enterprise had to adopt the Leninist credo in
toto, with no reservations and no backsliding permitted. There was
to be no friendly coexistence with heretics or conciliators. The
"church militant" had closed its ranks and recognized only those
in the category of the revolutionary upright and those in the
category of its enemies. This had nothing to do with Lenin or the
other Bolsheviks wanting to dominate personally the international
labor movements. The twenty-one points were the inevitable
organizational corollary of the political premises. If sanguinary
revolutions were the order of the day throughout Europe, the only
parties that could lead them were quasi-military parties captained
by professional revolutionaries of the Leninist mold. The reform
figures of social democracy, accustomed to the routine of social
welfare pressure politics, even when well intentioned, would only
be in the way.

At the time, the idea of revolution in Europe was not as
fantastic as it appears today. Many of the statesmen and observers
on the other side of the hill were apprehensive to the same degree
that the Soviet leaders were exultant. The Austro-Hungarian
empire was breaking up into its component nationalisms, and
Vienna and Budapest were the scenes of revolutionary rioting. The
Balkans were seething. Italy, which resembled more a defeated
country than a member of the victorious entente, was slipping out
of the hands of its rulers. In 1920 Italian workers hoisted the red
flag over the biggest factories and tried to run production. In
Central Europe, Germany was swept by revolutionary crises. For
a while, a Workers and Soldiers Soviet was meeting in Berlin. The
old military and upper-class elements managed to hang on through
the successive Social Democratic coalition governments, but it was
not until 1924 that a stabilization of sorts was effected. Even in
victorious and comparatively well-off France and England there
were stormy strikes, and the mood of the left-wingers went to ex-
tremes.

Nevertheless, the Leninist perspective was illusory. Not primarily
because, as the Russians were wont to explain the innumerable
miscalculations and defeats of their European cohorts, the young

Communist organizations lacked gifted leaders and seasoned troops. The horrendous errors of judgment and crushing setbacks were not even due, in the main, to the Comintern system of international direction which, instead of facilitating revolutionary strategy, produced a bureaucratic chaos. Had the Russian atmosphere of Czarist days existed in the postwar West, capable revolutionary leaders and effective parties would have been fashioned in time through a process of trial and error. But the upheavals of 1919–1921 were passing manifestations due to the devastation of the war and the consequences of the Versailles peace. They did not represent a fundamental transformation of the Western working classes. The suffering peoples, particularly in the defeated countries, wanted succor, but they continued to look to their traditional spokesmen and to constitutional methods of solution. The Communists were a minority voice in the nation. Once the worst of the war dislocations was patched up, the tide flowed back into its old channels.

The breakdown of the revolutionary strategy led to the triumph of Stalin's "socialism in one country" idea in Russia, and the degeneration of an international society of Communist firebrands into a power vehicle of the Soviet state. The Communist International succumbed, like its Socialist predecessor, to a national outlook. The passage occurred by a different route and for a different reason, but it occurred nonetheless. Ironically, the organizational structure of the world staff of the revolution, which had been designed to bar the way to national adaptations like those that had taken place in the prewar labor movements, became the agency for the changeover.

The formula of the world staff, in which all freely participate, was all very well, and it is true that in the first heroic years the Communist International congresses were the scenes of free and stormy debates, and Communists from all over the world dealt with the Russian leaders on terms of equality. But the laws of power operated in Moscow no less forcefully than in Geneva. Most of the foreign Communist movements were inconsequential, and even in the few sizable parties, the leaders were pygmies in comparison to the Russian leaders. The Russians dominated all proceedings because of their prestige and power. They had made a successful revolution, and they were the leaders of a powerful state. No one else could make either claim. The debates and maneuvers and caucuses veiled the true disposition of power. When the Russian delegation wanted to put through a policy, that decided the issue; and when the leaders of other parties were anxious to win the adoption of their viewpoints, they first tried to catch the ear of Lenin or Trotsky or one of the other Russian oligarchs, since the nod from the Kremlin was worth a bushelful of speeches in the open sessions. In consequence, the world general staff, while it included Communists from many countries, was a mechanism for Russian overlordship of the Communist movements around the world.

Strangely enough, when the hope for revolution in other countries waned and the Soviet leadership turned isolationist, the Communist parties did not loosen their ties with Moscow; instead, they turned into unabashed agencies of the Russian state, the defenders of every twist and turn of the Kremlin oligarchy. And at the next stage they became the apologists for the crimes of Stalin. The Communist parties were easily subverted from their original purposes and ideals, because as their own prospects went glimmering, the connection with Moscow became the most important attribute and boast for the Communist leader; and the Soviet state was the only substantial thing that the Communist faithful could cling to. When this bizarre evolution unfolded, the new internationalism lost all its independence and dignity. Long before its dissolution, it had become a laughing stock and byword to many of its erstwhile friends as well as to its enemies.


II

In the first heroic stage of the Comintern, the Communists adopted Lenin's implacable stand on war. It was exclusively the product of the class division of society. That meant that in the modern world war was the inseparable companion of capitalism and imperialism. It was ridiculous to think of war as the sin of humanity, or as part of the evil policies of a particular regime. The nature of the system and the changing balances of nations made wars between the powers inevitable, and assured fresh assaults against rebellious colonial nations. From this it followed that war would be abolished only when capitalism was overthrown. All other methods, theories, and proposals to counter war were a delusion and a snare, and had to be fought as such.

During this Leninist period, the Communists employed some of their most ferocious epithets against pacifists and pacifism, in which category they included practically every individual and tendency that sought, by one means or another, to abolish war within the existing social system. The Communists did not glorify or revel in war in the manner of militarists or Nietzschean ideologists. Peace was their ideal. They were convinced however that there was no way of arriving at this shining goal other than by ruthless class war and the proletarian dictatorship. They were incensed at such traditional pacifist proposals as arms reduction, peace pacts, and peace petitions because these could only divert the fighting masses from revolutionary tasks into these essentially frivolous gestures. It was for this same reason that they emptied their vials of wrath against all Tolstoyan declamations against violence. It was not that they worshiped or sanctified violence. Their ideal was a libertarian one, a world without compulsion of any material sort. But in accordance with the Marxian reading, all societies through all the epochs of history have rested on violence, and there was no other way of reaching the golden portals of the Socialist Nirvana. The proletarian dictatorship could not push on with its liberating mission except by employing the methods of its foes. There was no alternative to the violent seizure of power and the violent suppression of the resistance of the reactionary classes.

Lenin reverted to Marx's classification of just and unjust wars, which the Second International had never discarded but which it had in practice muted. Marx had been preoccupied throughout his life with adopting attitudes on national wars: which peoples had indigenous cultures and made up intrinsic national units; which national consolidations aided the process of clearing the grounds for socialist struggles. Lenin updated the concept by declaring that 1914 had ushered in the epoch of imperialist wars, and that these were unreservedly reactionary for all the belligerents and had to be opposed by all means. He insisted that progressive national wars were still possible, as witness the Easter uprising of the Irish in 1916. Basically, however, the national era had closed in Europe; the field had shifted to the colonial world where national upheavals could be anticipated. These anti-imperialist wars were progressive; they complemented the struggles of the socialists, and had to be supported. Finally, the wars of the proletariat against the bourgeoisie, or the war where the Soviet Union was defending itself against capitalist attackers, were holy wars for the socialist cause, and had to be treated as such.

The distinctions were clear-cut, and they fitted in well with the temper of the left-wingers of those days. But an ambiguity of

position arose after Soviet Russia broke into the international arena
with the Rapallo Pact in 1922, and after her diplomatic recognition by
other countries. Up to this time, her foreign relations had not been
sufficient to hamper her revolutionary crusading; the entente had
forced her into an iron ring of diplomatic isolation. With her
changed position, the contradiction became more apparent between
Moscow as the headquarters of world communism seeking the
overthrow of the rest of the European governments, and Moscow
as the capital of the Russian state which was attempting to establish
friendly relations with these same governments.

At the Genoa Conference of 1922, her plenipotentiaries laid on the
table a sweeping proposal for disarmament, and they were to repeat
this proposition on every possible occasion, climaxed by Litvinov's
virtuoso performance in Geneva in 1927. How did the Communist
denunciation of pacifism square with the Soviet government's
campaign for disarmament? How did the Communist organization
for class war square with the Soviet government's efforts for
coexistence? The ambivalence was not resolved, but as a matter
of fact was written right into the program of the Communist
International. In one section of the war resolution adopted by the
1928 world congress, the fifty-seven varieties of pacifists were
properly and unmercifully roasted again, and the line was heavily laid
down on how these pernicious heterodoxies were to be fought without let-up or quarter. ("Pacifism is being transformed from a mere
screen to conceal war preparations into one of the most important
instruments for these preparations"; "pacifism is acquiring a new
objective significance as the ideology and the instrument in world
imperialism's struggle against the progressing world revolution and
its stronghold, the U.S.S.R.")

In another section of the same resolution, the faithful were assured that "the proposals for general and complete disarmament
submitted by the Soviet government to the Preparatory Commission
on Disarmament called by the League of Nations in November,
1927, differ radically in aim, sincerity, and objective significance from
the phrases and schemes submitted by the imperialists and their
Social Democratic flunkeys." How do they differ? "The aim of the
Soviet proposals is not to spread pacifist illusions, but to destroy
them." Wasn't this a relapse into non-Marxian subjectivism and
idealism? The Russian theoreticians tried to get around the
difficulty with this rationale: "The Soviet government called upon
the imperialists who talk cynically about disarming, actually to

disarm; it tore down the pacifist masks from their faces. It goes without saying that not a single Communist thought for a moment that the imperialists would accept the Soviet disarmament proposals. Nevertheless, the Soviet government's proposals were not hypocritical; they were made in all sincerity, because they in no way contradict the domestic and foreign policy of the workers' government, whereas imperialist 'disarmament' phrasemongering contradicts the policy of bourgeois states." Stripped of its jargon, the explanation consists of two points: (1) We decided to call our opponent's bluff because we knew he was bluffing. (2) Our policies are by definition above reproach, because the social organization of the Soviet state is virtuous, and only virtuous policies can issue from such a state. (This was the syllogism which was later used to befuddle a generation about the Moscow frameups and blood purges.)

The Shavian discourse inaugurated by Litvinov at Geneva was not to end with a simple unmasking of the forces of evil. The ambivalence of the 1928 program was to be resolved, but not in the way the authors of the program had anticipated. The unbeliever who came to scoff remained to pray, or at least to put something into the collection plate. An abrupt shift on the international chessboard pushed the Soviet Union, and by implication, its shadow organization, the Communist International, into the thick of the League of Nations, described earlier by Lenin and his coadjutors as the "thieves' kitchen" and the "robbers' den." The shift was the Nazi emergence over Europe and the arms buildup for a new war.

There was a unique sequence of actions and reactions to bring about the startling reversal of Communist policy. When the Comintern lost its independence and began revolving like a satellite around the Soviet state, every reflex from the central star was automatically transmitted to every Communist party around the world. The politics of the Comintern became unreal as they became arbitrarily standardized, with the same slogans and propositions advocated from Greenland to the Cape regardless of local circumstances. That is how it came to pass that Stalin's leftward switch in Russia after 1928, when the country was turned into a forcing house of collectivization and industrialization, resulted in a Comintern response where the Communist movements abroad proclaimed that again revolution was everywhere the order of the day. Where this was passionately believed by the Bolsheviks in 1919, and the political situation in Europe at the time lent the perspective some

credence, the concocted radicalism a decade later was not taken
seriously by Stalin and his entourage, who were growing contemptuous of the Comintern and its noisemaking.

The revolutionary demagogy led to a series of bizarre encounters
and revolutionary peccadilloes, but it had tragic consequences in
Germany, the one country with a sizable Communist movement,
and which by 1930 was again experiencing a social convulsion.
Stalin never understood naziism. His big contribution to the
analysis of the phenomenon, repeated like the gospel in every
Communist movement, was that fascism and social democracy were
"not antipodes but twins." For him, Hitler was just another
bourgeois reactionary, and his rise as a major force on the scene did
not materially alter the components of German politics. So, in the
years that Hitler was readying his storm troops to crush the entire
labor movement, the Communists kept the fires of civil war blazing
within labor ranks, more intent on wiping out the influence of their
Social Democratic rivals than their Nazi enemies. The bankruptcy of
the Communist International was sealed when naziism was able to
take over, lock, stock, and barrel, and the strongest labor movement
on the continent let itself be strangled without striking a blow
in its own defense. There was far more to the story than just the
stupidity and irresponsibility of the Communists; others on the
scene were by no means blameless saints. But Communist culpability
was sufficiently large to justify the phrase current among German
radicals after the collapse that "without Stalin there would have
been no Hitler."

When Stalin finally woke up to the meaning of the Nazi victory,
particularly to the war danger that it represented for the Soviet
Union, Russian and Comintern policy took a violently rightward
lurch. His representatives soon sat in the League of Nations, Communists were calling loudly for collective security against the aggressors, and Russian diplomacy was at work to forge alliances with
the entente powers. At the Soviet Congress of January, 1934, Stalin
explained, "It is not for us who have experienced the shame of the
Brest-Litovsk peace to sing the praises of the Versailles treaty. We
merely do not agree to the workers' being flung into the abyss
of a new war on account of this treaty." Russia had joined with
France and England as an upholder of the international status quo.

By the spring of 1935, Russia had concluded alliances with France
and Czechoslovakia, and the Comintern was ordered to drop its
traditional antiwar propaganda in those countries which were

held to be friendly to Soviet foreign policy. Stalin announced the change of front to the European chancelleries with no attempt to conceal his disdain for his foreign Communist allies. On his return to Paris after concluding the Franco-Russian agreement, Pierre Laval declared that Stalin had authorized him to say that he sympathized with France's efforts to strengthen her armed defenses. This announcement not only undercut the French Communists who had been voting against military expenditures, but was all the more brutal since Stalin chose to convey his new policy through the mouth of an unscrupulous politician despised by every section of the French Left.

After the Seventh Congress of the Comintern, Communists became vociferous supporters of military defense in the democratic countries, and Stalin tried to lay the ghosts of the past when he repeatedly sought to assure foreign correspondents that all the fears of world revolution were the result of "tragi-comic" misunderstandings. The line of moderation was carried into the Spanish civil war. Russia demanded and was granted the power, in return for military aid to the Republican forces, to crush the more radical Syndicalist and quasi-Trotskyist contingents, and to keep the war limited to the defense of democracy against Franco.

To no avail. The ghost of revolution would not be laid that easily. Russia remained a society with an antipathetic economic and social system, and the Comintern tradition and impulse was Left despite the Communists' newfound enthusiasm for bourgeois democracy. It was in vain that the Popular Front in France and the Republican cabinets in Spain assured the conservatives in Europe that they were not interested in going beyond the defense of democracy against fascism. The two events frightened the middle classes, who feared that the Red specter was lurking nevertheless behind the democratic phrases, or concluded that once insurgent forces were brought into the political arena, no one could control them or could be sure where things would end. The policy of alliances with the democracies blew up in the Munich crisis, and Russia found herself completely isolated at the very time German expansion threatened her security. Even as a defender of the U.S.S.R., the Comintern "border guard," as Trotsky later contemptuously called it when he was in exile, was an unmitigated failure. It was ironical that the Soviet Union had been able to elicit more mass support in Western Europe against intervention in 1919 than it was able to set into motion after two decades of

Comintern agitation. If the Second International ended with a bang, the Third International went out with a whimper. It could not even give a good reason for its dissolution in 1943 other than Stalin's attempt to reassure his war allies.

The Trotsky opposition attributed the bankruptcy of the Comintern to the degeneration of the Soviet Union and to the fact that there were no real mass parties in the organization besides the Russian. If several additional strong parties had existed, they argued, it would have been impossible for the Russian party to seize monopolistic control. In that case, the democracy characteristic of the early congresses would have resulted in the Comintern reorienting Russia to an international revolutionary policy, or failing that, in the breakaway of the Comintern from the tutelage of the emergent Stalin dictatorship.

The line of argument has been shown by later events to be a superficial one. The assumption on which it rested was the naive faith that the rules of power which had affected and corrupted relations between capitalist states would not come into play when introduced in relations between Communist parties or Communist states. Alas, the god of power is no respecter of ideologies. He adapts himself to all sorts of ideologies. He is omnipresent, because he is the demiurge of physico-political relations whenever and wherever aggregates of humans gather. The Communist attempt to create a new international morality foundered for different reasons, but foundered no less conclusively, than did the attempt of the League of Nations. The international discipline devised by the Communist architects became the mechanism for the domination of the most powerful unit, and the ideology of internationalism became the rationale for the imposition of Russian national interests upon all Communist movements.

When, at the next turn of the wheel after the war, the Yugoslav and Chinese Communist parties became state powers, the absence of an international morality revealed itself in another way. It was no longer possible for the Russians to dictate to these other parties and to make them swallow the myth that what was good for the Russians was good for them. The attempt was then made to strong-arm the weaker powers by pressures, threats, and sanctions. First came Stalin's expulsion of Yugoslavia from the Cominform, accompanied by the organization of an economic blockade and an international campaign of vilification. More recently, when the Russian and Chinese leaders started to bicker, the quarrel quickly passed from words to ruthless power plays and economic sanctions. And the ally of the Chinese, tiny and weak Albania, was given the rubber hose.

Differences of opinion and heated debate between Communists can be a sign of democratic vigor in that camp as elsewhere. But the ferocity of the exchanges and the quick recourse to punitive measures dispels the easy assumption of an earlier day that once countries are governed by some sort of Marxist leadership, international cooperation would follow as a matter of course. The Communists, committed by their ideology to internationalism, have had as much difficulty in practicing it as their Socialist predecessors and their liberal contemporaries.

ALTHOUGH the United States had repudiated Wilson's commitment to the League of Nations, it was another American President who urged upon his war partners the need for a new international organization. Churchill was at best lukewarm, and Stalin went along to maintain the unity of the wartime alliance, and probably to prevent any consolidation of an anti-Soviet coalition. The drive and the initiative for the organization came from the United States. It was here that academics and government planners had given the most thought to it and, in the midst of the war, had drawn up elaborate models for the world-to-be. This was more than a case of history repeating itself. The Wilsonian vision had been premature. The United States had not been ready to take on the role of world leader, and her two Western allies were by no means disposed in 1919 to dispatch the crown overseas. As the peacemaking at Versailles made obvious, they had their own commitments and their own ideas how the world was to be organized, which did not necessarily conform to the interests and preferences of this country. By 1945, however, the world balance had altered: The United States was the uncontested leader of the West, and her spokesmen thought they could convince or pressure Russia to join her team as well. As the leader in fashioning the peace in the second half of the twentieth century, we could no more dispense with a world organization of the nations than the peacemakers of a hundred and thirty years before could dispense with a concert of European princes.

Jurists and social scientists had given a lot of study to the precise constitutional character that a new world organization ought to have in order to avoid repeating the "mistakes" which undid the old League. When the government representatives got down to the business of drawing up the statutes for the new organization, however, what they produced was little different than the constitution of the ill-fated predecessor. The procedural changes that were put through were of far less importance in the subsequent history of the organization and of the relations between states than the specialists had anticipated.

It is ironical to recall nowadays the hours of time that high government officials expended, the howls of anguish and dire accusations with which our own press and that of other countries belabored each other, and the shrill debates of the experts reinforcing the arguments with soaring moral principles, on such questions as whether Russia should be granted two additional votes in the assembly for the Ukraine and Byelorussia, and whether the United States must likewise claim three votes for herself—and all this, while the world was writhing in the shambles of its recently concluded slaughter. This example of the inability of governments and the press to show any more sense of proportion or history than the meanest of their citizens was of a piece with the solemn pronouncement of the Big Three at Yalta that all neutral states would have to declare war on Germany before March 1, 1945, or be refused admittance to the founding conference of the world peace assemblage. After the deadline, no more tickets were to be sold.

The two crises that Stalin kicked up before and during the San Francisco conference—on whether the veto in the Security Council applied to the right of discussion, and whether the General Assembly was to have the unrestrained right to take up any question—and the great show of intransigence on the other side for its particular formulations, were of not much greater moment. Of course, Stalin wanted to play hard-to-get because of Anglo-American recalcitrance over Poland, and he was ever on guard against granting any powers to an organization in which he assumed the U.S.S.R. representatives would be surrounded by an unfriendly majority. The Western powers were not above thinking of using their majority to mobilize public opinion for their point of view. And the smaller states were afraid that the big powers would try to hold them to the role of a Greek chorus, and not even permit them to try to bring moral suasion to bear. All the same, the excited debates over the wording, after the essentials of organization had been agreed to, were in the category of hairsplitting. They were a display of frivolity on the part of august statesmen.

In retrospect it would appear that the experts, particularly the Anglo-American experts, were too preoccupied with parliamentary punctilio and tended to interpret the League's failures too much in administrative terms. The differences between the League and the United Nations, where the Assembly could now make substantive recommendations by a two-thirds instead of a unanimous vote, and where collective security was allegedly improved by Article 43 of the U.N. Charter as against Article 16 of the League covenant, proved of small consequence. As events were to show, there were profound differences between the two bodies, but these were due to the two different international realities, not to the differences in the administrative mechanisms of the two organizations. The constitutional cogitations yielded meager results because what were defined as the League's "mistakes" were the inabilities of national states to transcend their nationalism, and what were considered "loopholes" in the machinery were not the result of careless craftsmanship, but of the refusal of national states to commit their destinies to a supranational authority. The only kind of international organization that the major armed powers would permit was a confederation of governments in which their freedom of action remained unimpaired. Just as in the case of the League, the national ambitions and egotisms were not removed, modified, assuaged, mitigated, transmuted, or sublimated—they were simply moved, in all their rawboned primitiveness, under the one roof of the United Nations.

## II

The Charter of the United Nations set out the same high purpose as had the League's covenant: "to save succeeding generations from the scourge of war"; but it could formulate no strategy to reach this promised land beyond the discredited "collective security" of its precursor. Many, yearning for a world of peace and friendship, seized upon the statements promising "equal rights of men and women and of

nations large and small," and "social progress and better standards
of life in larger freedom," without trying to consider the dispropor-
tion between the lofty ends and the pitifully inadequate means
devised to attain them. But outside of the one-world enthusiasts,
who among the informed really believed that "collective security"
could do more than stamp out peripheral conflicts of small nations?
The experience of the League had been conclusive on this score.

The architects of the United Nations understood this right along.
At Yalta, during the discussion of the veto right reserved to the
big powers in the Security Council, the following colloquy took
place, as reported by Edward R. Stettinius, our then Secretary of
State, in his book on the conference:

> The main task, the Marshal [Stalin] added, was to prevent
> quarrels among the three great powers and guarantee their unity
> for the future. The charter of the new world organization should
> have this as its primary objective. . . . Both the Prime Minister
> [Churchill] and I [Stettinius] insisted at this point that under the
> American proposal [which was finally accepted] the power of the
> world organization could not be directed against any of the
> permanent members. Stalin, however, seemed uncertain of this,
> and said that he feared any conflicts or disputes in the world
> organization might break the unity of the three powers. The
> Prime Minister admitted the importance of this argument but
> replied that he did not believe the world organization would
> eliminate disputes among the three powers. The settlement of
> these disputes, he believed, would still remain the function of
> diplomacy.

Churchill reported this conversation in his war memoirs in a
similar vein. When Stalin asked for guarantees that the new organization would not be used, as the British and French had used the
League of Nations against the Soviet Union, "Mr. Eden pointed out
that the American proposal would make it impossible." Dean
Acheson was also quite clear that collective security was something
for the big powers to use on the small ones, not against each other.
In *Power and Diplomacy,* he wrote that "it has always been plain
that the United Nations could not use force against a great power.
The veto in the Security Council was put there to prevent such
questions ever arising; and, as a practical matter, to attempt it
would only bring on a major war."

A collective security that both practically and legally could not be used against a great power was not much of a rock on which to rest the organization of the peace. We were to be treated to another round of Geneva cant, with this difference: where the illusion had persisted in many quarters during the League days that this was effective antiwar doctrine (at least until Japan invaded Manchuria and Italy invaded Ethiopia), the intrusion of the cold war at the birth of the United Nations reduced the proposition to a nullity in the new organization from the very first day. Here is what happened to the implementation of the relevant part of the Charter meant to secure the peace: to Article 43, which reads, "All members of the United Nations, in order to contribute to the maintenance of the international peace and security, undertake to make available to the Security Council, on its call and in accordance with a special agreement or agreements, armed forces, assistance and facilities, including rights of passage, necessary for the purpose of maintaining international peace and security"; and to Article 47, which sets up a military organization under the chiefs of staff of the permanent members of the Security Council, to be in a state of readiness, so that when diplomatic and economic means fail, the Security Council, as provided under Article 42, "may take such action by air, sea, or land forces as may be necessary to maintain or restore international peace and security."

In February, 1946, six months after the conclusion of the war in the Far East, the Security Council instructed the Military Staff Committee to prepare recommendations for implementing Article 43. The committee did not come back with a report until fourteen months later, and in its prolonged and arduous labors it had been able to do no more than codify the deadlock between Russia and her erstwhile allies. The Western powers wanted no limitation to the size of military forces that any power could bring under the Security Council; the Soviets wanted equality in both composition and strength of the national forces. The Western powers insisted on their right to garrison troops in foreign countries with the permission of the local governments; the Soviets wanted to confine garrisons of member states to their own territories. The Western powers wanted to leave it up to the Security Council when forces would be withdrawn from foreign territories after they had suppressed a threat or a breach of the peace; the Soviets wanted a specific time limit. The conflict of positions was extreme, the impasse complete. It was the military-technical expression of the political break between the two sides, and that each was trying to subvert the international machinery for its own national maneuvers in the cold war.

The United States, commanding at this stage of the game an overwhelming majority in the United Nations, wanted to use its strength to expand the powers of the council. The U.S.S.R., fearful of an anti-Communist majority, sought security by limiting council powers. The military disputations were echoes of the fundamental political debate going on outside of the U.N. committees where Churchill hurled the thunderbolt at Fulton, Missouri, that communism was "a peril to Christian civilization" and called for an Anglo-American crusade "while time remains." And Stalin answered in a *Pravda* interview that Churchill was beating the drums for war, and warned that if the Westerners tried to have a military test over Eastern Europe, "they will be thrashed just as they were thrashed once before twenty-six year ago."

It was a bit thick, even in the charmed world of diplomacy, to expect two sets of powers who were hurling war threats at each other to sit down in a quiet committee room and draw up, over a green baize table, staff plans for joint military forces to police the world. At the moment, both sides were mainly concerned with policing each other. The Military Staff Committee became defunct, the powers started building alliances against each other, and Article 43—the heart of the U.N. mechanism against war—atrophied away. When U.N. contingents were organized later during the Suez and Congo crises, they were set up under emergency *ad hoc* procedures. The forces of international politics had in effect rewritten the Charter of the United Nations. The documentations, discussions, and legal parchments of Dumbarton Oaks and Yalta were swept away in a matter of weeks by the bitter winds of the cold war. The new organization that emerged has its great importance and uses— but it is not the organization that had been projected in the blueprints of its founders. And the cold war and arms race is certainly not the peace that was promised humanity in the Four Freedoms.

Who was responsible for starting the cold war? It is like asking: who was responsible for the First World War? You can point to empirical events in the chain of sequences that led to the shooting. You can say it was Austria's arrogant ultimatum to Serbia. Or Russia's mobilization. Or Germany's invasion of Belgium. But in a larger sense, given the system of Europe's armed states, the military collision was inevitable. In the same way, when the Soviet state came out of the war as the world's second military power, and its armies sprawled into Central Europe, its contest with the West was decreed. Whether the West could have reconciled itself to a Czarist empire flinging its suzerainty up to the Elbe is a big question; in any case, the West could not reconcile itself to the Soviet system trampling underfoot both private property rights and its elites in territories embracing 125 million souls.

Walter Lippmann put the thing in a nutshell when he wrote in *The Cold War*:

> The British and Americans, of course, could not accept the permanent division of the European continent along the Yalta line. They could not accept a settlement in which Poland, Czechoslovakia, Yugoslavia, Hungary, Rumania, and Bulgaria would lose all independence and become incorporated as Soviet republics in the U.S.S.R. They had a debt of honor to the countless patriots in those lands. They realized that if the frontiers of the Soviet system were extended as far as the middle of Germany and Austria, then not only Germany and Austria but all Western Europe might fall within the Russian sphere of influence and be dominated by the Soviet Union. Thus for the best of reasons and with the best of motives they came to the conclusion that they must wage a diplomatic campaign to prevent Russia from expanding her sphere, to prevent her from consolidating it, and to compel her to contract it.

There have been endless references to the relevant clauses of the Yalta documents in which each party to the dispute has tried to demonstrate from scripture that his position conforms to the true intents of the agreement, and that it is the other side that has been guilty of the violations. The arguments on Poland particularly became exhaustive as well as exhausting and led to recrimination, and finally, to threats and attempted sanctions. The attempts to establish the rights and wrongs by quotations from original texts are totally unedifying because the agreement was deliberately written in vague and inconclusive language to conceal the inability of the wartime allies to come to firm political settlements. They left further decisions to future meetings, in the hope that events would somehow relieve them of embarrassing conflicts. Certainly none of the three plenipotentiaries at Yalta was unaware of troubles in store, not even Roosevelt, the most buoyant and hopeful of the three. When

Admiral Leahy warned Roosevelt at Yalta that the rubberiness of the accord reached on Poland would permit the Russians to make their own interpretation, the President could only wearily reply, "I know, Bill, I know."

But the fates were not kind. The tug-of-war over East Europe took on the most irreconcilable and exasperating form possible after the war. It was not just a matter of the Russians trying to extend their social system into their occupied zones. What was in Stalin's head on this score in 1945 is hard to say, and his conversations, as reported by Djilas, may have been only passing vagaries and boasts. The fact is he did not install regulation Communist governments in most of the East European countries until two years later when the cold war lines had become set. In the case of Poland, though, there was no chance of fabricating a government that was oriented to the Soviet Union—"a friendly government," as the Yalta formula put it—other than by installing his own quislings. The country's political spectrum held no intermediate alternatives. Poland's prewar ruling cliques were socially reactionary, politically anti-Soviet, personally fanatical. As their gyrations in the interwar years had demonstrated, they lacked not only flexibility but common sense. The United States, in its determination not to have the West frozen out of a third of Europe, was insisting on a strict adherence to democratic electoral principles that she felt no call to enforce in Greece, Turkey, or the Far East. The result was a power fight for strategic advantage exacerbated by ideological differences in which idealistic principles were the pawns.

While the United Nations Charter put reliance on collective security and said hardly anything at all about disarmament, the logic of the East-West conflict reversed the schema. No sooner did the powers enter into their days of wrath than it became inevitable that each side would try to mobilize public opinion behind its positions. Since every proposal for the reduction or elimination of armaments could count on eliciting a ground swell of mass support, and the nuclear bomb had raised the popular concern to a pitch of hysteria, it was a foregone conclusion that one or the other side would seize on the issue. When that happened, all the powers would willy-nilly get entangled in the web of disarmament debate. That is exactly what happened. In a sense, public opinion rewrote the design of the U.N. architects and made disarmament its instrinsic pattern. But the long heritage of the past, in the form of self-contained sovereign states, had its revenge by reducing the negotiations to barren exercises where the pot accused the kettle of insincerity, and the kettle accused the pot of indulging in propaganda—and where both the kettle and the pot were right.


## III

The first act of the grand opera was dominated by the Baruch Plan. This was a fulsome product of national arrogance and delusion. We thought the bomb, when added to our industrial and financial preeminence, put us in a position to dictate the terms of the world settlement at the end of the war. We thought Russia either would have to submit, or if her rulers remained defiant, would be thrust into internal crisis. The scientists who worked on the bomb warned that our monopoly would be short-lived, that there was no secret about it in the scientific sense. The message never got across to the statesmen and the press. When the Russians exploded their bomb in 1949, we went into a tantrum, convinced that spies and saboteurs were responsible for giving away our secrets.

It was this exaggerated estimation of our strength, powered by swollen national pride, that swayed Bernard Baruch when he dramatically announced to the United Nations on June 14, 1946, "We are here to make a choice between the quick and the dead," and outlined the now famous plan. According to its provisions, an international atomic authority was to be set up which would constitute little less than a world government. The authority was to have absolute control or ownership of all phases of atomic development from the raw materials to the final manufactured products all over the world. Its agents and inspectors could examine any activity anywhere which they considered suspicious, and no country could embark on any atomic energy projects for even peaceful purposes without specific license from the authority. For any violations, ranging from illegal possession of fissile material to interference with the activities of the authority, Baruch provided "an international law with teeth in it"—international sanctions against the offender, to be invoked outside the U.N. Security Council with its veto, by a simple decision of the international atomic authority.

After the world authority had taken over the atomic energy business of every country and had clothed itself with the full panoply of sovereignty in this field, the United States, if it was satisfied that it had a guarantee of safety "not only against offenders in the

atomic area, but against the illegal users of other weapons: bac-
teriological, biological, gas—perhaps why not? Against war itself"—
would then agree to stop her manufacture of atomic bombs, to
dispose of her existing stocks (apparently by transferring them to
the authority), and to turn over all technical information in her
possession, "subject, of course, to our constitutional processes."

Now, like all proposals not meant to be negotiable, the Baruch
Plan promised the millennium at its completion; but in its initial
stage, and through the subsequent stages up to the final one, it
shifted the power balance abruptly to the advantage of its own side,
and to the disadvantage of the opposing side. It provided amply for
the security of the United States at every stage of the game, but was
little mindful of the security of the Soviet Union. Here were a few
of the consequences of the Baruch proposals for Russia. She would
have to permit the authority inspectors—and thus possibly the
American chiefs of staff—to secure a complete target map of her
country in the course of making unlimited surveys for the raw
materials of atomic energy. She would have to make the atomic
power development section of her economic planning subject to
the decision of an international authority, which could on its volition slow or stop the development of atomic energy for industrial
purposes. All the while, the United States would be continuing to
add to her stockpile of atomic weapons, until such time as she was
satisfied that the authority was in full control and all other conceivable dangers to her safety had been satisfactorily removed.

This was an uneven bargain, particularly since American executives were in the habit of defining dangers to our safety in the
broadest terms. When Stalin delivered a speech in February, 1946,
in which he announced a new five-year plan of industrial expansion
and garnished his remarks with the usual boasts of superiority and
routine pejorative estimates of imperialism, James P. Forrestal, then
Secretary of the Navy, was convinced that it proved "that there was
no way in which democracy and communism could live together,"
and recorded in his diary that Justice William O. Douglas had called
the speech "the declaration of World War Three." William Bullitt
saw in the Soviet Union's plan to raise her annual steel production
to sixty million tons a proof of her aggressive imperialism.

The other part of the Baruch Plan that made it unnegotiable was
that the international authority would have been a West-dominated
institution. The United Nations was so dominated for the first years
of its existence. Our country's representatives in combination with

our allies were able to roll up the votes with deadly precision. In the General Assembly, Russia could count on only five votes out of fifty-one in 1946. In the eleven-man Security Council, Russia held one of the five permanent seats. The Secretariat personnel was largely in American hands. The key organizational subdivisions, like the Trusteeship Council, the World Bank, the International Monetary Fund, were under Western control. Outside of its own bloc, Russia had no supporters in those years, and no country that was thinking of negotiating a loan with the international bank or fund, or of getting a grant from Washington, could contemplate straying off the Western reservation. Russia was consequently being invited by Baruch to join an international authority where, in the words of P. M. S. Blackett, "she would have been subservient to a group of nations dominated by America." She would have consented to forego her own atomic energy program and, in effect, to accept permanent technological inferiority to the United States.

The Baruch Plan was an offshoot of the "containment" strategy of that time. It fitted into the concept that Russia, if sufficiently pressed and compressed, would begin to disintegrate internally of her own contradictions. Blackett related that in 1946 Lord Inverchapel, then British ambassador in Washington, told him that it was the general opinion that if Russia accepted the plan and opened her frontiers to agents of the projected international authority, the Soviet system would collapse. It was later claimed that the original Lilienthal Plan as conceived by the scientists was a farsighted and disinterested effort to channel atomic energy into peaceful purposes for the benefit of all mankind, but that when the security-ridden militarists and politicians converted it into the Baruch Plan by adding sanctions outside of the U.N. veto, they robbed it of its idealistic intent. Even this is overstating it. Robert Oppenheimer said at the time of his hearing that he was the main author of the Acheson-Lilienthal Plan, and that he never expected the Soviet Union to accept the proposition, because the Soviet system could not have continued to operate under it.

In the main, the military was opposed to any kind of international control, and it was freely predicted at the time that if Russia, by some unlikely miracle, accepted the plan, the Senate would refuse to ratify it. Baruch himself had many misgivings about international involvement and he admitted as much in a letter to President Truman, which the latter quotes in his memoirs. It is entirely possible that the final draft of the Baruch Plan was made as lopsided as it was in an attempt by those who opposed all international control, and who wanted to put reliance in an old-fashioned arms race, to block any possible action. This group had no sympathy with the spread-eagle international phraseology of Lilienthal and Oppenheimer. It is well to note that within several years, as the military establishment grew in power, Lilienthal was attacked as being soft on communism because of his part in the formulation of the plan. Similarly, Oppenheimer's contribution was used as a count against him in the subsequent hearings, which resulted in his humiliation and exclusion from access to security information.

Despite these and other divergencies of approach, both the out-and-out advocates of an unrestricted arms race and the advocates of international control shared the common illusion of the time that the bomb had made it possible to force through fundamental changes inside the Soviet Union either by threat, or failing that, by sanctions which would not precipitate a third world war. It was the military absurdity that a handful of atomic bombs (our arsenal was still small in those days) could subdue a great continental power quickly and cheaply that made "preventive war" so attractive to one group. This same absurdity was also responsible for the inclusion in the Baruch Plan of the threat against a great power of "instant and condign punishment" and the subsequent campaign to erase the veto provision of the United Nations Charter.


IV

The blanket rejection of the plan by the Soviet representatives followed expected lines. In the inundation of words evoked by Baruch's proposals, they based their criticisms on four major points: (1) The control and ownership provisions would give the United States a world monopoly of atomic energy and put branches of the Soviet economy under foreign control. (2) The absence of specific time limits in the plan's stages made it possible for the United States to prevent, on one or another pretext, its final implementation. While all others were policed by the authority, the United States could continue her own nuclear production. (3) The attempt to circumvent the veto was an attack on the United Nations Charter. (4) There was no provision for the ultimate destruction of existing bomb stocks.

Concomitantly, the Soviets tried to shift the discussion to their own counterproposals to prohibit all production and use of atomic weapons, to destroy within three months all existing atomic stocks, and only when that was done, to set up a system of control to ensure observance, and a system of sanctions against unlawful use of atomic energy.

Despite the strength of some of their objections, and the holes they succeeded in knocking into the Baruch Plan, the Soviet representatives were in an unenviable defensive position. The United States had succeeded in maneuvering them into a diplomatic box. The popular fears of the new dreadful bomb, when coupled with the irresistible majorities in the United Nations that the United States was capable of commanding, produced a general impression that this country had made a bold, imaginative, and generous proposal for a major breakthrough toward international cooperation, to which the Russians were offering only obstruction. People had neither the time nor the opportunity to wade through the voluminous documentation. They had little idea of the technical niceties, the power infighting, or the political consequences of the rhetorical positions. With the aid of the mass media, Western public opinion worked itself into a lather of self-righteousness, convinced that the Baruch offer was not only equitable but magnanimous.

Here were the Americans, the sole possessors of the bomb, offering to turn over their manufacturing know-how and existing stocks to an international body, and all they wanted in return was a system of international ownership and authority so that atomic energy could be used for the good of all, and safeguards against their own generosity being taken advantage of by any would-be aggressors. And here were the Russians, unreasonable, uncooperative, sullen, and nihilistic, repeating all their familiar anti-Western propaganda, standing in the way of international understanding, and by their disruptive conduct, leaving mankind defenseless against the new holocaust. The full fury of Western bitterness and frustration broke over the heads of the Soviet spokesmen, and left them morally isolated at a most inopportune time for themselves, a time when the United States was at the height of her power, and when the Soviet Union had scarcely begun to clear away the war debris. The demands for war on Russia were many and were by no means confined to militarists or chauvinists. How widespread was the mood of indignation, reinforced by the false belief that the West had Russia at her mercy, can be gauged from Bertrand Russell's call at the time to threaten Russia with atomic bombs unless she agreed to terms.

The Russians began to play for time. Inside their own laboratories they mounted a crash program to produce the bomb and break the American monopoly. Outside the U.N., they tried to mobilize public opinion against America with the propaganda to ban the bomb. Within the U.N., they drew the Western representatives into involved technical discussions, giving ground on details, as in their 1947 concessions on an international inspectorate—all of which discussions and marginal agreements made the stalemate and the bogus character of the proceedings more obvious. All the while, they tried to turn the Western flank and convert the debate into a free-for-all on general disarmament. As soon as the first momentum of the Western onrush had spent itself, they started to pound away on the instrument which they felt they could use more masterfully than could the other side. In October, 1946, Molotov introduced the new orchestration when he told the General Assembly that the time had come for a general reduction of all armaments, as well as for the prohibition of atomic weapons.

The Western delegations were slow in grasping the popular appeal in disarmament. While the Baruch Plan remained the center of attraction, they gave the Soviet spokesmen the backs of their hands on the issue. Sir Hartley Shawcross of Britain breezily informed Molotov that disarmament had to go hand in hand with collective security, and that control could only be ensured by doing away with the veto. Secretary of State Byrnes spread himself with the assertion that the peace-loving nations, far from being fearful that America was maintaining excessive armaments, were concerned that America had failed to maintain sufficient armaments.

To Gromyko's proposal in the Security Council for the establishment of a disarmament commission, Herschel V. Johnson, the American delegate, countered that "substantial progress in the crucial field of international atomic energy control is a prerequisite to success in the general field of the regulation of armaments." When the council nevertheless set up a commission, the working paper presented by the Americans, British, and Canadians read that arms reduction could take place only "in an atmosphere of international confidence and security," and that to get such an atmosphere, a number of propositions had to be fulfilled, such as a system of collective security as specified by Article 43, the Baruch Plan, peace settlements with Germany and Japan, and several others.

When Vyshinsky tried to mobilize the General Assembly against the Western powers by calling attention to their rising military expenditures, and proposed a one-third reduction of all land, naval, and air forces, the Western representatives countered with the offer that the commission start its work with the collection and verification of information of existing conventional armaments—the start of the charade which has become familiar over the years: shall we have inspection first and disarmament later, or shall we disarm first and inspect later?

Though the discussions dragged on in desultory fashion from one commission to another with no hope of achieving anything, the Western powers had dissipated their initial propaganda advantage, and were being increasingly belabored and pressed by the Soviet representatives with disarmament proposals. In 1954 they decided to turn the tables on their tormentors. The international picture was a far different one now than when the Baruch Plan had been first introduced. Both Russia and the United States had tested hydrogen bombs; notions that a swift and cheap preventive war could be waged had fallen by the wayside; and the Soviet and Western orators no longer addressed other U.N. delegations who understood that it was their part to be seen and not heard. The Bandung Conference of April, 1955, signalized the emergence of a new force composed of nations committed to neither of the military blocs, deeply concerned about disarmament of the great powers, and watchful of their maneuvers.

The opening gambit was the memorandum submitted by the British and French on June 11. It had been the unspoken assumption in all previous discussion that Russia had stronger land forces, with the imbalance righted by the American atomic monopoly and, later, by America's larger nuclear stockpiles and superior array of delivery vehicles. All proposals to ban the bomb, accompanied by across-the-board percentage reductions of conventional forces, were consequently viewed by the West as giving undue advantage to the Soviet side. The new draft proposed to meet this problem, while taking cognizance of Soviet objections and requirements. The six principles of the scheme were: (1) Stop all increases in manpower and military budgets as of December 31, 1953; (2) complete one-half of the reduction in conventional armament and armed forces to levels to be stipulated; (3) stop the further manufacture of nuclear weapons upon completion of step two; (4) finish the second half of the conventional reduction; (5) ban the use of the bomb and

destroy existing stocks upon completion of step three; (6) set up a
control body to enforce each step.

These six principles introduced some crucial innovations. There
was a cutoff of the manufacture of nuclear weapons when half of
conventional armaments were eliminated. Conventional arms reduction was no longer meshed with the Baruch Plan, but with the
banning of the bomb. From this point on, the Western delegates
continued to add specifics and sweeteners to their package, and to
relentlessly press the Soviet delegates to agree, or confess their
refusal to come to a disarmament agreement. On March 29, 1955,
the British and French proposed numerical limits of armed forces
of one to one and a half million for the United States, the U.S.S.R.,
and China, and 675,000 for Britain and France. The American
delegate figured this meant a 53 per cent to 69 per cent reduction of
United States forces, much more than the old one-third proposal of
the Russians. On April 19 the British and French improved the
offer by suggesting that instead of postponing the prohibition of
nuclear weapons until the completion of conventional arms reduction, the prohibition should become effective upon 75 per cent
completion. On May 3 they passed from appeals to peremptory
demands. The French delegate declared, "It is now for the Soviet
government to say whether it maintains its original position in its
entirety, and therefore bears the responsibility for the failure of
these talks, or whether, on the contrary, it recognizes that we have
gone halfway to meet it and consents to follow suit." The American
delegate called attention to the fact that "fifteen days have elapsed
since the Franco-British proposal," and that if they got no answer,
he and his colleagues could "arrive at no other conclusion than that
there is no desire to negotiate."

A week later the whole elaborate and over-clever house of cards
they had built collapsed around their ears. The Soviets did the
unexpected and accepted the main provisions of the Western offer.
Of course, there were still plenty of things unresolved to haggle
about for months and years to come. But the negotiations were
taking a turn that the Americans found intolerable. The first reaction to the great news that they were drawing closer toward an
agreement was for the Westerners to vote, over Russian objections,
for a good, long recess. The disarmament subcommittee did not
meet again until August 29.

In the interval, the Summit Conference was on at Geneva, and
according to the testimony of his authorized biographer, Robert J.

Donovan, in *Eisenhower: The Inside Story,* the President went to the conference with no clear intention of introducing anything on arms control. Only after Bulganin urged disarmament did Eisenhower decide to counter it with the open-skies plan. At the last moment, Nelson Rockefeller and his staff of psychological strategists were ordered to fly to Geneva posthaste to explain the plan's details —and the issue was neatly tied up in knots for the nonce. When the disarmament subcommittee met again, the American delegate shamefacedly announced that all the "pre-Geneva" propositions were withdrawn, and tried to divert discussion to aerial reconnaisance and exchange of military information. At the tenth session of the General Assembly, Sir Percy Spender of Australia inadvertently let the cat out of the bag when he declared that he, and the many others who thought like him, viewed the disarmament negotiations as psychological warfare exercises.

In the final debate, Krishna Menon of India summed up the results to that date: "We are in the ninth year of this disarmament debate and we have to ask ourselves whether, as a result of our endeavors, a single weapon of war has been abandoned, whether there has been the limitation of any of the stocks, conventional or otherwise, and whether there has been any progress in the agreements in regard to this. And the answer is 'no'; that is to say, the disarmament debate, so far as we are concerned, is only an annual performance. . . . While the assembly talks about disarmament, the world prepares for war."


V

After the 1955 debacle, disarmament discussions were conducted half-heartedly until the fall of 1957, at which time, after another embarrassing reversal and the recall of Harold Stassen, they were virtually suspended until 1960. The actors in the drama went about their chores by rote, without conviction, as if asking the audience not to blame them for the poor script they were forced to work with. When one or another delegate would toss in a new proposal, or agree to a demand that had been made by his opposite number, it would change nothing. It only underlined the fact that the technical discussions were irrelevant to the real sources of disagreement.

There had been a lot of talk of restricted actions, unilateral or otherwise, to build confidence. But when the Russians put through substantial reductions in their armed forces in 1955 and 1956, there was no elation in the Western camp. The American leaders looked on them as parts of a modernization program which would not affect Soviet strength. When the United States proposed reciprocal reductions in the stockpiles of fissionable materials held in reserve for future manufacture of weapons, the Russians shrugged their shoulders. By this time, the American stockpile had grown so large that discarding surpluses would not subtract from her nuclear strength. In the prevailing cold war, concessions that would not disturb the power balance were regarded as meaningless gestures or hoaxes. Concessions that would alter the power balance, neither side was willing to make.

The juggling with committee structures did not break any deadlocks, either. Up to 1958, the Russians had negotiated in disarmament committees in which they were a minority of one and the West was a majority of three. That year, in response to what they considered was the changed balance between the two sides, the Russians refused to go along any further with these arrangements. They successively forced through a disarmament commission composed of all U.N. members, then a ten-nation commission with parity for East and West, then later, a still larger commission with a representation of neutral nations. All to no avail. The stalemate remained unbreakable.

The recent phase of what might be called the disarmament battle, or the disarmament cold war, opened when Khrushchev donned Litvinov's old mantle, and on September 18, 1959, set the United Nations assembly agog with his call for "general and complete disarmament." Over a period of four years all military establishments were to be reduced to agreed-upon levels of internal police forces, all rockets and major weapons of warfare were to be junked, all nuclear weapons were to be destroyed and their further production terminated. An international control organization would be set up to "function in conformity with the stages by which disarmament should be effected." This was the proposition, and there is no question that it electrified the world. By this time, the fears and hopes of the man in the street had been so sensitized that no statesman who figured on pursuing his trade for a while would dare to openly oppose disarmament. The assembly unanimously adopted a resolution to express "the hope that measures leading towards the goal of general and complete disarmament under effective international control will be worked out in detail and agreed upon in the shortest possible time."

American officials tried at first to meet this Soviet onslaught with customary diversions garnished with ideas borrowed from the "arms control" school. Secretary of State Herter, in an address delivered three months after the passage of the U.N. resolution, reiterated the Eisenhower open-skies plan and made portentous references to "controls over armaments" and moving "toward a more stable military environment." At the ten-nation committee which convened in Geneva in March, 1960, the Western powers presented Dulles' 1957 program, dressing it up with a final stage of disarmament. After four months of wrangling, the Soviet bloc delegation walked out of the committee meeting accusing the NATO powers of using disarmament negotiations "as a cover for intensifying the arms race."

When the Kennedy Administration took office, the decision was made to talk as fiercely about disarmament as the Soviet Union was doing. America would no longer permit herself to be undercut by far-reaching Russian proposals. In the words of an unnamed official quoted by a *New York Times* correspondent, Washington was henceforth going to compete with Moscow for the "propaganda high ground." American spokesmen boldly and repeatedly declared themselves in favor of "general and complete disarmament." On September 25, 1961, President Kennedy addressed the United Nations assembly with an impassioned plea for world peace which included such aphorisms as "The weapons of war must be abolished before they abolish us"; "The goal of disarmament is now a practical matter of life and death"; "The risks inherent in disarmament pale in comparison with the risks inherent in an unlimited arms race"; "Together we will save our planet or together we shall perish in its flames." Five days later, John J. McCloy for the United States, and Valerian Zorin for the U.S.S.R., signed a statement of principles for general and complete disarmament because "war is no longer an instrument for settling international problems."

If one were not acquainted by this time with the underlying dynamics of international disarmament negotiations, one would be tempted to say that a sound foundation had been laid for the work of the seventeen-nation committee that met at the Palais des Nations in Geneva in the spring of 1962. Unfortunately, agreement on general principles was only the new formula to register disagreement on concrete actions. Under the Russian plan, the final stage of disarmament was to be completed in four years, while under the American plan the date was unspecified. Although both agreed that when we entered the final stage, armed forces of nations were to be reduced for the sole maintenance of internal order, the American plan envisaged a United Nations police force with unchallengeable power enforcing an international law, while the Russian plan proposed that member states would place needed formations at the disposal of the Security Council.

In different guise, we had returned to the deadlock that had frustrated progress all along. The American plan was unrealistic and non-negotiable because it presupposed a community of world law which did not exist. Clearly, neither Russia, nor China, nor, for that matter, the neutral countries of Asia and Africa, would agree to a world gendarmery dominated by the West—which is what a United Nations police force would be at present. The Russian scheme was based on great-power unanimity, the principle that the Soviets have upheld since the United Nations was established. But since the great powers rarely saw eye to eye on the big questions of international politics, it meant the world police force or authority would be helpless to act in the case of many or most of the crucial conflicts that would arise. The differences in organizational and juridical formulas simply expressed the power and strategic deadlock. Hence, all attempts to get around the difficulty by juggling with the administrative propositions have proven useless and pointless. Until and unless a new element comes into the world equation, and there is a new way of thinking about the ordering of world affairs, disarmament is doomed to remain a chimera.

The great powers could not even agree to scale down armaments. The Russians proposed, as the first stage, to scrap all missiles, planes, artillery, and delivery weapons; to discontinue further weapons production; and to demolish all proving grounds. An international control authority was to function within six months of the signing of the treaty, and the first stage was to be completed in fifteen months thereafter. The authority was to recruit its own staff and make all substantive decisions by a two-thirds majority. Only in the case of sanctions was the Security Council to take over.

The American first stage was more limited and cautious on disarmament, and more demanding on inspection and international authority. The first stage was to be completed in three years, and was hedged with the provision that the permanent members of the Security Council had to agree unanimously that the stage had been satisfactorily fulfilled. Its main points read: Reduce United States and Russian armed forces to 2.1 million each; reduce all non-nuclear arms and delivery systems by 30 per cent; limit all new production to an agreed allowance for specified categories; stop new production of weapons-grade fissionable material, and transfer small amounts from existing stockpiles to peaceful purposes. An international authority was to be set up with the signing of the treaty which would verify disarmament, and which McCloy had previously explained in a letter to Zorin meant broad rights for comprehensive inspection of all aspects of the military establishments. There was also to be a United Nations observation corps to check on possible conflicts; the parties would be obligated to accept compulsory arbitration by the International Court; and they would prepare for the setting up of a United Nations police force which would begin to function at the second stage.

Even with this wide disparity of proposals, both sides could have come to some partial and meaningful agreements for arms reductions were there a disposition to come to grips with the war system. But the disposition was not there. The bargaining immediately assumed the farcical pattern of the previous years. The Americans amended their plan so that the permanent members of the Security Council no longer had to agree unanimously to proceed from one stage to the next; the transition could be made by a two-thirds vote of the projected disarmament control body, provided both the United States and Russia agreed. The Russian delegate accepted the American proposition of a 30 per cent reduction in conventional weapons provided mortars and small arms, which the Americans had left out, were included.

There followed the more serious psychological bombardment. In September, 1962, Foreign Minister Gromyko announced in the United Nations assembly that the Soviets were amending their plan to meet Western objections. Both sides could retain a strictly limited number of intercontinental missiles, antimissile missiles, and ground-to-air missiles until the end of the second stage. Thus, both sides would be under a "nuclear umbrella" to guarantee them against each other's aggression until they were ready to move to the final stage of complete disarmament. The Westerners felt that this would give the Russians an advantage and would shift intolerably the military balance. William C. Foster, our delegate, told the Geneva conference that Washington's plan for percentage across-the-board cuts in all major categories was the "simplest, the fairest, and the best way to assure that neither side gains a military advantage over the other" during the disarmament process.

Then, in the summer of 1963, American officials proposed that both sides scrap their obsolete bombers, 480 of the American B-47's for 480 of the Soviet TU-16's. The open door was too inviting for the Soviets to resist entering. They countered with the proposal to scrap *all* bombers. They were even more magnanimous, and modified this proposal to scrap all bombers of only the major powers, while exempting the smaller countries. The *New Republic* tartly observed that "instead of seeking to test the sincerity of this Soviet counterproposal, the West backed off like a horse from a rattlesnake." At the end of the year, the Russians tried another tack. Khrushchev offered a treaty for all nations to reject force to solve any and all territorial disputes. Thereupon, President Johnson countered that such a treaty had to include rejection of "subversion" as well, in his message to the new opening session of the Geneva conference on January 21, 1964. Johnson threw another American proposal into the hopper: a freeze of nuclear and defensive vehicles with full inspection. On March 2, 1964, *Pravda* ran a half-page interview with Gromyko in which he characterized the Geneva discussions as an exercise in futility. He went on to accuse the United States of offering pseudo-disarmament measures that amounted to "a proposal for stepping up the arms race."

This was the balance sheet of the over 150 sessions of the disarmament conference since the spring of 1962.*

---

* Some might view this conclusion as unduly one-sided and pessimistic. They can point out that in this very period there has been a détente in the cold war, both sides have announced minor cuts in their next war budgets, a partial test ban treaty has been signed, a "hot line" has been set up between Washington and Moscow, and several other small but possibly significant steps have been taken by both sides to lessen tension and promote trust. However one judges the import of the current détente, it is undeniable that the plans for disarmament, or meaningful arms reduction, have gotten nowhere, and that the arms race is moving ahead under its own gathering momentum.

The present lull in the cold war is a product of the October, 1962, Cuban missile crisis, when both the United States and Russia alerted their armed forces for action, and a petrified world watched the two superpowers poised for the grand thermonuclear exchange. The crisis was resolved when Russia backed down and agreed to remove her intermediate-range missiles and bomber planes from Cuba, and the United States pledged in return not to launch any armed invasion of Cuba. In a major speech a year later, General LeMay explained that we had forced Russia to back down in Cuba, as well as in Berlin, because we had greater nuclear muscle, that our buildup of "superior counterforce strength" was paying off. Fortunately, the Kennedy

The basic reason why the two sides could not arrive at any disarmament agreements—even small ones—was that their statesmen did not believe in them. The two states could not see their way clear of any disengagement from the war system. The argument of percentages versus absolute cuts recreated the well-worn game where each side makes non-negotiable proposals that would shift the balance in its favor. The American rationale for its disarmament strategy was explained by Henry Kissinger in a revealing interview that he gave over the B.B.C. network on September 5, 1962. Kissinger explained that the present strategy of the West "relies on strategic nuclear superiority to counterbalance Soviet local superiorities, particularly in Europe. Therefore our disarmament proposals have a tendency to freeze our strategic superiority throughout the period of disarmament, and this provides very little incentive for the Soviet Union to agree to a plan that would keep them in their position of inferiority for about ten years."

Administration estimated the results of the encounter more soberly and did not seek to overplay its hand.

The lull in the cold war is a tenuous thing nonetheless, because the only substantial agreement both sides have been able to reach has been the partial test ban—and no further agreements are in sight. The cuts in the two defense budgets are slight, and the American budget for 1965 will still run a quarter higher than during the Eisenhower years. The détente does constitute a recognition on both sides that the arms race and the cold war have reached a dead end. This recognition is not producing as yet any ability to alter the dispositions of the power conflict.

The most hopeful aspect of the lull is the loosening up of the two blocs. In an attempt to reestablish her influence in that part of the world, France is boldly seeking a political solution in Southeast Asia. The newly installed British Labor government may well seek an amelioration in Central Europe. If the relaxation continues for a number of years, the rigid cold war lineups of the past will very likely be demolished.

CHAPTER 14   Years of Wrath and Frustration

It is impossible to distill good cheer out of this eighteen-year record. The ingredients are not there. The United Nations would appear to be as great a failure in securing the peace as the forerunner League of Nations. This opinion has nothing in common with the fulminations of know-nothing factions who oppose the United Nations on grounds of unbridled nationalism. It is not to deny its indispensability as a meeting ground, as a negotiating center, as a world forum, as an umpire in small disputes, as an administrative convenience, as a clearing house of the nations as they are presently organized, constituted, and led. Nor is it to question the yeoman labors of some of its humanitarian agencies. But the organization, under the tutelage of the world's major powers, seems incapable of realizing its declared and overriding objective, "to save succeeding generations from the scourge of war."

There have been various theories and subtheories constructed to explain the strange conduct of statesmen who seem intent on driving themselves and their nations to the point of no return, who can declaim in Ciceronian periods on Sundays about the irrationality and wickedness of arms diplomacy, and who are unable on workdays to mitigate by a jot or tittle the thrust to war. For a number of years Western propaganda has attributed the absence of progress to Soviet rejection of adequate inspection systems. The Russians, it would seem, are pathological in hugging their military secrets to their bosoms; they won't permit an opening up of the military establishments for verification that no one side is cheating, and consequently it is they, and they alone, who have been responsible for blocking any advance toward beating swords into ploughshares.

The lessons of recent history are supposed to be clear as crystal on this score, and serve to emphasize the importance of thoroughgoing inspection as the indispensable guarantee for good faith and honest performance. Germany is said to have violated the disarmament provisions of the Versailles treaty because of the trusting nature of the peaceful democracies who thought that because they had good will, everyone else did too, only to pay the price of Hitler's aggressions for their gullibility. Japan's unannounced and treacherous attack upon the United States at Pearl Harbor allegedly furnishes another proof of the need for international controls to make sure that all sides are keeping their hands on the table and are not preparing any foul blows from ambush to disadvantage those who are righteously and conscientiously living up to their commitments.

The Russians counter that the West is not really interested in disarmament, but in fooling the public. That is why the Western representatives continually introduce plans whose initial stages call for merely token or marginal or inadequate reductions of armaments accompanied by extensive inspection schemes, the sole purpose of which is to break the security of the Soviet military establishment. Were these to be accepted, the military balance would shift against the Soviets in the opening stage and make it easy for the United States to launch a crippling attack, while the second and remaining stages of the disarmament plans would never see the light of day. The Soviet plans, in contrast, make inspection fit the amount of disarmament, and at the conclusion of the plan, when disarmament becomes total, inspection will become total as well. Under this kind of arrangement no one need fear that the legalized espionage will be used by one side to prepare an aggressive blow against the other.

A number of students of the question have taken these arguments to heart and have concluded that inspection is the touchstone of the difficulties, since it has been on one or another aspect of this principle that the disarmament talks have foundered from the time of the

Baruch Plan to the 1962–1964 Geneva parleys, and that this point and counterpoint have run like red threads through the welter of arguments of over eighteen years. They have proceeded to apply their ingenuity on how to break through the syndromes of little disarmament with unlimited inspection countered by unlimited disarmament with limited inspection, or as the popular parlance has it, Western plans for control without disarmament, and Soviet plans for disarmament without control.

The most extensive investigations were conducted by a group of scholars at Columbia University during 1957 and 1958, and the results were issued in a study containing eighteen papers, *Inspection for Disarmament,* under the editorship of Seymour Melman. These papers cover the entire range of inspection possibilities: aerial inspection, detection of underground nuclear explosions and high-altitude missile tests, disclosure of biological warfare production, direct inspection of factory operations, fiscal and records analysis, psychological techniques including the utilization of the native populations, and even studies of possible methods of evading disarmament agreements. This opus of love and labor, a veritable store-house of useful information and ingenious techniques, remains, alas, an academic exercise, because it technically assumes what has been politically unattainable: a comprehensive agreement permitting unhindered access by an international inspectorate.

Another ingenious and more politically pointed scheme has been offered by a keen student of the disarmament question, Louis B. Sohn, professor of law at Harvard University. Mindful of the dead-lock among the disarmament debaters and of their inability to get past the hurdle of their incompatible plans, he has tried to devise a method which would satisfy the objections of both sides.

It would seem desirable [he has argued] to combine the good features of the two groups of proposals and to eliminate their deficiencies. . . . It is not likely that the inspection system in the first stage will be so efficient as to guarantee complete compliance with the provisions of the agreement. A margin of safety would be necessary, therefore, and each of the sides might wish to keep a number of means of delivery roughly equal to the hypothetical number of means of delivery which might have been hidden by the other side and which are not likely to be discovered immediately by the international inspection teams. (Since an aggressor needs more than a 200 per cent superiority in weapons to destroy the ability of the other side to retaliate, a number of weapons equal to the size of the possible error in inspection checkup should constitute sufficient insurance against a premeditated attack.)

Having thus satisfied American demands for guarantees against a surprise attack, Sohn gets around the difficulty of Russia's insistence that controls be proportionate to disarmament with the suggestion of phasing controls on a zoning basis. Each side would divide its territory into a number of areas in each of which there would be an equal number of delivery vehicles. One of these zones would then be picked at random, and inspection teams would be stationed temporarily on all borders beforehand to prevent sudden shifts of armaments out of the selected zone. Even if the system did not work with 100 per cent perfection, "in the early phases, a certain amount of possible evasion is not too dangerous, as the other side would still retain most of its retaliatory force." The scheme made a strong impression on a number of experts, and it was incorporated in the 1962 American disarmament plan. Unfortunately, when adopting Dr. Sohn's inspection system, the American document did not incorporate at the same time his disarmament proposals, which in some respects are even more drastic than those of the Russians. So another astute and well-devised plan left the arms race unaffected.

The reason the different inspection projects have gotten nowhere is that it is more than doubtful that inspection is the culprit holding up the wheels of progress. It is definitely the stick with which we have been belaboring the Russians, but many of the best informed Washington newspapermen do not believe that the United States Senate would confirm most of the inspection propositions demanded by the different American negotiators. The problem has not arisen because inspection has been attached to other measures of such proven unsatisfactoriness to the Soviets that no one has had fears that the proferred packages might be snatched up by our opponent. Richard J. Barnet has observed in *Who Wants Disarmament?*:

Comprehensive inspection represents a substantial sacrifice of national sovereignty. There have been a number of individuals and groups in the United States that have been bitterly opposed to permitting foreign inspectors into our atomic plants. . . . As President Eisenhower posed the question in his press conference of July 6, 1955: "Are we ready to open up every one of our factories, every place where something might be going on that could be inimical to the interests of somebody else?" . . . No more than British firms or Soviet state-owned factories, would American industry welcome the disarmament inspectors into their laboratories, especially if the intruder happened to be a national of a commercial rival. Writing in the relatively optimistic days of the "spirit of Geneva," Sir John Slessor, Marshal of the Royal Air Force, observed that neither the British nor the Americans nor the Russians would accept within the immediately foreseeable future an inspection system under which the agents of the international control organ would be "free to go literally anywhere they chose."

That inspection has become the bête noire of disarmament has been due to the public relations exigencies of the debate rather than to its compulsive importance to the matter at hand. It had been pushed to the fore even in the negotiations for a ban on nuclear testing, a field where it has only marginal significance, and where the attempts of interested establishment men to befuddle the issue with far-fetched theories of undetectable explosions in underground caves have exposed its artificial character. In the test ban negotiations, each side had promiscuously taken over each other's arguments, like changing partners at a barn dance. At one time Western representatives argued that a test ban could only be considered in indissoluble relation to a general disarmament agreement. Then they dropped that and argued that it could best be negotiated as a separate agreement. The Soviet diplomats went through an identical performance. The necessary symmetry of the dance was achieved at both times, however, because at each point the two sets of diplomats were in perfect disagreement, deftly exchanging each other's arguments. An equal flexibility was shown in the infighting. When the Russians were ready to set off their test explosions in the fall of 1961, the Americans and British offered an uninspected ban agreement on all atmospheric tests, which the Russians rejected. When the West was ready to begin its test series in the spring of 1962, the inconvenient proposal was summarily dropped. When the United States was completing its test series, the proposal was disinterred again. When the state of technology and political expediencies made a test ban advisable, Russia and the United States signed a treaty without long preparations or debates, and without any manned inspection procedures over each other's territories.

As a matter of fact, the entire litany of thought—wherein it is conceived that the nations will agree to a disarmament pact, and then one party will successfully fool the international inspectors and secret away enough missiles and nuclear warheads to threaten the other party with instantaneous destruction unless it capitulates —is a product of the icy fanaticism of the military intellectuals, and of the hysteria engendered by the arms race. Germany's secret violations of the Versailles disarmament provisions is an example that speaks against them, not for them. First, Germany's secret rearmament under the Weimar Republic was a case where the nation had been forcibly disarmed by its conquerors against its own will, and where the clandestine rearming was viewed with satisfaction and connived at by the German populace. Second, all the allied chancelleries had shrewd suspicions that the Rapallo treaty with Russia contained secret military clauses. They were aware that Germany was violating the Versailles disarmament dispensations. Third, the surreptitious rearmament never amounted to much beyond the inherent potential of a highly industrialized country to rearm. By its very nature, serious rearmament cannot be put through secretively. It involves the activities of masses of people, and the telltale movements of mountains of material and equipment. Despite all the violations, in 1930 Germany was still virtually a disarmed power. When she really moved to rearm under Hitler, her government openly repudiated the Versailles treaty, occupied the Rhineland, and demonstratively voted large military budgets.

II

What then is the key to the disarmament deadlock? It is not inspection, and a Russian psychopathic addiction to secrecy. It is not that the Russians are wicked and we are virtuous, or vice versa. It is not that supreme earthly power will be seized by a crowd of Cesare Borgias who hold out on their disarmament pledges by hiding a parcel of nuclear bombs in their aunts' closets. It is simply this: the governments do not want to disarm because they do not believe in it. They cannot see disarmament as a practical proposition in this day and age.

By the very nature of their calling, government leaders are consolidators rather than innovators. They adhere to the social arrangements that are familiar; they feel they are discharging their duties responsibly and prudently when they cling to time-honored simplicities and assumed securities. They understand the sovereign national state. It has been with us for the past four hundred years, and in a more general sense, for several thousand years. They have seen it operate; they have experienced its gravitational pull; they have lived under the sway of its laws and devotional symbols; they know it is a solid social reality that both demands and receives the loyalty of its subjects. They take for granted that national patriotism can always be counted on to stir the citizens to the depths of their souls. ("And how can man die better, than facing fearful odds, for the ashes of his fathers, and the temples of his gods?")

They also understand armaments, armed hosts, and war. These have been with us since civilization's dawn. This has been the nature of the world and the way of man. This has been the way our fathers and our forefathers, and our sires before them, settled their quarrels and slaked the thirst of their lusts. But a world without armaments, without the *ultima ratio* of war to cut the Gordian knot of contending claims, and to render the final and irrevocable verdict beyond the power of any mortal to dispute or upset—this they cannot visualize. What will replace the arbitrament of the sword? Can anything replace it? They dread the unknown. They are skeptical of what they have not seen. And they cling to the familiar, which because it is familiar gives the comforting feeling of being realistic and safe.

Despite the fire-eating of some of the militarists in and out of uniform, the civilian governments of the major armed powers, mindful of the realities of the nuclear age, do not want war. Among them are no Alexanders nor Caesars, no Napoleons nor Hitlers. But the importance of their wishes is diminished by their continuing to lust for the usufructs of war, and their knowing no other statecraft than that issuing out of the war system. The consequences may be just the same as if they were conquerors at heart, for in 1914 nobody really wanted war, either, not even the "two third-rate men," as George Bernard Shaw called the Kaiser and the Czar, "one little more than an imbecile, the other hardly sane." Lloyd George, who had ridden the tides of the period, wrote: "The more one reads of the memoirs and books written in the various countries of what happened before August 1, 1914, the more one realizes that no one at the head of affairs quite meant war. It was something into which they glided, or rather staggered and stumbled."

That the United States does not view disarmament as an *actuel* proposition is understood by all students of the question and attested to by a wide diversity of authorities. It was all but admitted during the Acheson and Dulles tenures in the State Department. In his paper appearing in the Fall, 1960, *Daedalus* issue on arms control, Sayville R. Davis, managing editor of the *Christian Science Monitor*, talked of the "harmless" American tradition, beginning with the 1920's, of paying lip service to disarmament. "This tradition of the white lie carried over into the nuclear age, when the need for arms control revived and caused great havoc before it was exposed. For in the mid-fifties the nuclear arms race began in earnest, and the need to check it began to override the incessant struggle to build a better deterrent. For several critical years the habit of pretending to work for disarmament served to mask the fact that the political leadership of the United States did not want disarmament." Indeed, in his July 22, 1957, speech delivered over the air waves, Dulles tried in all frankness to set the matter straight for the public. He said, "Let me first of all make clear that we do not, of course, use the word 'disarmament' in any literal sense. No one is thinking of disarming the United States or the Soviet Union or any other nation." What the government meant by disarmament, he explained, was certain minor reductions pending political settlements. A week later the United States was a party to the Berlin declaration which stated, "The Western powers do not intend to enter into an agreement on disarmament which would prejudice the reunification of Germany."

After Khrushchev made his proposals for total disarmament, Professor William Langer, a distinguished historian, stated in his contribution to the report of the President's Commission on National Goals: "It is unthinkable that anything approaching complete disarmament can be achieved in the foreseeable future. To be sure, the Soviets have proposed the speedy abolition of all armaments, but this proposal is so patently illogical and impractical as to stamp it a cynical propaganda fraud." Professor Langer's evaluation was not formally accepted, and the American government underwrote the "illogical" and the "impractical." But did it? In a little while Louis B. Sohn was to say: "While our government has accepted in the last two years 'the goal of general and complete disarmament under effective international control,' there is a strong feeling in this country and abroad that we are paying only lip service to the idea." A year later Senator Joseph S. Clark stated to the Intercollegiate Conference on Disarmament at Swarthmore College, "Not more than a handful of my colleagues in the Senate are fully familiar with the McCloy-Zorin agreement and the

President's disarmament plan. A majority of them think total and permanent disarmament is the rosy dream of a few impractical idealists."

Do the Russians take disarmament any more seriously? In 1928, as we have seen, they viewed it not as a negotiable issue but as psychological warfare. They did not believe the capitalist states could or would disarm—and the capitalist states, it may be added, obligingly danced to their Marxian tune. Hence, their crusade for disarmament was designed to expose their opponents' bad faith and predatory intentions. It was meant to capture for the Soviet Union the aureole of peace. Two things have substantially altered under Khrushchev since the days of Litvinov at the League disarmament conferences. At that time many of the Westerners thought that the Soviet proposals, to the extent that they were not unadulterated propaganda, stemmed from Russia's industrial and military weakness; that the commissars were trying to carve out equality with the capitalists by cutting the latter down to their own military size. Such a motivation can no longer explain Soviet disarmament campaigns. Today Russia is a first-class military power, and were the missiles, planes, and bombs scrapped, she would be in a position to contribute an impressive total to the disarmament bonfires and dumping grounds.

The other big change is the revision of Leninism to the effect that it is no longer inevitable for the capitalist nations to make war. Is this an honest change of ideology, or is it a diplomatic formula? The evolution of Soviet Marxism has pretty much destroyed the distinction. Once Marxism became transformed from a critique of capitalist society into a state religion of Soviet society, the sacred texts were systematically manipulated to justify the going policies of the day. As the unlimited monarchs of the past used to make no distinction between the public purse and the privy purse, so the Soviet leaders confounded their empirically determined state policies with their ideological traditions. So ingrained has this habit become that it was carried on by the Titoists after their break from the Kremlin: when relations with their erstwhile Big Brother were bad, they downgraded the Soviet Union in their Marxian sociology to the status of state capitalism; when relations improved, they upgraded it to the status of socialism.

For practical purposes, therefore, it can be assumed that the Khrushchev revision of Lenin apropos the non-inevitability of war is a legitimate part of the presently accepted exegesis, especially since it is a reasonable theory from the present Soviet outlook. After all, Khrushchev has not said that the capitalist nations will definitely not make war. His modification of Lenin goes only so far as to say that war is no longer inevitable—not because the capitalist states have had a change of heart, but because the power balance between East and West has made war a possibly prohibitive adventure. It can also be taken for granted that since the arms race places a far greater burden on Russia's smaller industrial complex than it does on the larger American one, and Russia is short of capital for her ambitious plans, her rulers would welcome at least an abatement of the armaments contest. Because all her investments are government-determined in any case, and her war production more intermingled with civilian production than is the case in this country, she has not built up the counterpart of our own specific vested interests in an arms economy.

How much do these propositions weigh in the overall balance of policy? Not much. Arms buildups are not invariably tied in with make-work considerations. The pre-World War I arms race occurred in a very prosperous decade, when government executives thought of it as a drain on a rising economy, not as a shot-in-the-arm for a sluggish one. The grim fact is that the epoch of the cold war has been inhospitable to Tolstoyan principles on either side of the Iron Curtain, whether job considerations are present or absent. Once the two divergent systems collided politically, and menaced each other strategically, it followed as a matter of course that they would proceed to arm to the teeth. In the circumstances, Russia's insistence on disarmament, while continuing relentlessly to pursue her international claims, means that she too views disarmament as an objective that is not destined to be realized in this vale of tears for a long time to come, but the disarmament campaign must be waged without letup to capture the good will of the peoples around the globe. Disarmament has become not a negotiation to end or mitigate the cold war, but another aspect of the cold war.

III

There are social scientists who believe the disarmament tumult is caused by the hysteria of statesmen, or by unworthy pandering on the part of governments to the ignorance of the mob. They reason that armaments are not the cause but the effect of conflicts between nations. They compare the attempts to do away with armaments while leaving the conflicts intact with the method of quacks who try to bring down a fever with ice-packs while ignoring the raging disease that brought the fever on.

In the course of the second great war, E. H. Carr wrote in *Conditions of Peace* that one of the lessons of the League experience was that peace is not and can never be a direct object of policy, that it can only be a by-product of a healthy and continally advancing social organization. "Everyone who followed the history of the League of Nations knows the stifling effect exercised at Geneva by the word 'security' on any progressive movement. . . . [International peace] cannot be achieved by the signing of pacts or covenants 'outlawing' war any more than revolutions are prevented by making them illegal. A generation which makes peace and security its aim is doomed to frustration." Raymond Aron spoke in a similar vein in his 1957 essay *On War*, saying that disarmament was impossible so long as predacious national states remained in conflict. "After 1918, pacifists believed that the cause of war had been an armed peace. On the assumption that there are no genuine issues at stake, that conflicts arise from misunderstandings, that no state is prone to expansion, that war psychosis and war itself are created by the accumulation of arms on either side of a frontier, then disarmament by its very nature would ensure peace. By abolishing the instruments of warfare one would automatically abolish the will to fight. No one today would uphold so naive a view."

Were we to follow through on this line of thought, we would abandon the misguided efforts to secure disarmament and concentrate our energies on removing those economic, political, social, and strategic causes of conflict which have led to the cold war, and which are responsible for the arms race. Such an idea might have appeared ultrarealistic and ruthlessly practical in the thirties because in that decade, consciously or unconsciously, social meliorists were wont to see the relation between social imbalance and war as a direct one. Remove social inequalities, clear up the slums, give people opportunity, supply good hot lunches for the children of the poor, and you will have removed the causes of international brigandage, and the armed establishments will proceed to wither on the vine. When the national state is in harmony internally, it will have no reason to engage in adventures abroad. This was a modern transposition of the argument of the bourgeois radicals of the nineteenth century who said: Do away with kings and princes who are interested in dynastic quarrels and are obsessed with chivalric notions of honor, establish stout republican governments concerned with trade and the welfare of the people, and you will have abolished the effective causes for wars between nations. The post-World War II world has established the inadequacy of this type of sociology.

The main armed powers of our day are a long way from having perfected social justice on their own grounds, but all of them—the United States, Russia, Britain, Germany—have established high living standards in comparison with conditions of fifty years ago, and all enjoy unparalleled social peace within their own homes. Yet these are the very powers who are arming as never before, and who are responsible for frightening mankind with the prospects of a disaster. The social tensions and struggles that are boiling up in the poor countries would threaten no one outside their own borders were it not for the interference and conflicting claims of the great powers. So it is not enough for a country to have a loyal and possibly contented population at home; it must also function in a favorable international setting. But any formulas for making the world safe for democracy, or making the world safe for communism, are obviously formulas for a third world war, not for organizing the peace. We are therefore called upon to turn our attention to the various conflicts between the nations, and particularly between the two war blocs, to see if these can be dispelled, or ameliorated, or adjudicated, to the end that the armed camps can feel free to demobilize and cease their threatening gestures toward each other.

Unfortunately, the minute we examine any of the outstanding political disputes—Berlin, German unification, Taiwan, Cuba, South Vietnam—we discover that the conflict between East and West is not the sum of the individual disputes, but that the individual disputes are only symbols and symptoms of an underlying disagreement as to which bloc and which system is to lead the world. We see that when one of the specific points at issue is eliminated—as when Russia withdrew her troops from Iran and permitted that country to adhere to the West, or when Austria was given its independence, or when North Vietnam joined the Communist camp —this does not tranquilize the international climate. The powers are able to concentrate their energies on the other boundaries of the encounter, or several new disputes arise out of the hostile confrontation. Nothing is accomplished by cutting one head off a

hydra-headed monster, especially when it is capable of growing
new heads to replace those it has lost.

Paul Nitze provided excellent insight into how the international
positions and the conflicts of the cold war are all made or unmade,
not because of their intrinsic worth, but in response to the master
question: "Who shall be top dog?" In discussing the change in
United States attitude about a free zone in Central Europe, he wrote
(Klaus Knorr, Ed., *NATO and American Security*):

> Those in the Policy Planning Staff who favored disengagement
> [in 1948 and 1949] were of the view that if Russian forces were
> withdrawn behind the Bug, a very substantial political reorienta-
> tion was certain to take place in all of Central Europe. It was our
> hope that this reorientation would take place gradually and with
> discretion. We did not see how reunification of Germany in a
> form acceptable to the Bonn government could be prevented if
> Russian military forces were not directly present in support of
> the East German regime. Far from wishing Germany, or any
> other part of Central Europe, to become part of NATO, it was
> our thought that the influence of the NATO powers would be
> directed to keeping Central Europe a buffer area incapable of
> disturbing the security of the West or of challenging the East.
> The United States monopoly of atomic weapons was considered
> a sufficient strategic guarantee to ensure that the U.S.S.R. did not
> violate the agreement. Today the correlation of forces is quite
> different. . . . In 1948 it was our purpose that the intervening
> area would come to be governed by regimes responsive to the will
> of the peoples of Eastern Europe—in other words, that it would
> be in the power zone of the free world—even if it were militarily
> neutral. If the Soviets had indicated a willingness to withdraw
> their troops at that time, we would have interpreted it to mean
> that they accepted such a political solution to the problem of
> Eastern Europe. Today an evacuation of United States troops
> from Germany or from Europe would probably be interpreted
> by the Soviet Union, and by many Europeans, as acceptance by
> the West that all of Continental Europe was thereafter to lie
> basically in the power sphere of the U.S.S.R. The U.S.S.R. for
> many years might well make no very direct demands upon the
> individual European nations, but the essential question of who
> is to decide the most basic issues—those potentially involving
> war or peace in the area—would, in their view, have been

decided. The situation of Europe would then be comparable
to the present position of Finland.

This being so, we have made no progress at all by following the
advice of those who say, "It is necessary to straighten out the
political differences before you can have disarmament." We meet
the same difficulties in political debates that we have encountered
in the eighteen-year debate over disarmament, and it is no easier to
settle the one than the other. Even when the United States gave
up its initial postwar illusion that it could more or less easily pressure
Russia out of her enlarged sphere of influence and lock her up
behind the prewar borders, there was no escaping for either side
from the vicious circle of the cold war. Neither East nor West
could change its behavior until trust was restored, and trust could
not be restored while behavior remained unchanged. Neither side
was or is willing to reconcile itself to an evolutionary victory over
the other. Both maintain that they have faith in the future, but
whenever the chance presents itself, or can be manufactured, each
wants to help history along to do the right thing. That is why it is
relatively easy to write learned brochures on how reasonable men
in 1861 could have gotten together across the bargaining table and
avoided the American Civil War, but very hard to induce two
sets of men similarly placed to avoid a world war a century later.
No one has yet hit on how to resolve by methods other than war
the kind of question that was always resolved in the past by war.

IV

There is no beneficent social arrangment which will automatically
make peace fall into our laps as a bonus for good behavior. It may
have seemed right in 1941 to say with Carr: "If the victors in the
present war are able to create the conditions for an orderly and
progressive development of human society, peace and security will
be added unto them." In the postwar world we have to turn that
around and say: To get a world without war, we have to directly
and specifically devise new institutions and arrangements which
will permit nations to settle conflicts by other means than those
used for the past six thousand years. Otherwise, we will have another
war of world dimensions and of fatal consequences.

Even if we were able to whisk away the specific conflicts stem-

ming from the clash of rival social systems and return the world to
the ideological harmony of 1913, and even if we were to postulate
a far superior concern for social justice within the states, we would
still be far from the Eden of international peace. For conflict and
change are the laws of history. If there is any rule that has withstood
the wear of time and tide, it is this. No prince, no ruler, regardless
of the ferocity with which he extirpated all opposition, or the watch-
fulness with which he attempted to isolate his subjects from outside
influence, has been able to freeze his social system. The resourcefulness of the human has been superior in the long run to the whip of
the tyrant. Any new order that is to have viability must allow for
change, and no instruments have been fashioned, or are likely to
be fashioned, which can differentiate ahead of time between irresistible social trends and the subversive antics of disordered or unruly
minds. The one can be differentiated from the other only in practice.
Social arrangements that might appear virtuous and forward-looking
to one generation are oppressive and iniquitous to a succeeding one.
What is revolutionary in one age becomes reactionary in another.
The new upholders of the status quo are likely to be just as obdurate
and as blindly self-righteous in resisting change as were the Royalists of the eighteenth century, or the feudal barons of the sixteenth
century. In the absence of new relations between men, such resistance would inevitably lead to new conflicts, and when peaceful
pressures have failed, such conflicts would necessarily lead to war.

Skeptics say this is not a good time to try to construct a new
*ultima ratio.* We are not engaged in bending a sapling, but in
redirecting the growth of an aged and hardened tree of civilization,
and it is not realistic to try to do so while two hostile social systems
are locked in mortal combat. Unfortunately, the clash has reached
its climax concomitant with the scientific revolution in warfare,
and whether the time is opportune or not, the operation will have
to be performed within the next generation—or calamity is liable
to overwhelm us.

Everyone who has delved into this matter knows that at the
hub of the problem is the nationalism of conflicting sovereign states
which recognize no morality beyond their own borders. Everyone
who has studied it understands the need to bend the wills of the
separate nations through some form of world government or
international authority. There are already several dozen elaborate
projects for world government on the market, and it would be

fatuous to present still another one in the naive hope that it would accomplish what all the others have failed to accomplish. While some of the plans ignore all political realities of our own age, or of any age, a number are drawn with exceptional skill, and attempt to avoid granting any advantage to any side or nation beyond its present position. A particularly impressive document, in which is worked out in the most meticulous detail a constitution for a revised United Nations, was drawn up by Grenville Clark and Louis B. Sohn in *World Peace Through World Law*. The trouble with this document, as with all the other ones, may be summed up by what the Emperor Frederick cynically wrote in a letter to Voltaire about Abbe Saint-Pierre's *Project for Perpetual Peace*. He said it was perfect in every way; all it needed was an amendment on how to get the various heads of state to agree to it. Until circumstances and social influences show the way to break through the political monopolies presently exercised by the sovereign armed powers, the memoranda, documents, and draft constitutions for world government are destined to join all unbaptized infants in limbo.

In their impatience to get on with the job, there are One World enthusiasts who confuse steps toward world government with moves in the cold war. They figure that the fates are weaving the threads, even if they are working in somewhat mysterious ways. They view the United Nations attempt to impose sanctions on an aggressor in the Korean War, and its dispatch of troops into the Congo, as links in an evolutionary chain of the future, in which the obstruction and resistance of the recalcitrants will be subdued, the veto in the Security Council will be abolished, and the structure of a sovereign world authority, majestic and unchallengeable, will emerge. The more visionary devotees gratuitously assume that Western ideas and predilections are the sole and proper basis for world law. This is an old Anglo-Saxon failing, as when Woodrow Wilson declared that American principles were the principles of mankind, or when Arnold Toynbee discovered that the security of the British empire was in "the supreme interest of the whole world." Count Sforza commented wryly on "that precious gift bestowed upon the British people—the possession of writers and clergymen able in perfect good faith to advance the highest moral reasons for the most concrete diplomatic action, with inevitable moral profit to England." The gift of identifying the good of mankind with one's own national interests is granted only to imperial aristocrats in an aristocratic age. It is of no use to any concept of international morality in our own mass age when no single nation has hegemony.

To equate Western victories against the Soviets inside the United Nations as steps toward world government can be done logically only if one envisages the new world authority being imposed by a conqueror, in the way the Caesars carved out a world state and forcibly instructed the inhabitants thereof in the Roman peace and the Roman law. However, if one visualizes a supranational authority coming into being by agreement and the pressure of circumstances, somewhat analogous to the way the thirteen independent American states were incorporated into a federal union—and that is the only way it is likely to come, if at all—then the history of the United Nations reads less optimistically.

In terms of an evolution toward world government, or simply, some international authority, the history of the United Nations has been a tale of frustration and sterility. Strangely enough, that is because the United Nations is a more formidable experiment in international collaboration than was the League of Nations. The League never attained universality; once the United States decided not to join, it was reduced to a primarily European institution; and even as a European institution, it was inadequate. For a long period of time, neither Germany nor Russia was in its councils. Designed to uphold the status quo of the Versailles system, it was dominated throughout its career by the two major European victors, France and England. But the two victors soon drifted apart when England reverted to her traditional diplomacy of opposing domination of the continent by any single power. Then, the United States, as the emergent creditor and trading power, was interested in maintaining social stability and an open-door policy without becoming involved in the particulars of European territorial claims and settlements. Finally, once recovered from the shock of war, Germany, Russia, Italy, and Japan were out to revise the existing settlements. The result was that the main international puruits were taking place outside the League, and the thrust and counter-thrust of international diplomacy was not even adequately echoed in its debates. Many of the League proponents began to wonder whether provincial Geneva, situated outside the main arteries of Big Power movement, had been after all the right choice for the League site. It was less its faulty geographical location, however, than its political inadequacy that was responsible for the League's becoming isolated from the leading currents of international life.

The United Nations was saved this fate by enlisting from the first the support of the two superpowers of the post-World War II epoch. Though it still lacks universality because of the exclusion of Communist China and of Germany, it began in 1955 to take cognizance of the colonial independence movement by admitting to membership all of the newly founded states until today it has twice its original membership. The United Nations has consequently become a sounding-board for all of the conflicts, disputes, maladjustments, and aches and pains of seething humanity, and there is scarcely an issue of international significance, from disarmament and Red China, to Apartheid and the Congo, which has not at one time or another been exhaustively aired in its discussions. But since the two superpowers split immediately after the war, and each has sought to enlist all other nations in their quarrel, the United Nations became paralyzed as an executive institution, and was better able to mark at each stage the fever chart of the cold war than to do anything about the cold war. When the big powers found themselves stymied inside the international organization, they took the line of least resistance and bypassed it. The main thrust of Western and Soviet diplomacy moved toward regional bilateral military alliances; money loans and grants were made primarily on a nation-to-nation basis; and the United Nation's leading financial institutions, to the extent that they were employed, became instrumentalities of Western policy.

V

For the first decade of its existence, the United Nations was dominated by the West, and above all, by the United States, the banker and armorer of the Western bloc. Of the 51 original foundation members, or the 60 members up to 1955, the Russians could muster only the half-dozen votes of their own and of their East European satellites, while the United States, with its hold on Latin America, and with the aid of its West European allies and their supporters, could mobilize overwhelming majorities in both the General Assembly and the leading committees. The United Nations' administrative machinery was also in Western hands. The bulk of the Secretariat personnel was Western in origin and outlook, and Trygve Lie, the first Secretary General, was, in the words of the *New York Times* correspondent, C. L. Sulzberger, "our man both spiritually and politically." The Soviet bloc tolerated this minority role to which it had been assigned, because it was protected from hostile sanctions by its veto in the Security Council, because it felt that it could better carry on psychological offensives inside than outside the United Nations, and because its unfavorable position reflected America's preponderant position in world affairs in the initial postwar years.

The first attempt to break the paralysis of the United Nations came with the Korean War in June, 1950. By an accidental conjuncture, the Soviet delegates were at this time boycotting the Security Council to protest the council's refusal to seat Communist China. The American representative took advantage of this to secure the passage of a resolution which branded the North Koreans and called into being a United Nations army to repel their aggression. This was followed up in November by the passage in the General Assembly of the "Uniting for Peace" resolutions, under which the assembly could be called into emergency session on 24 hours notice, and which empowered the assembly to advise member states of the existence of an aggression, and to come to the military aid of the victim.

For those enamored with the formal aspects of international institutions, a blow had been struck to free the United Nations from its debilitating veto, and the creation of an army under U.N. auspices had saved the organization from the fate of the League of Nations when the latter had failed to stop the Japanese or the Italians. For those who looked at the substance of the matter, no evidence of a growing international law was visible. While it was generally accepted that the North Koreans had set off the spark, it was also accepted in many circles of public opinion that MacArthur's threatening strategy had brought the Chinese into the combat. Although the American forces, supplemented in the main with troops of their Turkish client, fought under the U.N. banner, to the nation outside the war blocs, and particularly to the peoples of Asia, the Korean War represented not the apolitical forces of international morality arrayed against the dark powers of international rapine, but the eruption of the cold war into a hot one.

In any case, the attempt to vitalize the United Nations by a dose of military action, and to shift power to the assembly, was a failure. Trygve Lie's alignment with the West led to a crisis within the U.N. His reelection in 1950 was vetoed by Moscow, and when the West nevertheless overrode the veto with questionable legality in the assembly, the Russians boycotted the Secretary General and forced his resignation two years later. The next Secretary General was not from a NATO country. Dag Hammarskjold came from neutral Sweden, and while he was decidedly a Western man in outlook and cultural training, he was of a more independent mold than his predecessor. To quote Mr. Sulzberger again, "Dag Hammarskjold was no more ours politically than is Sweden, but spiritually he was a democrat as we understand that word's meaning." When the West tried to utilize the "Uniting for Peace" rule in 1956 by securing the passage of a resolution in the assembly which called on Russia to end its intervention in Hungary, it was a propaganda coup for the West, but it symbolized the continued impotence of the United Nations. The deadlock between the two superpowers had led to the deadlock of the U.N., and no manipulation of the U.N. constitution could change the reality. The international organization was an amalgamation of sovereign states, not a world parliament of man. The U.N. could exercise no more authority than the major powers were willing to confer upon it.

The next crisis of the United Nations came in 1960 with the Congo and Hammarskjold's ambitious attempt to break the U.N.'s paralysis by shifting power to the Secretariat. By this time the U.N. situation had changed again in several respects. The power balance between the two war blocs was more equal than it had been in the recent past, and it was reflected in the changed composition of the U.N. votes. While the West could still, by exerting itself, muster majorities on most important issues, these majorities were no longer as overwhelming or as automatically won as before; and a congery of neutralist nations, standing outside the two major blocs, was bringing to bear an independent influence in the direction and style of U.N. affairs, and forcing the major powers to bid for their support.

Hammarskjold began to feel his way cautiously toward utilizing the new balance to gain elbow room for the U.N. administration. His first step was to create a more decisive role for the office of the Secretary General. In 1957 he dispatched a mission of conciliation to Cambodia and Thailand without reference to either the council or the assembly. In 1959 he sent a functionary to Laos as the Secretary General's personal representative to establish a "U.N. presence"—this time in the teeth of the public displeasure of the Soviets. He justified his conduct by a concept of the "implied powers" which he held were vested in his office. As he explained it,

"I believe that it is in keeping with the philosophy of the Charter that the Secretary General should be expected to act without guidance from the Assembly or the Security Council should this appear to him necessary toward helping to fill any vacuums that may appear in the systems which the Charter and traditional diplomacy provide for the safeguarding of peace and security."

The full reasoning behind this forceful policy was laid out in his annual report issued in September, 1960, when he was already being buffeted on all sides by the Congo affair. Because the international organization, he said, exists in a split world, "it is extremely difficult for the United Nations to exercise an influence on problems which are clearly and definitely within the orbit of present-day conflicts between power blocs." The Council, Assembly, and Secretariat can therefore do little in conflicts "within that orbit." What then can the U.N. do? Its main field of useful activity is "in keeping newly arising conflicts outside the sphere of bloc differences." This he proposed to do by "preventive diplomacy" and "preventive action" in order to fill "power vacuums" so as not to "provoke action from any of the major parties." In other words, when a new weak nation or scene of instability was liable to tempt Russia and the United States to makes lunges to bring the area into their respective spheres, the U.N., in the person of the Secretary General, would step in as a neutral above the battle, fill the vacuum, and thus forestall the major belligerents. The U.N. would thus stand guard over that vast indeterminate area not tied up by the military blocs, to prevent any part of it from becoming another Spain or Korea or the starting point for a new world war.

The doctrine proved totally untenable. The attempt to create a secretariat with sovereign powers of its own, against the wishes of one of the power blocs (and if it had ever come to the actual point of decision, it would not have been countenanced by the other power bloc either), went to smash in the course of the Congo crisis. It was all very well to talk about a supranational United Nations military force intervening as a neutral, only "to maintain law and order," and desisting from becoming a party to any internal Congolese conflict, but the very nature of its military presence in a country wracked by chaos and civil war meant that it was going to be sucked into the conflicting intrigues. Anything it did, or failed to do, would necessarily strengthen one faction and weaken another. There was no such thing as an apolitical intervention.

When U.N. representatives closed all major airports and the

Leopoldville radio station, they undercut the position of Lumumba, and to that extent, that of his Soviet ally, and made possible the acquisition of power by Kasavubu, thus enhancing the position of his Western patrons. Later the U.N.'s decision to send troops into Katanga weakened the position of Tshombe; a howl of rage and indignation went up from his Belgian and British patrons, and an organization to support "the Katanga freedom fighters" was even formed in this country.

The savage public denunciations of U.N. activity by the Soviet representatives, and the equally vindictive if more veiled attacks by the West European representatives, might have been shrugged off if there had been such a thing as an international common law and an international public opinion which Hammarskjold and his staff were working to enforce. For contrary to Soviet assertions Hammarskjold was no flunky of any foreign office or power bloc; he was a high-minded civil servant who thought only to build a U.N. authority for the good of mankind; but there was no international morality or law to sanctify his *ad hoc* and necessarily arbitrary interventions. He had nothing with which to fill the vacuums of power. In effect, he arrogated to himself the right to interpret true international morality. But what appeared to him as fair and proper was conditioned by his Western upper-class background, education, and associations. And finally, no one had authorized him to become the conscience of mankind, if for no other reason than that mankind had not yet agreed on what its conscience ought to be. His accidental death in an airplane crash eased the way to resolve the U.N. crisis that his doctrine had provoked, and to end the contest which, had he lived to be challenged, he could never have won. The new Secretary General, U Thant of Burma, came not from a neutral Western country, but a neutralist Asian one, and again according to Sulzberger, "is not our man in any way." He has not yet disengaged himself from the embarrassing Congo legacy that had been left him, but Hammarskjold's unsuccessful thrust proved that if mankind, in its present circumstances, is to make a marriage with international morality, it will have to be done by consent; it will not be done by rape.

CHAPTER 15   Caesars and Saints

THE first duty of the political analyst is to expose the hollowness and the sham of the diplomacy and military system that is supposed to save us from war. To understand that humanity is standing on a quaking bog is the precondition for purposeful orientation. Nothing can be gained by pretending, or by cheerful idiocy. But it is precisely when we have arrived at this point that we have to stop being "practical," if we hope to see anything practical issue out of the cold war dilemma. To be practical as the *realpolitikers* are practical means to cook up projects that will be acceptable to the political directorates in charge of the status quo. That means to reconcile ourselves to the status quo, and the status quo includes the arms race. For the political craftsmen who lead our governments are not playing the war game because they are more wicked or insane than the rest of us, but because the status quo of national states rests on age-old premises, which once accepted, lead necessarily to acceptance of the war system. To eliminate the war system means to change the fundamentals of state power, both within and without. That can only come from a profound new idea seizing multitudes of humanity and becoming transmitted to governments. It will not originate with governments, for governments are bureaucracies, and bureaucracies cannot risk the unknown. They have not been trained and fitted out for such efforts. They are equipped with antennae and limbs to administer the estate entrusted to their care.

In the first excitement over Hiroshima and Nagasaki, some people were convinced that the atom bomb would quickly affect thinking; that it would lead to a revolution in the techniques of government. The anticipation has been borne out to the extent that the bomb shook up the thinking of vast numbers and produced a recrudescence of peace movements around the world. However, it has not changed the dynamics of governments, because the actions of states can be transformed only when states are supplied with new institutional organs. The governments are helpless to extrude these organs by their own creativity, when it is a question of such decisive innovations.

That is why the academics' well-intentioned advice to opponents of the war system that they stop shouting simplistic slogans and become expert in the literature of the military analysts, and in that way be better able to get the ear of men in power, is naive. It is like advice to Luther on how to establish better intergroup communication with the Vatican. The mechanics of social innovation do not work that way. Governments will become convinced of the soundness of the peace idea only when, like the Emperor Constantine in his conversion to Christianity, they are impressed with its social influence. Of course, research in the subject is of high importance as all true scholarship is of high importance; and depending on its breadth, depth, and conscientiousness, the results may enrich our cultural heritage and affect the political thought and action of the age. But it will do that only to the extent that it fuses with the social drifts of a militant idealism.

Although the history of mankind is the history of power and the struggle over power, the concept of a world without moral foundations or high purposes is ultimately repugnant to man. The most cynical and vulgar of politicians recognize the need in their profession for dressing up their meanest actions with glistening moral principles. The matter goes beyond worldly men exploiting the aspirations and visions of unworldly dreamers. Even a Machiavelli, who wrote a political science by turning himself into a machine without soul or emotion, and who tried to view the movements of history as amoral chess problems, ended his treatise with an impassioned plea—inconsistent with everything that went before— to cleanse the holy soil of Italy of the foreign barbarians.

Man insists on endowing life with meaning and purpose. Causes and emotions are as much a part of his history as are the building of cities and the fighting of battles. When rulers or systems rob human existence of meaning and purpose, they set in motion angry human tides which sometimes do not exhaust themselves until they have demolished cities which have become prisons, and have released the human spirit from bonds grown oppressive. The idea, given a cynical twist, was expressed by one of our leading secular theologians, Reinhold Niebuhr: "Without the ultrarational hopes and passions of religion, no society will have the courage to conquer despair and attempt the impossible; for the vision of a just society is an impossible one, which can be approximated only by those who do not regard it as impossible. The truest visions of religion are illusions, which may be partly realized by being absolutely believed."

If we seek to reduce all history and politics to power, we end by reducing power to a sterile metaphysic. Power, like nature, abhors a vacuum. It can take on the substance of historical meaning only by embracing ideology. It can operate in the world of men and affairs by representing some set of ideas. Just as the most vacuous individual must believe in something beyond self, so the most naked power must absorb some piece of human aspiration, else it is unable to function in the world of the living. But even in periods when humanity yearns for a renascence of the human purpose, seeking new ideas as a thirsty man craves water, and when the dialectic of history swings away from the Caesars and towards the Saints, man's quest is governed by his strong discriminatory tastes. We can accept only those new ideas which are in the flow of his history, and which have been granted substance by the junction of past events.

The idea of a world governed by other mechanisms than war falls into this category. It arises out of the drift of past history and conforms to man's present needs. At the same time, the idea is sufficiently unsettling of past practices and folkways as to require the profoundest social renovations. Marx had written that all past revolutions had simply transferred power from one minority to another minority, whereas his proletarian revolution would for the first time in history transfer power to the majority. We have not yet seen that kind of revolution, but the thought can be paraphrased for the present proposition. All past revolutions retained the war system in the transference of political power from one group to another. The peace revolution envisages nothing less than the outright replacement of the war system.

How is the start to be made? How will we break out of the vicious circle where the nations refuse to disarm in the absence of international law, and where no international law can arise while the sovereign marauders remain at large? How are we to change an international scene where eminent jurists assembled in a world court have no cases to decide, and because of the absence of common concepts of equity, remain, in the past words of Alfred Zimmern, "an array of wigs and gowns vociferating in emptiness." Do we need a world police force first? The same forces which make it impossible for the world court to adjudicate major international disputes operate against the setting up of an international police force.

The Communists believe they would be criminally stupid and irresponsible if they consented to the formation of a capitalist-dominated international military force. The Westerners give equally short shrift to the idea of a Communist-dominated international military force. Were we to resolve to rise above these parochial outlooks and propose to set up an international force, staffed by honest men, dedicated solely to the welfare of all mankind and deciding all disputes exclusively on the basis of justice and equity, what would that mean exactly? Can an international community be imposed by a Bonapartist assumption of authority? Dag Hammarskjold tried something like it, and he did not get very far, because unlike all hitherto successful Bonapartes of history, he did not have his own military force to lend weight to his ideas of the common law.

Ingenious devices have been suggested to get around this difficulty. One plan proposes to create an international gendarmery divorced from national politics and unidentified with national loyalties through staffs of mixed nationals, with a central agency reassigning troops and weapons to meet the defense requirements of the participating nations. This is another variant of the administrator's dream that he can straighten out anything if only the demagogic and troublemaking politicians are kept out. Unfortunately, politics arise wherever people enter into public relations, and a non-political army would be as much of a curiosity as a headless rider. Very likely, some idea of an exclusively technical international military force was in the mind of Hammarskjold, but when the idea was implemented in the world of wicked men, it also became embroiled in their political contentions and convictions. The many proposals which may be meritorious in and of themselves, when lifted out of memoranda and dumped into the brutal environment of the cold war, get entangled in the underbrush of state intrigues and hostilities and transmogrified into cynical catch phrases or self-serving ploys put forward by one or the other of the belligerents. Like the comely maidens of Shangri-la, they turn hideous when they leave their original habitat.

## II

In an attempt to break out of this cul-de-sac, bold spirits have come up with the Solomon judgment of unilateral disarmament. Where the world seems petrified before the problem of apprehending the cheater, the difficulty is dissolved by putting everybody on the honor system. Where the military and diplomatic plenipotentiaries are wracking their brains for ways to reduce armaments without upsetting existing power balances, the unilateralists dispose of the obsession by asking their own government to leave itself militarily naked and give the world a moral example and lead. Let us be done, the pacifists cry, with all the pharisaical disputations to which there is no end. Let us cut through the conundrums of the military gamesmen and the tangles of the political gamesmen and offer a clear and straightforward answer which can be understood by all and which does not require the agreement of any other government to be put into effect.

A modicum of thought, they say, will immediately demonstrate to all and sundry the compelling logic as well as the sound morality of the proposition. Since we are arming and risking a nuclear war to preserve our free and democratic institutions, and since these most certainly cannot survive a nuclear war, we will have lost the very things we have gone to war to save—not a very sensible procedure. If we disarmed, there would be no war, and thus the extreme calamity would be averted in any case. At the worst, even if the opponent were to impose his tyranny upon us, we would still be able to fight back, and as time went on, to regain our free institutions; whereas if civilization were destroyed in a nuclear war, it would be the end for all time of free institutions. Though communism is an abhorrent system, it is, like all social systems, transitory; but life, once wiped off this planet, will not return. The case for unilateralism is thus clinched on practical as well as moral grounds.

It is symptomatic of the grimness of the international scene, and a proof of the crisis of traditional politics, that a school of thought which despairs of all the ordinary remedies of diplomacy and politics has arisen in England and has evoked echoes of response in various countries including our own. It has to be kept in mind, though, that its considerable support in England, going far beyond pacifist opposition to war on grounds of Christian conscience, is the result of a peculiar juxtaposition in that country. England is no longer a first-class power, and the attempts of her governments to keep up the military pretenses have proven beyond her strength. The attempts of both Tories and Laborites to achieve an independent nuclear deterrent have come to nought. Her shrunken empire can no longer stand the financial and personnel strain of present-day nuclear militarism.

Consequently the question that is asked most frequently on all levels of British society is whether the country, on strictly utilitarian grounds, would not be better off ditching its nuclear pretensions, getting out of the East-West arms race, and as a neutral, trusting to a policy of maneuver between the two superpowers. It is noteworthy that a man like Sir Stephen King-Hall, son and grandson of admirals, a graduate of both the Navy and Army Staff colleges who has had a distinguished naval career—a man combative by both temperament and training—should decide that unilateral disarmament was the right answer to Britain's dilemma. Liddell Hart also has said that the disarmament campaign "is basically sound common sense." It is this widespread feeling that has produced an army of so-called nuclear pacifists. When these converts to neutralism joined hands with the conscience pacifists, the supporters for nuclear disarmament swelled into a mass movement.

Where England's special circumstances do not exist, unilateralism appeals only to the small bands of high-minded and alienated who have contempt for the world of power and who are indifferent to its passions and prizes. That is probably why its adherents are oblivious of the flaw in their Aristotelian syllogism. It is true that the democracies have armed to the teeth to preserve their way of life; but their way of life is not limited to their democratic political institutions. Besides these are the power positions

and privileges, at home and abroad, of their nationals. Since the
Western nations have thus far found it impossible to compromise
the conflicting claims with their opponents, how are they going
to be persuaded to surrender their claims?

For one must assume that in the event of one side disarming,
the other would gain world hegemony by the exertion of ordinary
diplomatic pressures, even if Soviet troops were never to appear
off the coast of Newfoundland—which is the actual probability
of it. But the idea of putting oneself at the mercy of an opponent
is repugnant to the pride of a nation and demeaning of Western
training and values. While any kind of international agreement
and order will necessitate revised modes of thought and behavior,
the unilateralists are asking for a Tolstoyan renunciation that has
heretofore been congenial to only an insignificant fraction of the
human species, and which the generality of mankind shows neither
the disposition nor the ability to adopt.


III

The instinct of humanity has not played it false, however, when
it has passed up other issues and seized on disarmament as the
way to reverse the engines of war. Not that national armaments
are independent entities, or that military establishments are separate and apart from the legal structures and sovereign claims of
national states and the furies of conflicts of the cold war. They
are mistaken who try forcibly to tear apart the militarist from
the diplomat and to assign priorities of moral culpability.

But the military establishments are not mere passive beneficiaries
of the struggles of nations; they are ringleaders and provocateurs
in the arms race. Lop off the munitions arm of the nation state,
and you will have forced the organism to change its mode of
existence in its foreign relations and its domestic affairs. Demobilize the armed forces and reassign the personnel to productive
labors, and you will have damped down the war fevers, and altered
the *modus vivendi* of governments and citizens. Because the war
system is imbedded in national economy, national law, national
folkways, national morality, its elimination is tantamount to a
transfiguration of the national state. Whether the end of foreign
policy or of armaments is tackled has to be determined not by
principle but by practice—which end is the most susceptible to

pressure; which proposition can best enlist the passions of a people. In practice, it will be found that disarmament and political settlements are two sides of the same coin. The first serious attempt on the part of the major powers to adopt agreements leading to disarmament will be accompanied by equally serious attempts to compromise outstanding political conflicts.

The reason the popular imagination has centered its attention on disarmament is that the arms race presents the immediate point of danger, and it appears more susceptible to a solution. There is no need to enroll millions of people in seminars in group dynamics, communications and motivational research, cold war theology, or arms control metaphysics before you are able to mount a resistance. There is no need to elaborate arcane theses about the interrelationships of arms strategy and national security before you can try to roll back the forces of war. Some are suspicious of disarmament proposals precisely because of that. They feel that here is an attempt to oversimplify a complex and rarefied sociological problem. There is a class among the arms necromancers that seeks to keep the common public away from the sacred portals by pretending that only years of cloistered study of these black arts entitles one to express an opinion, and that any attempt of the untutored and the unwashed to meddle with these mysteries will lead to dangers if not outright disasters. This is the familiar snobbish denial of experts that democracy can work. This is the mumbo-jumbo of guildsmen trying to stake out a craft monopoly. Of course, the technical aspects of disarmament settlements require expert knowledge. But the principles of settlement can be grasped by all intelligent laymen. As the noted military historian Walter Millis said, "This notion of the 'difficulty' of the subject is an illusion. Given a desire by all the great powers to disarm, there would be nothing very complicated about disarming," but given the desire to cling to the assumed simplicities and supposed securities of the war system, "the problem becomes one which all the technical and intellectual *expertise* in the world is unlikely to resolve."

The difficulty is not in devising the proper techniques or legal plans of which we already have an oversupply, but in changing political habits and social organizations. This is difficult indeed. But it is no more difficult in the matter of disarmament than it is in any of the other major questions that plague humanity today. Since any changes of this magnitude will never come to

pass without great masses of people getting swept into the fray
and becoming passionate about solutions, it is reasonable to center
popular thought along lines which are comprehensible, and to put
the kind of demands to governments and statesmen which cannot
easily be evaded or obscured. There is no chance of disarmament
until many political relations change. But disarmament is the best
shorthand expression for a new international morality and the will
to reeducate the nations.

Although war arose out of the needs and lusts of civilized societies, once generated it is self-breeding. The war system suffuses
all the mores of nations with the colors of paranoia; it excites
and exacerbates all differences; it turns opponents' fears into sinister threats to oneself; it frequently brings on the catastrophes it
was designed to avoid. Once nations are fully caught in the coils
of the war system, they may go to war over parcels of real estate
which are economically useless and financially a burden, but whose
possession is deemed strategically important against the rival. Nations may even go to war for useless malaria-ridden pieces of
territory, not because they are of strategic importance to themselves, but because it is intolerable that the enemy should have them.

International relations are consequently turned into a vicious
game of trying to manipulate and balance off other nations, who
are doing the same to you, and to prevent any one country from
getting such riches and strength which would make her overwhelmingly formidable in a possible future war. Fear of the future, anticipatory intrigues which are considered the hallmark of
prudent statesmanship and patriotic devotion, the urge to deprive
a potential adversary of contingent advantages in a conceivable
conflict—these rather than present needs have been the authors
of more than one war, and have bedeviled relations between countries in the modern world as they did in the ancient. The great
perils which nations resist with war are often the creations of
the war system itself.

The Rush-Bagot agreement of 1817 is an example of how disarmament can alter the political relation between two states. The
war of 1812 between Britain and this country was a stalemate,
and the Peace of Ghent two years later resolved none of the
issues that had led to war, nor did it temper the pioneering ex-
pansionism of the American war hawks. The war had clearly
demonstrated, however, that the strategic situation on the Canadian
frontier depended almost entirely on the command of the Great

Lakes, and egged on by the military advisers on both sides, the two governments began a costly and dangerous naval race. This disrupted the commerce that both wanted to promote and threatened to produce a new military blowup. It was a time of great tension. Finally, in 1816, Castlereagh, the British Foreign Secretary, who previously had been overruled by the military, was able to reopen negotiations, and a short and simple agreement was rapidly reached for mutual disarmament on the Lakes. It was both Castlereagh's and Monroe's great good fortune that there were no operational research staffs in their day.

The two governments forthwith dismantled or sunk all the warships on Erie and Ontario. And although there were long, acrimonious boundary disputes for the next fifty years, the disarmament agreement held inviolate. The two sides were able to peacefully fix a frontier that stretched for 4,000 miles and had no natural boundaries. The British historian G. M. Trevelyan wrote, "If there had been armaments there would sometime have been war." As the passage of time and events changed the character of society on both sides of the border, the politics between the two nations changed likewise, and the original dispute disappeared into the pages of history.

Thus there is a lot to the theory that if a start could once be made at disarmament, new rules and customs of international usage and conduct would sprout and grow and begin to entwine and interlace the spokesmen of nations. National patriots would find themselves in the grip of more encompassing traditions and influences, and it would not be easy to go back to the old methods of fang and claw. Naturally, the Rush-Bagot agreement only illustrates a point. It is an example of a possibility, an instance where a decline of armaments mitigated political divergencies. Further than that the argument is not meant to stretch. The Canadian-American conflict of 1817 is not analogous to the cold war of the 1960's.

The implacable competition between the Western and Communist blocs is occurring within a generalized national revolution unprecedented in its social depth and universal sweep, and aggravated by the force of a scientific revolution. This has produced antithetical tendencies. On the one hand, the great powers are arming themselves to an extent that dwarfs the preceding activities of Alexander, Caesar, Genghis Khan, Charles XII, Napoleon, and Hitler combined. In no other era dominated by the great

conquerors of history have the military establishments penetrated
so thoroughly into the fabric of civilian life. In no epoch of empire have arms threats and arms blackmail so dominated the international landscape. On the other hand, the saturation parity of
the arms race has sterilized military power. The race for nuclear
supremacy has produced what Liddell Hart has called "nuclear
nullity." Despite the blood-curdling yells and incitations issuing
from the two military camps, the ability to destroy each other
has immobilized the military machines. The belligerents maneuver
against each other, they spy on each other, they flaunt their battle
flags, they rattle their weapons, but the missiles remain on their
pads and the planes at their stations.

Willy-nilly, the two belligerents have been led to attempts to
turn each other's flanks by arming their allies and clients and
unashamedly peddling arms in an attempt to win friends and
influence people. This is no hardship for them on the economic
plane, since the arms race has led to the accumulation of mountains of obsolescent military junk which has to be disposed of
through one means or another. But the standoff of the two superpowers makes the encouragement of peripheral wars equally ineffective. There are strict limits as to how far each side can commit
itself, for every peripheral war may escalate into a nuclear world
war. And the attempt to dominate the world through clients is
self-defeating. How much success have the great powers had in
thwarting national movements by military force? France and Holland brought their superior might to bear in Indonesia, Indochina,
and Algeria, and they lost, as the European powers lost in
Egypt, and as America is losing in Laos and South Vietnam
today. From the time of the American Revolution of 1776 to the
insurgent struggles of today, it has been demonstrated that an
organized, militant, and popular guerrilla force cannot be finally
defeated when it is able to obtain substantial arms and aid from
another power. The successes of England in Malaya or of Portu-
gal in its African colonies are only delaying actions. The countries
of Africa and Asia have a manifest destiny to independence.

It is an illusion to think that the end result of the present
struggles, alarums, and confusions will be a world eventually
dominated by Western-style capitalism or Russian-style communism.
The most important of the newly arisen nations are wary of both
superpowers. They try to get aid from both sides, and they bor-
row from the social systems of both sides. But they want to stay

neutral. The Western powers are precluded from imposing their system on the new nations because of their long history of racism and exploitation, and because these nations have unique problems in trying to make the leap from medievalism to the twentieth century. The Communists lost their international banners and credentials during the bloody years of Stalinism, and they will never regain them. The split in the Communist camp has broken its pretensions to universality. Western hopes to regain the allegiance of the East European countries may be vain, but the Communist bloc is clearly dividing along national lines. Humanity is not headed toward a unitary system; it is entering an age of diversity and pluralism.

The ideological split in the world, and the rise of numerous young states jealous of their new-found independence, will make for a long era of centrifugal impulsion and nationalist assertion. Technics have established a rudimentary world community of mutual dependence, but politics have kept it split—and will keep it split—ideologically. That is why, unless all the nations were threatened with a simultaneous invasion from outer space, the conditions cannot be recreated that impelled theocratic Massachusetts, Quaker Pennsylvania, Catholic Maryland, and Anglican Virginia to federate into a single and centralized union. The political drift is away from a unitary world state or world government. That makes chimerical for the immediate generations ahead the creation of a world police force (aside from marginal forces for incidental conflicts) which cannot be a purely administrative artifact, but is necessarily an arm of a world community.

But there is the strong undercurrent of conviction around the world that we are in an impossible situation, that things cannot go on as at present, that some method must be found to free humanity from the danger of nuclear extinction; and that unless some method is devised, nuclear war is sooner or later inevitable. The disarmament negotiations of the past decade and a half, for all their farce and insincerity, have been a response to this strong surge of peoples. In that sense, they are a towering fact of the historical process of our times.

It is impossible to extrapolate from the present social dispositions any possible disarmament agreements of the future because these involve nothing less than a revolution in human thoughts and state arrangements. But certainly any abolition or meaningful reduction of the war system would have to include a settlement

of the most pressing political conflicts and the creation of a limited
world authority to supervise the destruction of weapons of mass
annihilation. A world treaty of this kind—were it approved by all
governments and nations—would not usher in the millennium.
Sovereign states would continue to exist. Animosities and maladjustments would remain. It would still be a world of strife, of
turmoil, of contention—and of power. Factions within the nations
would still organize to displace existing governments, and other
states would still give aid and comfort to dissidents abroad. Strife
and struggle are the fate of mercurial man and the method of
social evolution. But the supreme threat would have been removed,
and the preconditions laid down for the slow emergence of world
law, and a more integrated, a more humane, and a more attractive
community.

How could we be sure that the other side would not cheat and
secretly rearm? While fears of this kind have a greater place in
the thinking of governments and peoples than fears of a nuclear
holocaust, there will be no elimination of the war systems. The
change will come when these fears appear as either unrealistic or
secondary to the need of removing the Damocles' sword above our
heads. Once an international authority had come into being, and
all or most of the missiles and nuclear warheads had been junked,
a popular opposition of incalculable force would probably gather
to overwhelm any government and any nation that attempted to
break the disarmament covenant and return the nations to the
nuclear jungle from which they had but recently emerged. After
a number of years of disarmament, the very idea of any nation
proposing to transfer its scientists and engineers from fruitful pursuits to arms research and production would be as preposterous
and quixotic as an oil baron or cattle king fitting out a private
army of gunmen to challenge in this second half of the twentieth
century the suzerainty of our federal government.

Who would gain under this arrangement, the West or the
Soviets? Probably neither side in the sense that victory is conceived of today. In truth, the whole nature of the international
struggle to carve a new world order and a social stability out
of the volatile materials of twentieth century industrialism and
science and nationalism would metamorphose the internal regimes
of both blocs. We have to gain the long view that nothing is
permanent, that the current arrangements of the West as well
as of the East are not the last word and will in any case disappear

down the deep caverns where rest the remains of past civilizations of man, and that under relatively non-military international folkways, many of the strategic and ideological conflicts which exercise us today will fade away and become incomprehensible to a new generation of earth dwellers.

So long as the thought of governments and peoples moves in cold-war channels, so long as the risk of nuclear annihilation appears more bearable than the risk of social changes, so long will all attempts be abortive to move out of the rut of the arms race. The grand lunge will be made when peoples and nations come to feel that it is intolerable for their generations and succeeding generations to live under the balance of nuclear terror, that things cannot be permitted to go on in the way they have been proceeding for the past two decades, that it is impossible to battle out with nuclear weapons the issues of our times, and that another way has to be found to conduct the affairs—as well as the quarrels—of mankind.

# INDEX